What If Boomers Can't Retire?

How to Build Real Security, Not Phantom Wealth

Thornton Parker

16
EasyRead Large

RHYW

Copyright Page from the Original Book

What If Boomers Can't Retire?

Berrett-Koehler Publishers, Inc.
235 Montgomery Street, Suite 650
San Francisco, California 94104-2916
Tel: (415) 288-0260, Fax: (415) 362-2512
www.bkconnection.com

Ordering information for print editions
Quantity sales. Special discounts are available on quantity purchases by corporations, associations, and others. For details, contact the "Special Sales Department" at the Berrett-Koehler address above.
Individual sales. Berrett-Koehler publications are available through most bookstores. They can also be ordered directly from Berrett-Koehler: Tel: (800) 929-2929; Fax: (802) 864-7626; www.bkconnection.com
Orders for college textbook/course adoption use. Please contact Berrett-Koehler: Tel: (800) 929-2929; Fax: (802) 864-7626.
Orders by U.S. trade bookstores and wholesalers. Please contact Ingram Publisher Services, Tel: (800) 509-4887; Fax: (800) 838-1149; E-mail: customer.service@ingrampublisherservices.com; or visit www.ingrampublisherservices.com/Ordering for details about electronic ordering.

First Edition
Hardcover print edition ISBN 978-1-57675-112-1
Paperback print edition ISBN 978-1-57675-249-4
PDF e-book ISBN 978-1-60509-808-1

2010-1

Interior Design & Illustration: Gopa Design & Illustration
Copy Editor: Sandra Beris
Indexer: Paula C. Durbin-Westby
Proofreader: Henrietta Bensussen
Production: Linda Jupiter, Jupiter Productions
Cover Design: Richard Adelson

Set in 16 pt. Verdana

TABLE OF CONTENTS

To my wife, Eugenia, and our favorite boomers in the order that we met them—Linda, Jim, and Diane.

Foreword

This book is welcome relief to those many of us who invest for the long term and value a healthy society and environment, as well as sound economic returns. Socially responsible investors approach their assets and portfolios with this broader vision and use criteria including environmental impact, labor relations, product safety, human rights, corporate citizenship and community reinvestment. As it turns out, such investments now account for $2.1 trillion of capital invested in the United States alone, with over sixty mutual funds offering such products for individual investors, 401(k)s, and other pension and trust funds. Returns are comparable or often higher than with conventional funds, and the Domini Social 400 Index has consistently outperformed the Standard & Poor's Index for over five years.

Such investors will resonate, as I did, with Thornton Parker's experience and deep wisdom on the nature of Wall Street today. As of mid-year 2000, there has been a healthy correction from the unsustainable "bubble" that greeted the new millennium. Yet, aspects of our nation's financial markets are still troubling: the focus on short-term returns and capital appreciation, momentum day trading, playing to the analysts with "creative" accounting, and the premature initial public offerings (IPOs), not to mention the Internet revolution's continual restructuring of securities markets themselves. All of these sweeping changes are now covered in real time by the plethora of new TV channels, Web sites, and news sources such as Reuters, Bridge, Bloomberg, and others—all amplifying the casino atmosphere.

Adding to the general concern, the drive to please Wall Street analysts leads to a mad dash to hype stocks and the rush to "bulk up" with me-too mergers and acquisitions. Analysts themselves join in the frenzy by giving information to big investors ahead of small ones, and only some 1 percent recommend selling the stocks they cover. Even the big accounting firms are accused of conflicts of interest, such as owning the stocks of companies they audit, while some are being sued for bad, incompetent consulting advice. The major stock exchanges have been the targets of SEC investigations for anticompetitive practices. Even the Mafia has infiltrated Wall Street.

Even if and when all these problems are addressed, there remains the instability of globalizing financial markets, which led to the Asian meltdown and the Russian default crisis that rocked the world's markets in 1997 and 1998. Earnest calls by the world's central bankers and finance ministers for a new international financial architecture have led to little in the way of concrete change. Currency markets now trade $2 trillion per day, some 90 percent of which is speculation unrelated to trade. This unregulated global currency trading is rife with "bear raiders" who attack weak currencies with herd behavior, driving these currencies down so as to buy them back at the bottom. Such speculative attacks make it difficult for even the smartest, most democratically elected governments to manage their domestic economies and retain their social safety nets. This means that interest rates must be hiked, causing bankruptcies, unemployment, and loss of savings—all of which affect the poor and the vulnerable, who are mostly women and children.

The good news is that there is no dearth of remedies for all this—at the international, the national, and the corporate level—not to mention at the level of individual investors. And as Thornton Parker points out, if we don't begin making some of these needed changes—right on Wall Street and in our own U.S. capital markets, the great expectations of baby boomers to sell their stocks and realize their gains for a comfortable retirement may simply evaporate.

At least the debate has begun, started perhaps by Alan Greenspan's famous phrase about Wall Street's "irrational exuberance." Now the title of a serious book published in 2000, author Robert J. Shiller warns of the growing stock market bubble and the unrealistic expectations driving investors. I have written my own warnings—as has archcapitalist George Soros, who also identifies the problem of "herd behavior," where investors bid stocks up and then all panic at the same time. This has at last dented the unrealistic economic theories of "perfect markets" that efficiently allocate capital to the most productive uses. In reality, such mathematical economists have been proven wrong, particularly the two Nobel Prize-winning "rocket scientists" who lost millions in the near-collapse of the Long-Term Capital Management hedge fund in 1998. A red-faced Nobel committee awarded the 1998 prize in economics to Amartya Sen, who studies poverty. After such debacles and the Asian meltdown, ordinary people and small investors have learned the phrase "moral hazard," as hosts of speculators were bailed out by taxpayers.

Just as being a socially responsible investor can be prudent in the long run, so can the reforms in financial markets advocated by Thornton Parker in this book make these markets sounder and protect retirement incomes. You will come to appreciate the inner workings of our current markets and the hidden fragility that many "new economy" boosters ignore. Such advocates highlight the new equity economy typical of Silicon Valley, where many start-up companies often "buy" their office space, equipment, and outsourced services with stock and options rather than cash—in the same way they compensate their employees. All this is fine while these companies' stocks are inflating, even allowing the huge acquisition sprees of companies such as Amazon.com and America Online. But these new stock certificate "currencies" inflate the money supply, as does the ballooning credit card debt, leaving central bankers even less in control of the nation's monetary policy. And when dot-com stocks tumble, employees' stock options become worthless and venture capitalists remain the few winners—if they have managed to float these stocks in previous IPOs.

A surprising effect of all this and the inroads being made by the Internet sector (which is for real and still growing) is that money is becoming less important—just at the time when it appeared to have conquered all other values. Billions of dollars were thrown at Internet start-ups, which grew on debt and further infusions of cash in the pie-in-the-sky hopes of growing by simply capturing customers, even at a loss. To date, even the benchmark of the dot-com sector, Amazon.com , has yet to earn a profit. In their 1999 book *Internet Bubble,* Anthony B. Perkins and Michael C. Perkins, the editors of *Red Herring,* exposed the underside of Silicon Valley's "vulture capitalists" and cut-throat, money-crazed, adolescent culture, and explained how it would lead to the shakeout that finally began to occur in May 2000. Their Appendix, "Calculating the Bubble," convinced me. "The average Internet company in our set of 133 publicly traded companies (as of June 11, 1999) with equity market capitalizations greater than $100 million will need to generate revenue growth of approximately 80 percent every year for the next five years—in other words, revenues will need to increase by a factor of over 18 times by the first quarter of 2004."[1]

Today, even with so many burned investors, money still pours into Wall Street from all those individual retirement accounts (IRAs), 401(k)s, and company pension plans. Many Wall Street–related interest groups have joined with conservative think tanks and worried young voters in urging that Social Security be partially privatized, adding to the billions of pension dollars pouring into the coffers of Wall Street's money managers. This book will shed light on the fundamental issues underlying the crucial debate over Social Security. From my perspective, there is already too much cash chasing too few really intelligent companies and business plans.

Meanwhile, important new enterprises in the budding twenty-first century economy remain underfunded because they are off the radar screen of conventional investors, asset managers, and financial media. These are in the promising new clean energy sector: solar, wind, tidal power, fuel cells, flywheels, and the shift from fossil fuels to hydrogen and renewable sources. Other opportunities await in holistic health, organic foods, the Internet, and media sectors to link concerned "global citizens" in sharing new approaches to their local economies and community challenges, and thereby becoming a part of the great global transition to more sustainable economies for our human future.

The good news is in exploring all the dammed-up inventions, innovations, creativity, and entrepreneurship searching for highly conscious investors, angels, and venture funding. Many of the Internet sector's best and brightest are now exploring all these new investment opportunities in restoring and enhancing our environment. These offer a much richer legacy for their children than money and more mindless consumption. Many, including Bill Gates, Robert Glaser, and Joe Firmage, have started nonprofits focused on health, alternative clean energy, environmental protection, and quality-of-life indicators, similar to the Calvert-Henderson Quality of Life Indicators, which I co-created with the Calvert Group, Inc. family of mutual funds. Others, including James Fierro, founder of Vancouver-based Venture Resources, are incubating companies that are breaking new ground in cyberspace. James and I are both investors in wet v.com , the Internet partner of WETV, Canada's global, public access TV network, which will be its platform for ecological commerce, socially responsible business, and investing for a TV series I have developed for WETV called "The Ethical Marketplace." Another innovation is Barter.com , which will provide money-free, electronic barter for all those 2 billion people left out of the world's banking and money systems.

The spiritual aspect of the current situation can be seen precisely in the amount of money being thrown into human expectations, ideas, and even half-baked business models. This is the evidence that capitalism has morphed into a new form so that money now follows information and ideas—if not yet wisdom. Intellectual capital is now arguably a company's most important asset, and accountants are now grappling with proper ways of measuring knowledge. The highest human values—wisdom, love, and spiritual striving—cannot be captured by accountants or money-coefficients, any more than humans can evaluate fully Nature's role. But we can move toward much greater understanding and certainly beyond our current practice of setting the value of such priceless aspects of our existence at zero—as in our Gross Domestic Product national accounts. Knowledge is the newest factor of production to enter economic theory and it resides not in land or factories, but in the heads of employees. Thus, shifts continue occurring in the way enterprises are structured, toward partnerships, cooperating and sharing with all stakeholders—not only stockholders. As I wrote in my first book, *Creating Alternative Futures* (1978, 1996),[2] there is no "divine right of capital," just as King John learned in Britain in 1215 that kings did not possess such a right.

So conscious investors, employees, and citizens are changing the rules of the market game and raising the ethical floor under the global "playing field," and many concerned Wall Street insiders are joining them. Some investors and entrepreneurs, myself among them, are now so cognizant of Wall Street's current dysfunctionality that they are vowing *not* to go public. Who wants an IPO that throws their socially visionary young company into shark-infested waters? Instead, they are forming private networks, based on the pioneering Social Venture Network and similar groups it helped catalyze. Instead of losing control of their higher purpose and mission to today's greed-based financial casinos, they are extending their relationships into cyberspace via electronic barter and information-based trading systems, providing their own pools of socially conscious "liquidity."

When you have read this book, you will better appreciate this enormous shift now quietly occurring in our capital markets. Using Thornton Parker's research and suggestions for enabling this healthy evolution of capitalism, you can become a participant in these shifts toward economic and ecological sustainability. This will be an investment in your own future and even more in the futures of your children and grandchildren. Today, the move toward corporate codes of conduct and a more ethical marketplace are becoming a pragmatic necessity. On a small, interdependent planet, all our self-interests turn out in the long run to be identical: survival and a more humane future.

Hazel Henderson

Preface to the Paperback Edition

As I write the Preface to this edition, the cover of *Time* magazine asks, "Will you *ever* be able to **retire?"** *The Wall Street Journal* prints the front-page headline "For Investors Near Retirement, Stock Fall Poses Stark Choices." *USA Today, The New York Times, The Washington Post, The Boston Globe,* and other papers have told about baby boomers whose retirement plans have crashed and of retirees who must go back to work. Enron, Global Crossing, WorldCom, fraud and padded numbers, options, layoffs, conflicts of interest among auditors and stock analysts, and legislation to prevent all this from happening again are front-page news.

The global investment adviser Wilshire Associates reports that stock portfolios lost $8.2 trillion after their March 2000 peak. But was that money ever real? In a rational world, how could a company like Enron, said to be the seventh largest of the Fortune 500 companies, go bankrupt in less than a year after it was supposedly worth $62 billion? And how could 98 percent of WorldCom's capitalized value of $41.7 billion vanish in six months?

This book tells why that money, which was based on stock prices, was just *phantom wealth* and why the waste and abuses it caused would show up after it vanished. The book also explains why boomers can only build real security by ignoring phantom wealth, making realistic plans, and living in vibrant, healthy communities.

Some think that today's stock market problems are due to a "few bad apples" or are like a "hangover" after a "binge." But as the book explains, the picture is much bigger. We are seeing just a preview of what can happen if enough Americans don't learn why they should plan to work and support themselves for more years than previous generations have done. This book explains how boomers' retirement plans have helped inflate stock prices and how they could depress them even more. That would hurt everybody.

Financial experts and political leaders are missing the most important lessons. They say, for example, that workers who suffered the largest 401(k) plan losses owned too much of their companies' stock and the problem can be fixed with more diversification. But that that ignores the mistake of depending too much on any stocks to pay retirement incomes. For two decades, the problems caused by retirement plans were overlooked, until portfolio balances plunged.

After 401(k) plans were started in 1982, record amounts flowed into pension and mutual funds, whose managers were expected to make the money grow. They pressed companies for higher stock prices, and this led to years of cost cutting, downsizing, merging, promoting globalization, laying off domestic employees, reducing support for communities, exploiting the environment, and buying back stocks. Most people still do not understand how much of the pressure for higher stock prices—and rewards for executives who produced them—came from outside of most companies. Much of it started with retirement plans.

And retirement plans can end it all with a bang. As this book explains, now that few stocks pay significant dividends, they are just things to buy and hope to sell at a profit. But no one has explained who will be able to pay enough for the stocks that the boomers' pension and retirement accounts will have to sell to produce retirement income. These accounts hold half of the country's traded stocks, and the most likely buyers are members of the younger, relatively smaller Generation X. Few boomers realize how much they will be depending on younger workers for their retirement income. The United States is literally betting its future on a concept that has never been explained.

AARP publications, *Consumer Reports,* and others are starting to tell their readers to plan to work longer. That is a switch, and it is good advice. Some brokers and financial advisers are now giving similar advice to their clients. I hope that enough boomers will understand and act in time to reduce the risks of expecting too much from stocks without triggering massive sales that could lead to a disaster. The trick will be to prevent the boomers' boom from becoming the boomers' bust, and we won't have much chance of pulling it off if we don't understand it.

Many boomers will need appropriate and fulfilling jobs for their later years. They will also need strong communities that provide services that they will not be able to provide for themselves. Yet, today, pension and mutual fund managers encourage companies to cut these jobs and the costs of supporting communities in order to increase stock prices. But lean and mean is just backwards. It pits workers against retirees and boomers' hopes for their later years against their own present and future needs.

The mindset that made inflating stocks the primary goal of public corporations has led to failure. For several decades, companies concentrated on what Wall Street wants and ignored what Main Street needs. That formula was wrong and its failure is behind many of today's headlines.

Large companies are like states and countries in their size and the range of interests they serve. They must have balanced goals. One goal should be to help their employees, who are stockholders, to enjoy their later years while working to contribute to their own support for as long as they can. Companies and institutional investors are the most powerful economic forces in the country. If they help make this transition, they will be part of the solution. If not, they will continue to be part of the problem.

The book explains how the stock bubble, the "new economy," globalization, corporate scandals, and the drive for growth by pension and mutual funds are all related to America's flawed retirement system. By looking at the whole system, it is easy to see how it can fail and could lead to a depression. That doesn't have to happen, but the longer the whole picture is ignored or denied, the more likely it becomes.

Why This Book Was Written

The book is intended to be a balanced, responsible warning about a serious problem that few people yet see, even today. It was written primarily for ten groups of readers, many of whom may be in more than one group:

- *Baby boomers* and others who are buying stocks directly and indirectly through pension and mutual funds to help pay their retirement incomes
- *Younger workers*
- *Parents of baby boomers*
- *Wealthy people* who are arranging their estates
- *Visionary leaders* who are working to reduce the contemporary emphasis on materialism and find a better balance of values and goals
- *Financial professionals* who sell or manage pension and mutual funds, advise individuals and organizations about retirement investments, or evaluate the financial condition of organizations and retirement accounts
- *Corporate directors, executives, and managers*
- *Government officials* of federal, state, and local governments who are concerned about the future financial condition and retirement plans of their jurisdictions
- *Professors* of economics, government, and business administration

- *Heads of philanthropic foundations* who have unique opportunities to help the country as they advance their own programs

How It Is Organized

The Introduction gives a brief overview of the book. It lists the book's five main messages and explains that they apply to individuals, retirement plans, and the economy as a whole. It also lists the twenty-six Highlights, or key points of the book.

The book is divided into three parts. Part I, which includes Chapters 1 through 4, concentrates on baby boomers and their retirement plans.

Chapter 1 begins with a discussion of Social Security because most people know that the program has a problem. But many people don't understand the problem and very few realize that it is just the tip of the retirement iceberg. The chapter explains the problem and why past proposals to use stocks to solve it are unlikely to work.

Chapter 2 goes on to explain why all retirement plans that expect to sell assets or take money from younger workers to pay retirement incomes have the same basic problem as Social Security does. The chapter explains why stocks probably can't help millions of boomers to retire and what could happen if the country fails to recognize that in time.

Chapter 3 briefly summarizes eight other books that differ with or support the positions taken in Chapters 1 and 2. It explains why all of these authors' opinions can't possibly turn out to be right because they conflict among themselves.

Chapter 4 discusses what may happen to individual baby boomers as they age. It classifies the boomers into seven types to show the magnitude of the national problem that relatively few people see and to help individual baby boomers reading this book to think through their own situations.

Part II, which includes Chapters 5 through 8, concentrates on how stocks are used to create phantom wealth. It introduces explanations and simple analysis techniques that are not normally used by economists or financial professionals.

Chapter 5 sets the stage by examining two different investment approaches and describing five classes of companies that are used for the analyses that follow. Chapters 6 through 8 explain some of the positive and negative effects of stocks, how stock prices are set, and problems that are caused by the drive to increase stock prices.

The current processes for creating and using phantom wealth are unstable and destructive in many ways. Even without the retirement plan issue, sooner or later they will have to be modified. But the fact that retirement plans have been built on the processes makes the need to change them more urgent. Retirement savings have flowed into these plans and they drove stock prices to record heights, but that was just the first half of the cycle. When the plans will need to sell stocks to pay retirement incomes, they may cause an equally historic market reversal.

Part III, which includes Chapters 9 through 12, identifies future needs and how to meet them. It suggests different ways of thinking in order to help people escape today's mindset, which fosters the phantom wealth economy. The suggestions are made to trigger readers' creative thought and exploration. They are not intended to be recipes or how-to lists.

Chapter 9 is the watershed chapter. In it, the discussion shifts from problems to opportunities. It explains how we in this country can use the knowledge of what may happen if current practices are not changed to redirect the power of investing to help meet the needs of all people, including the growing number of seniors.

Chapters 10 and 11 discuss what individuals and organizations can do to help themselves and create a more sustainable society and economy.

And finally, Chapter 12 provides a broad view of how to change the investment system from producing phantom wealth to meeting real needs.

"We"

In general, I use "we" when I'm speaking of the author and the reader. "I" shows up from time to time when it seems appropriate, but in the main, the book is intended to explore issues informally and collegially. I hope it will encourage and help readers to think about the future without being dull or preachy.

Thornton Parker
August 2002
Washington, DC

Acknowledgments

This book would not have been possible without the encouragement, ideas, interest, and practical support of Steve Piersanti, the President, and Jeevan Sivasubramanian, the Corporate and Editorial Administrator, of Berrett-Koehler Publishers, Inc. It was an honor to be accepted by them and a pleasure to work with them. As one author told me, "If Berrett-Koehler will do your book, you'd be a fool to look anywhere else!" He was right.

I am indebted to Hazel Henderson, Donald Lee Rome, Carl Henn, David Korten, and Maya Porter, who encouraged me to write a book and gave me all sorts of help along the way.

I am also grateful to Stephen J. Butler, Jonathan Forman, Gail Gormley, Thomas H. Greco, Jr., Sara Jane Hope, John McIntyre, D. Bruce Merrifield, Marlene Silva, Joseph A. Webb, Mavis Wilson, and Paul Wright for their insightful reviews and invaluable suggestions for improving the earlier versions.

Finally, I want to thank Linda Jupiter, project manager; Sandra Beris, copy editor; and all the other team members for their kind advice, assistance, and professional contributions.

Introduction

Beware of Phantom Wealth

The idea of using stocks to solve the Social Security problem seems like a "good, long-term, quick fix." The idea is so alluring, it just keeps coming up. But before jumping to that conclusion, we should be sure that we understand the problem, retirement plans in general, and what stocks really do.

The Five Main Messages of This Book

This book was written to present five major messages.

1. Much of the country's economy and many of its retirement plans are built on a structure of phantom wealth that depends on stock prices.
2. Stock prices are based on projected future events or what people hope will happen, not on actual corporate accomplishments. Using stock prices to measure wealth is like counting chickens before they've hatched.
3. The drive to create phantom wealth by inflating stock prices helps some people, but it distorts the economy and hurts society as a whole.
4. Demographic trends and retirement plans are helping to build the phantom wealth structure. But unless the structure is replaced with one that is more sustainable, those same trends will

eventually make it fail, and that in turn will drag down the retirement plans and the economy.

5. Individuals and organizations can help prevent retirement plans and the economy as a whole from collapsing—or protect themselves in case there is a collapse—by creating real wealth based on work, earnings, and solid accomplishments, instead of just hopes. But doing this requires a different mindset that includes new values, goals, and ways of thinking about living, aging, investing, and running companies.

These five messages apply to individuals and their retirement plans, to all the country's retirement plans in the aggregate, and to the whole economy.

What Is Phantom Wealth?

A *phantom* is something that appears to be but has no real or physical existence. Like an apparition, a shadow, a dream, or a vision, a phantom is not what it seems to be.

Throughout this book, we use the term *phantom wealth* to refer to the returns from corporate stocks that are based on market prices. Individuals, companies, investors, retirement plans, and the country as a whole are ignoring the transient or ephemeral nature of trillions of dollars of phantom wealth. The opposite of phantom wealth is *real wealth,* and it has very different characteristics. We will explore how phantom wealth is created, how unreal it is, and how quickly it can vanish.

Will Baby Boomers Have Enough Money to Retire?

Nearly everybody knows the conventional explanation of how capitalism works. It starts with people saving money, which they invest in companies, which use the money to build plants, buy tools, develop new products, and create jobs. The companies grow, their stock prices go up, the investors are happy, the economy prospers, and all is well.

Based on that explanation, millions of American workers—who can expect to live longer than any previous generation—are being told that their formula for years of comfortable retirement is simple: just be guided by the history of the stock market, buy stocks, and retire on the gains. Companies, state and local governments, and many other employers are using the formula to reduce the costs of pensions that they have promised their employees.

But the explanation is insidious. It sounds right and it seems to explain why the economy is doing so well. The concept has endured for decades. It has few detractors and even the collapse of the Soviet Union increased its general acceptance. It is particularly appealing to those who are benefiting the most from today's stock-driven economy. And it contains enough truth to save it from being labeled fiction.

For many reasons, however, the explanation has gradually become more fiction than fact. One reason is that little of the money that most people use to buy stocks for retirement accounts ever gets to the companies. Instead, it goes to previous stockholders through trades that often help increase stock prices, thus increasing the base on which phantom wealth is built.

As we will see, there are few positive links between the stock market and large companies. There are negative links, however, that work backwards from the conventional explanation. Important parts of the economy are running *in spite of* the stock market rather than because of it.

Even the prevailing formulas that are used to manage retirement accounts have a fatal flaw. Based on these formulas, baby boomers are buying large quantities of stocks and inflating the prices. But nobody knows what prices they will receive when they have to sell their stocks for retirement income. We will explain why there are serious risks that the stock-based retirement formulas may turn out instead to be formulas for an economic depression.

Money Isn't Everything

We in this country are constantly being bombarded by magazines, television programs, Internet sites, investment advisory services, brokers, and even banks purporting to explain how easy it is to make money with stocks. The financial services industry has large advertising budgets to convince us that if we save and invest in stocks, we can plan to enjoy years of retirement. All we need to do is buy enough of them soon enough and build a kitty that is large enough.

If you sense that something is missing in all this advice, you are right. As this book goes to press, the appealing idea that one can get something for nothing and create wealth out of thin air is working. But for baby boomers' retirement plans, the idea is fundamentally flawed, because it rests almost entirely on phantom wealth and transfers of money from workers to retirees.

Some members of the baby boom generation will have enough money to retire in comfort when they choose to. But as we will discuss, millions of other boomers will have meager retirement incomes, and many of them who hope or expect to retire will find that they have to work well beyond their mid-sixties.

It is important to understand that a sustainable system for older people involves a lot more than just money. It must provide adequate supplies of the things that money is used to buy, including the broad array of goods and services that are needed by most people of limited means. The economy now serves affluent people of all ages better than those who are less well-to-do.

A sustainable system must provide opportunities for millions of people to work at jobs that are appropriate for their interests, capabilities, and limitations. As a growing fraction of the country's adults live longer, they will have to help make the pie from which they will receive their slice.

Finally, a sustainable system must encourage people to find satisfaction and fulfillment by living more simply and within their means, limiting the amount they consume. This will be both an economic and an environmental necessity. Indeed, the consequences of this country's aging population will reinforce points that environmentalists have been making for decades.

Related Views

Many books have already discussed some aspects of what we will discuss here. Three of the best present a triangle of concerns.

- In *The Post-Corporate World,* David C. Korten explains in extensive detail how large corporations are shaping the world to serve their own ends and the ends of their stockholders as opposed to communities, society, and the environment.[1]
- In *The Emperor's Nightingale: Restoring the Integrity of the Corporation in the Age of Shareholder Activism,* Robert A.G. Monks explains how large corporations are out of control from a social standpoint and suggests that large institutional stockholders such as pension funds should bring them into line to better serve society.[2]
- In *Gray Dawn,* Peter G. Peterson explains how the populations of most developed countries are aging even faster than America's, and he discusses the social, political, and economic dislocations

that may be expected to occur throughout the developed world.[3]

These are strong books by responsible authors who have wide business experience and deep concerns for this country. They have different ideas about what should be done, but in combination they show the need to review where the country is today, where it is going, and why effective actions must be taken while there is still time to prevent disaster. The themes about corporations, investments, and aging populations that run throughout these books provide a good background for the five main messages of this book.

The Challenge

Those three books present the country with a challenge, but the challenge is even bigger. In *The Fourth Turning,* William Strauss and Neil Howe explain five hundred years of Anglo-American history as a series of cycles.[4] Each cycle includes four seasons or turnings. As the authors describe them:

- The *First Turning* is a *High,* an upbeat era of strengthening institutions and weakening individualism, when a new civic order is implanted and the old values regime decays.
- The *Second Turning* is an *Awakening,* a passionate era of spiritual upheaval, when the civic order comes under attack from a new values regime.
- The *Third Turning* is an *Unraveling,* a downcast era of strengthening individualism and weakening

institutions, when the old civic order decays and a new values regime is implanted.

- The *Fourth Turning* is a *Crisis,* a decisive era of secular upheaval, when the values regime propels the replacement of the old civic order with a new one.

The authors say that the cycles tend to be repeated roughly every eighty to one hundred years because no one lives long enough to remember and avoid the mistakes that were made during the corresponding phase of the previous cycle.

Strauss and Howe assert that, at the beginning of the twenty-first century, the United States is about to enter the Fourth Turning, or the crisis phase, of the current cycle. This cycle began as World War II came to a close, just before baby boomers started to appear. The authors predict that the next crisis phase will be similar to the crisis phases of the two previous cycles: one that included the Civil War and the other that included the Great Depression and World War II.

They predict the next crisis will start early in the twenty-first century—just when demographic trends are going to roil most developed countries, according to Peterson. Strauss and Howe don't think the next crisis can be prevented because they don't believe people can learn from the earlier crises and act to prevent it.

They may be right. But do they have to be?

What If Boomers Can't Retire? was written in the belief that if enough Americans understand what is happening and where their actions are leading them, they will be able to make the changes necessary to prevent another crisis that could include the depression that Strauss and Howe predict.

This country is exceptionally lucky as it enters the twenty-first century for three reasons:

- Rarely is it possible for people to see an impending national disaster in time to prevent it from happening. This is one of those few times.
- As the five major messages of this book show, the present situation is easy to understand.
- America has a history of responding to challenges.

Will the United States rise to this challenge as it has risen to challenges so many times before?

Highlights

Each chapter in this book includes one or more *Highlights,* brief summaries of important points made in the chapter. The Highlights form a logical chain to support the book's five major messages. The following list of chapters and their Highlights provides a summary of the book.

Chapter 1: Social Security: The Tip of the Retirement Iceberg

1. Today, there are about 35 million people over age 65. By 2030, that number is expected to double.

2. The Social Security problem is that more people are living longer and expecting to receive retirement benefits during their additional years that will have to be paid by relatively fewer workers.
3. Stocks can't solve the Social Security problem because to help pay retirement benefits, they would have to be sold to the same workers who can't continue the program as it operates today.
4. The so-called solutions that would use stocks to solve the Social Security problem would have far worse consequences and would make the program even weaker.

Chapter 2: Can Stocks Help Baby Boomers Retire?

5. The stocks-for-retirement (SFR) cycle has a front, or build-up half, and a back, or selling half. Today everybody is concentrating on the front half and ignoring the back half.
6. Demographic projections and stock-buying patterns indicate that only about half of the workers who will be contributing to Social Security will have enough income to buy retired boomers' stocks.
7. System-failure analysis shows that the stocks-for-retirement cycle probably can't work for most baby boomers because the most critical requirement of the cycle—adequate buying power—will be missing.

8. There are just two possible sources of returns from stocks—from within a company and from outside. The difference is critical.

Chapter 3: Views from Eight Other Books

9. Investment advice varies widely and is often contradictory.
10. Much investment advice for boomers is irrelevant or wrong.

Chapter 4: How Baby Boomers' Later Years Will Unfold

11. Many boomers are going to find themselves surprised when they learn they can't retire as they anticipate.
12. The effects of aging baby boomers may cascade throughout the economy.
13. The trend toward retirement self-sufficiency will force many boomers to decide how long they expect to live. That is the Impossible Decision.
14. Before the country increases its dependence on the stocks-for-retirement cycle, it should do and publicize a due-diligence, system-failure analysis that shows how the cycle can work.

Chapter 5: Stocks, Wealth, and Phantom Wealth

15. Productive investors provide money that companies use to create real returns and real wealth. Parasitic investors don't know or care who gets their money, and the returns they seek come primarily from outside the company as phantom wealth.

Chapter 6: The Drive to Create Phantom Wealth

16. Phantom returns can make a few people appear very rich—at least for a while.
17. The drive to create phantom wealth hurts people, companies, communities, and society.

Chapter 7: Why Stock Prices Don't Create Real Wealth

18. Only shares of a public corporation's stock that trade set the price, but all shares are treated as being worth the price of the last trade.
19. Stock prices result from the balance between supply and demand, but the balance is not as freely determined as market theorists say it is.

20. Stock prices aren't a realistic basis for evaluating either companies or retirement portfolios.

Chapter 8: How Phantom Wealth Hurts the Economy

21. The drive to create phantom wealth has many hidden costs.

Chapter 9: How We Can Meet Our Real Needs

22. The phantom wealth structure is based on false expectations. The way to replace the structure is to remove the expectations.

Chapter 10: What Individuals Can Do

23. Millionsof individuals can help change the course of history by looking ahead and acting in their own interests and the interests of the country.

Chapter 11: What Organizations Can Do

24. The most important steps that organizations can take are to evaluate the national stocks-for-retirement cycle and, if they find that it

is unreliable, to evaluate retirement portfolios realistically.

25. There are vast opportunities for organizations that pioneer new types of sustainable investments, investment instruments, financial institutions, and business organizations.

Chapter 12: Conclusion: How to Change a Very Big System

26. The key is to change a few critical things that will cause many other changes to ripple out and eventually to cascade.

PART I

Baby Boomers and Their Retirement Plans

Life can be delightful on a volcanic tropical island—until the volcano erupts again. The situation of millions of Americans today appears to resemble life on that island.

They are following the formula that says they will be able to enjoy years of comfortable retirement if they work hard, save enough while they are working, and use their savings to buy stocks. After all, that's the American Way.

Unfortunately, they are ignoring the volcano. And it's rumbling.

Part I of this book looks at the volcano from the standpoint of individual baby boomers and their retirement plans. As we will see, when too many people follow the same formula—that is, rely on stocks to pay for their retirement—they create problems with the formula and, in a broader sense, they create problems with the concept of retirement itself.

The discussion in Part I is on two levels. The first, of course, is the financial or technical level. The second is the conceptual level—the prevailing mindset.

People are following the formula because they have been led to believe, and they want to believe, that it is sound. Moreover, few good alternatives to the formula have been developed or made available for people to see and use.

As we will see, however, the conceptual foundations of the formula are very weak.

CHAPTER 1

Social Security: The Tip of the Retirement Iceberg

The basic idea of Social Security is simple. Started during the Great Depression, it was devised to help all Americans prepare for their later years, particularly older people who had little chance of helping themselves.

The program takes in money from workers and their employers through payroll taxes and then pays most of it out to beneficiaries. It is called a *pay-as-you-go* or *pass-through* program because most of the money that comes in goes right back out again. It is also called an *intergenerational transfer* program because, in the main, the younger, working generation transfers money to the older, retired generation.

Social Security really includes two programs, Old-Age and Survivors Insurance (OASI) and Disability Insurance (DI). OASI pays monthly benefits to retired workers, their families, and survivors of deceased workers. DI pays monthly benefits to disabled workers and their families. About 85 percent of all Social Security benefits are paid by the OASI program. In this book, we will treat the two programs as one (OASDI).

America's Aging Population and the Social Security Problem

Figure 1-1: America's Aging Adults, 2000–35
(In percent)

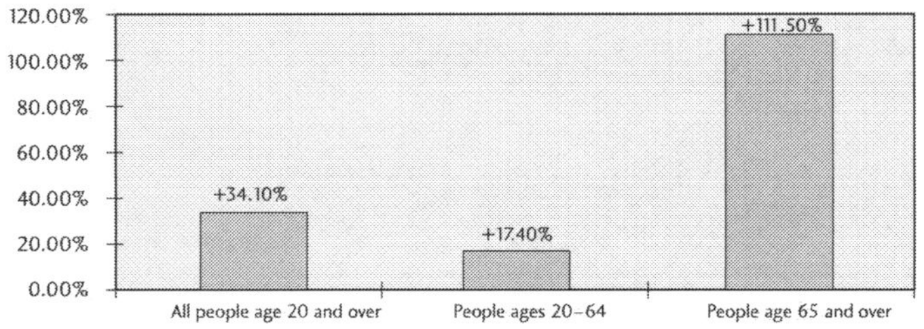

Source: U.S. Bureau of the Census, Resident Population of the United States, 1996

HIGHLIGHT 1: Today, there are about 35 million people over age 65. By 2030, that number is expected to double.

Americans today are living longer. As stated in the American Academy of Actuaries' *Public Policy Monograph No. 1,* 1998, "Financing the Retirement of Future Generations,"[1]

> When Social Security began paying benefits in 1940, only about half of 21-year-old men could expect to reach 65 to collect benefits, and those who did could expect to collect benefits for 12 years. By 1990, nearly 75 percent of them could expect to reach 65 and collect benefits for 15 years. These trends are expected to continue at least until the middle of the 21st century. At that time, an expected 83 percent of 21-year-old men will reach 65, and they can expect to live another 18 years.

Table 1-1
America's Aging Population 2000–35
(In millions)

Five-year age groups	Population as of July 1 2000	2005	2010	2015	2020	2025	2030	2035
100 and over	0.1	0.1	0.1	0.2	0.2	0.3	0.3	0.4
95 – 99	0.4	0.4	0.5	0.6	0.8	0.9	0.9	1.1
90 – 94	1.2	1.4	1.6	1.9	2.0	2.0	2.3	3.0
85 – 89	2.7	3.0	3.4	3.5	3.5	3.9	4.9	6.5
80 – 84	4.9	5.5	5.6	5.4	5.9	7.4	9.6	11.1
75 – 79	7.4	7.4	7.1	7.7	9.4	12.1	14.0	15.8
70 – 74	8.7	8.3	8.9	10.9	13.9	15.8	17.8	17.9
65 – 69	9.4	10.0	12.1	15.4	17.5	19.6	19.6	17.7
60 – 64	10.7	12.8	16.2	18.4	20.5	20.5	18.5	17.4
55 – 59	13.3	16.8	19.1	21.2	21.2	19.0	17.9	18.3
50 – 54	17.2	19.5	21.7	21.6	19.4	18.2	18.5	20.2
45 – 49	19.8	22.0	21.9	19.6	18.4	18.7	20.4	21.5
40 – 44	22.5	22.4	20.0	18.7	19.1	20.7	21.9	22.6
35 – 39	22.2	19.8	18.6	18.9	20.5	21.7	22.4	21.9
30 – 34	19.5	18.2	18.6	20.2	21.4	22.1	21.6	21.7
25 – 29	17.7	18.1	19.7	20.8	21.6	21.0	21.2	22.1
20 – 24	18.3	20.0	21.1	21.9	21.3	21.5	22.4	23.6
15 – 19	19.8	21.0	21.8	21.2	21.3	22.3	23.5	24.4
10 – 14	20.1	20.8	20.2	20.4	21.3	22.5	23.4	23.9
5 – 9	19.9	19.3	19.5	20.4	21.5	22.4	22.9	23.5
Birth to 5	19.0	19.1	20.0	21.2	22.0	22.5	23.1	23.9
All ages*	274.6	286.0	297.7	310.1	322.7	335.1	346.9	358.5
20 – 64*	161.2	169.6	176.8	181.4	183.4	183.4	184.8	189.3
65 and over*	34.7	36.2	39.4	45.6	53.2	62.0	69.4	73.4
% over 20 who are over 65	17.7	17.6	18.2	20.1	22.5	25.3	27.3	27.9

shows those born before 1946.
shows those born 1946 through 1964 (the baby boom).
shows those born 1965 through 1979 (most of Generation X).
shows those born 1980 through 1999 (the last year of Generation X).
shows projected births for 2000 and later.

*Totals may not add because of rounding.

Source: U.S. Bureau of the Census, Resident Population of the United States, 1996.

Figure 1-1, which is based on Census Bureau projections, shows how the percentage of people age 65 and over is expected to increase in relation to those ages 20 to 64.[2] This trend will have important effects on the economy, society, and the country as a whole for decades.

Table 1-1 shows the same picture in more detail. Bands of shading show five major population groups as they advance in age from the year 2000 to 2035. The group shown in the darkest band includes the baby boomers, who were born during the years 1946 through 1964.

The table is divided into three large sections for those ages 65 and older, which includes retirees; those ages 20 to 64, which includes most workers; and those under age 20, or the young. Obviously, some people's lives don't fall neatly into these groups. Many college students are in the working-age group, some people retire before they turn 65, and others work well beyond that age.

The dark band that contains the baby boomers shows how the number of people in the 65 and over age range will grow as the boomers age. The public discussion of the Social Security problem and how to fix it is a direct result of this demographic trend.

As members of the younger groups age, their numbers are projected to increase. This is due to anticipated immigration.

The summary under the body of the table shows that from the years 2000 to 2035:

- The total resident population of the country (all ages) is projected to grow from 274.6 million to

358.5 million, or by 83.9 million people (30.6 percent).

- The number of people ages 20 to 64 is projected to grow from 161.2 million to 189.3 million, or by 28.1 million people (17.4 percent).
- The older population of people ages 65 and over is projected to increase from 34.7 million to 73.4 million, or by 38.7 million people (111.5 percent).
- The combined effect of these increases in the population groups will be that the percentage of adults over age 20 who are 65 and over will rise from 17.7 percent to 27.9 percent. (See again Figure 1-1.)

Census Bureau projections are affected by changing immigration rates and mortality rates, and they will be revised by the 2000 census.

Nevertheless, the estimates of the number of people who will be 65 and over by 2035 are quite reliable because all of these people are alive today. The estimates for the people who will be born after 2000 (shown at the lower right of the figure) are more tentative.

HIGHLIGHT 2: The Social Security problem is that more people are living longer and expecting to receive retirement benefits during their additional years that will have to be paid by relatively fewer workers.

Now that we have a feel for how the population is expected to age, we can see how the aging population will affect Social Security. Today, retirees are receiving Social Security benefits from taxes that are being paid by the large number of working baby boomers, so the program seems OK. But this situation is not expected to continue.

Every year, the Social Security Administration publishes three projections of how the program may operate for the next seventy-five years. Figure 1-2 is based on the year 2000 intermediate, or most likely, projection.[3] The double bars show how the number of Social Security beneficiaries (short bars) will increase at a faster rate than the number of contributing workers (tall bars). (To clarify, it should be noted that by *workers' contributions* we are referring to the payroll taxes that workers and their employers pay.)

Figure 1-3 depicts graphically how the number of contributing workers will decline in relation to the number of beneficiaries.

Table 1-2 provides the numbers on which Figures 1-2 and 1-3 are based. The right-hand column shows that, on average, the Social Security payments to each beneficiary in the year 2000 come from the contributions of 3.4 workers. But because the number of beneficiaries is expected to increase faster than the number of contributing workers, there are expected to be only 2.1 workers per beneficiary by 2030, when the last of the baby boomers reach age 65.

Figure 1-2: Projected OASDI Contributing Workers and Beneficiaries, 2000–75
(In thousands)

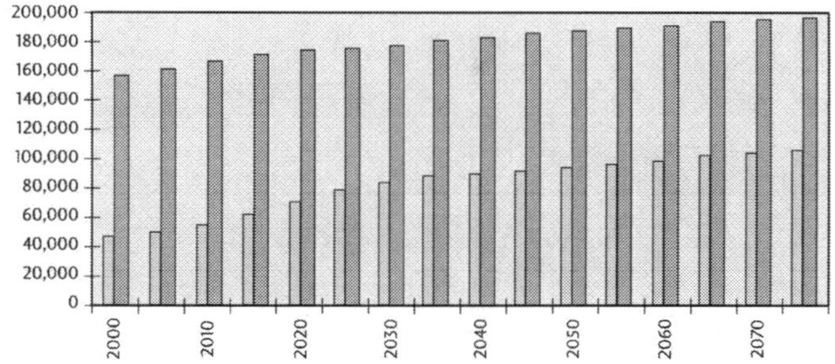

Source: Social Security Administration, Annual Report of the Board of Trustees, 2000.

Figure 1-3: Projected Contributing Workers per Beneficiary, 2000–75

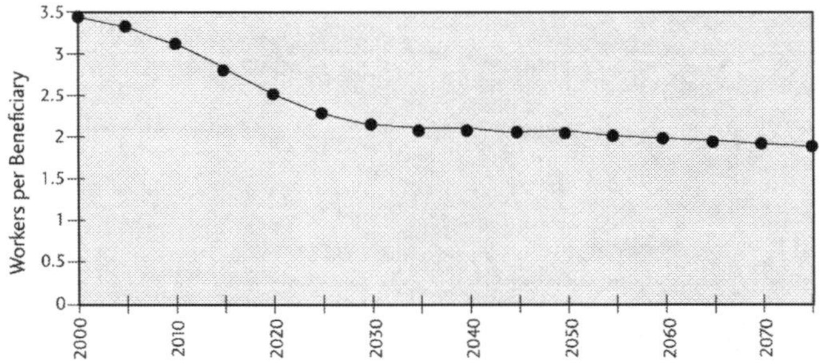

Source: Social Security Administration, Annual Report of the Board of Trustees, 2000.

Some observers have likened the baby boom generation to a pig in a python. That was the image that came to mind when schools had to be opened for the boomers and then closed once they graduated. The python analogy is not valid for Social Security, however, because boomers will affect it differently. According to the projection shown in Table 1-2, as they pass through their midsixties, between the years

2010 and 2030, the number of workers per beneficiary will decrease rapidly.

But unlike the schools that had to be closed after they graduated, the workers-to-beneficiaries ratio will not return to what it was before the boomers passed through; that is, it is not expected to go back up. This is because most younger people who are following the boomers are also expected to live long lives. As far as anybody can see, longer life spans are here to stay. Thus, for Social Security, the boomers are more like a step up to a higher plateau of operations than a passing blip on a radar screen.

Baby boomers did not cause the Social Security problem. Rather, it was caused by people living longer than they did when the program was established in the 1930s *and* expecting to spend their additional years in retirement. Indeed, the problem could even have occurred if birth rates had remained stable and there had not been a baby boom.

Table 1-2: Projected OASDI Contributing Workers and Beneficiaries, 2000–75

Year	Contributing Workers	Beneficiaries	Contributing Workers per Beneficiary
2000	153,560	44,819	3.4
2005	159,274	48,141	3.3
2010	164,900	53,322	3.1
2015	169,123	60,536	2.8
2020	171,935	68,803	2.5
2025	173,948	76,617	2.3

Year	Contributing Workers	Beneficiaries	Contributing Workers per Beneficiary
2030	176,126	82,705	2.1
2040	181,619	88,341	2.1
2050	186,120	91,780	2.0
2075	195,274	105,143	1.9

Note: Contributing workers and beneficiaries in thousands. Source: Social Security Administration, Annual Report of the Board of Trustees, 2000.

After Social Security established the idea of retiring at 65, it was used as a precedent for thousands of labor contracts and retirement plans. As people who were born during the 1930s and early 1940s started living longer because of improved health care and lifestyles, many of them retired or will retire in their mid-sixties. Boomers will defer the problem as long as they continue working, but they will make it arrive quickly if they too retire in their midsixties and expect to spend many years receiving benefits.

The Financial Aspect of the Social Security Problem

In financial terms, the problem will occur when baby boomers, who are pouring record amounts of money into the program through payroll taxes, stop contributing and start receiving benefits. Anyone who has an income from a salary or wages, has savings that earn interest, and pays living expenses can understand how the program works. In a year when there is more income than expenses, there is a surplus to add to the savings. If the expenses are greater than the income, there is a deficit and the savings go down. That's how Social Security's finances work. In this case, the accumulated savings are called *the trust fund.*

Figure 1-4 is based on the year 2000 Social Security report and provides a quick glimpse of what can happen from 2000 through 2035. The bars show the number of contributing workers per beneficiary. The curving line shows how the balance of the Social Security trust fund is expected to peak and then decline.[4]

Table 1-3 provides more detail on the financial ramifications. It shows annual projections for every fifth year. The annual surplus (deficit) column shows the Social Security problem.

The largest annual surplus is projected to occur between 2010 and 2015. By 2015, when boomers are expected to begin shifting from contributors to beneficiaries, the annual surplus will start to decline. Then, by about 2025, the outgo will start to exceed the total income, there will be an annual deficit, and the trust fund balance will start to decline.

The trust fund is projected to be fully depleted by 2037. The dates when events like the depletion are projected to occur change a little every time that Social Security updates its figures. For example, the 1999 projection indicated the trust fund would be depleted in 2034. The 2000 projection pushed depletion back to 2037. This was heralded by some as showing that the problem had become less serious.

Figure 1-4: Contributing Workers per OASDI Beneficiary and Year-End Trust Fund Balance, 2000–35

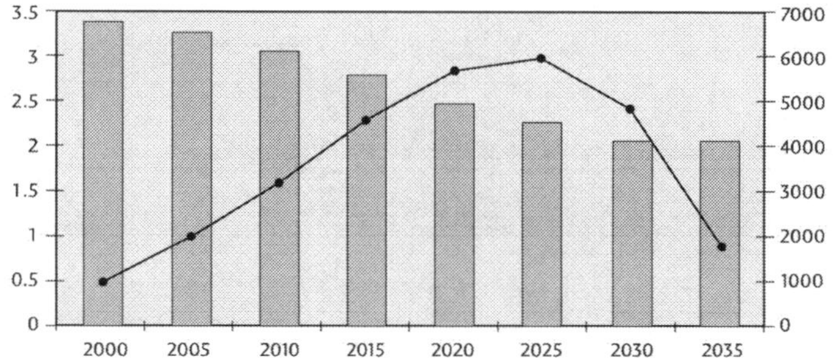

Note: Bars show contributing workers per beneficiary; line graph shows current dollars in billions.

Source: Social Security Administration, Annual Report of the Board of Trustees, 2000

Table 1-3: Social Security Financial Projections, 2000–35 (In billions of current dollars)

Year	Income Excluding Interest	Interest Income	Total Income	Outgo	Annual Surplus or (Deficit)	Year-End Trust Fund Balance
2000	500.7	64.9	565.7	410.3	155.4	1,051.5
2005	635.1	120.1	755.3	538.6	216.7	2,022.0
2010	810.3	194.0	1,004.3	737.2	267.1	3,262.9
2015	1,034.5	280.5	1,315.0	1,045.2	269.8	4,640.4
2020	1,309.9	352.2	1,662.1	1,491.5	170.6	5,738.7
2025	1,649.8	376.0	2,025.9	2,065.7	-39.8	6,007.7
2030	2,077.9	316.2	2,394.0	2,762.4	-368.4	4,866.2
2035	2,620.4	136.3	2,756.6	3,571.7	-815.1	1,726.6

Source: Social Security Administration, Annual Report of the Board of Trustees, 2000.

But the pattern is consistent. Under current law, the program is expected to take in more than it pays out until sometime in the twenties, then change and pay out more than it takes in. Regardless of *when* it happens, that change will be the most important event. The annual deficits are expected to continue through 2075, or as long as Social Security makes its projections. The projections show that the problem can't be expected to just go away.

When the program was created it was known that annual income and benefit payments could not be projected accurately, so a reserve for contingencies was set up to handle the difference. That reserve was called the trust fund. But the term has turned out to be misleading. It implies more durability than is really there. At its projected peak near 2025, the trust fund will have only enough money to pay benefits for about three years.

But despite the claims or fears of some, Social Security will not just go broke and quit. It could still limp along even if it is not changed and the trust fund balance runs out completely. Based on the year 2000 projection, in 2037 the total income would still be sufficient to cover about 72 percent of its annual payments.

As noted, nobody can predict the exact date when Social Security will shift from surplus to deficit. Each year, the program uses different assumptions for the Gross Domestic Product (GDP), inflation and interest rates, the unemployment rate, growth of the labor force, and other factors to make its projections. The data in Table 1-3 are from the intermediate, or most likely, projection made in 2000. The low cost projection made that year indicated that there wouldn't be a problem because the outgo would not exceed the income for the next seventy-five years. In contrast, the high cost projection showed that the trust funds would be fully depleted by 2025.

Social Security and the Federal Budget

The federal budget has two main parts or subbudgets—the operating budget and Social Security. Either can have an annual surplus or deficit.

Imagine for a minute that the Social Security trust fund was your own money. If you earned more than you spent, you could protect some of your savings by buying government bonds. This is what many pension plans do with some of their funds, and it is what Social Security is required by law to do with its annual surpluses.

If the operating budget has a deficit when Social Security buys bonds, the program's purchases help offset the operating deficit and so the combined budget deficit is reduced. This happened during the latter part of the twentieth century, when the operating budget had deep deficits and the trust fund was being built up, supposedly to have boomers pay for their own retirements. If the net of the two subbudgets is a surplus, then the federal budget has a surplus; this is what appeared to be the case in early 2000.

The important question is what will happen when boomers retire, the ratio of workers to beneficiaries declines, and the bonds in the trust fund must be cashed in. Table 1-3 shows that in the single year 2030—when the youngest of the boomers will start to retire—Social Security will have to cash in bonds worth $368.4 billion to get money to pay its beneficiaries (in current dollars). Where will the Treasury get the money to pay for the bonds?

There are four possible sources for this money.

- Social Security payroll taxes on workers and their employers can be increased.
- Operating programs like defense and disaster relief can be reduced to transfer money from the operating budget to Social Security.
- General taxes (other than Social Security) and user fees can be increased.
- The Treasury can sell bonds to the public.
- Now, consider how each of those sources will work.
- If Social Security payroll taxes are increased, the cost of retirement benefits will become a direct levy on workers.
- If operating programs are cut while general taxes and user fees are maintained, those who pay the taxes and fees will pay for the retirement benefits. Because most taxes and fees come directly or indirectly from those who are working, workers will

pay for the benefits that are provided to retired older people.

- Similarly, if general taxes and fees are increased to pay the retirement benefits, they will largely be paid by workers.
- Finally, if the Treasury sells bonds, the primary domestic buyers will have to be people with disposable incomes, who are, of course, once again workers. (The reason why foreign buyers may not fill the gap will be explained in the next chapter.)

All four alternatives will have the same result. In each case, workers will have to pay more to provide benefits to retirees, and Social Security will remain a pay-as-you-go, pass-through, intergenerational transfer program.

Stocks and Social Security

There have been proposals to privatize Social Security by using some or all of the money that is flowing into it to buy corporate stocks. The reasons that are offered for doing this include the following:

- Stocks have historically produced higher returns than bonds.
- The country should encourage long-term investments in its wealth-creating private sector.
- Using retirement savings to buy stocks would be a step toward severing connections between Social Security and the government's operating budget. Some see this as a desirable step toward reducing the role of government.

- Some believe that government assistance to retirees should be replaced with retirement plans that would operate entirely in the private sector.

As this book goes to press, however, there has been no adequate, publicized explanation of how any of the proposals to buy stocks could work.

Stocks provide returns in only two ways—through dividends and price increases. We will briefly examine each way here and then consider them more extensively in the next two chapters.

Dividends

Today, most companies pay small if any dividends. In 1998, Social Security paid $382.3 billion to OASDI beneficiaries. Federal Reserve Board data show that companies paid a total of $279.2 billion in dividends that year.[5] Thus, even if Social Security had owned every share in the country that paid dividends, the sum of all the dividends would have been less than three-quarters of the benefits it actually paid.

Social Security obviously could never have acquired all those stocks. So it seems that dividends can't be much help in solving the problem.

Stock Price Increases

Advocates of privatization say that stocks could help Social Security through price increases. However, there is a glitch that few of them seem to recognize or mention. If the Social Security program buys stocks, the only way it can get the money it will need to make benefit payments would be to sell the stocks.

HIGHLIGHT3: Stocks can't solve the Social Security problem because to help pay retirement benefits, they would have to be sold to the same workers who can't continue the program as it operates today.

In other words, the Social Security program's selling of stocks would raise the same basic question as its cashing in bonds to the Treasury: Who will have enough money to buy them? A possibility might be wealthy people, but most of them will already own securities and have little uninvested cash lying around. Therefore, the primary source of domestic buying power must be workers with adequate incomes. But when stocks are sold to workers to pay retirement benefits, the amounts of money that workers pay to buy them are pass-through intergenerational transfer payments.

HIGHLIGHT 4: The so-called solutions that would use stocks to solve the Social Security problem would have far worse consequences and would make the program even weaker.

The history of trying to put Social Security on a sound foundation is revealing. As John B. Shoven wrote in his paper "The Retirement Security of the Baby Boom Generation," published in the *TIAA CREF Research Dialogues:*[6]

> In 1983, Congress adopted Social Security amendments suggested by the Greenspan Com-

> mission. At the time, it was thought the changes would keep Social Security solvent until 2063, when the youngest of the baby boom survivors would be almost 100 years old.
>
> The idea behind some of the amendments was that the baby boom generation would pre-fund a portion of their own retirements. The Social Security system departed from being almost completely pay-as-you-go and adopted a plan that collected more taxes than were needed to pay contemporaneous benefits, at least during the work lives of most of the baby boomers.
>
> The initial forecasts in 1983 were that the system would accumulate a massive $20.5 trillion trust fund by roughly 2040, which would then be decumulated, finally being exhausted in 2063. Even though the system would ultimately require increased taxes or reduced benefits, 2063 was sufficiently distant that it could be legitimately claimed that the Social Security system was set for the long run.

Unfortunately, as the preceding figures and tables show, the changes made in 1983 didn't work as well as expected.

Like the 1983 revisions that failed to put Social Security on a sound financial footing, using its funds to buy stocks will not change its basic nature as a pay-as-you-go, pass-through, intergenerational transfer program. However, buying stocks will subject the funds to the vagaries of the stock market and remove the guarantee that money will be available when it is needed.

When baby boomers retire, the actions of all their retirement plans are more likely to cause stock losses than gains, as the next two chapters will explain.

What You Can Do to Raise Awareness of the Problem

Before your senators and congressional representatives allow Social Security funds to be used to buy stocks, the best thing you can do is to ask them to explain to you how stocks could solve the Social Security problem. There are five main questions to ask them.

1. Is there any way that stocks could help Social Security pay retirement benefits without the stocks being sold?
2. If the program buys stocks that must be sold, who could the primary buyers be, other than those who are still working?
3. If the primary buyers must be workers, why will Social Security not continue to be a pay-as-you-go, pass-through, intergenerational transfer program that continues to put the burden of retirement benefits on workers?
4. If the burden of paying retirement benefits would still fall on workers, what would buying stocks accomplish?

5. If workers must buy most of the retired baby boomers' stocks, to whom would the workers sell them when they retire? Why would that not be a pyramid scheme that would eventually fail?

If you ask these questions, you may be told about how in the past stocks have done so much better than other types of investments, including government bonds.

Don't accept that answer. Never before has the U.S. government attempted to make money in the stock market. As the next two chapters explain, nothing in the history of the market has ever come close to the planned waves of selling that virtually all boomers' pension plans and retirement accounts are designed to do. And as Part II of this volume explains, never before has so much of what this country considers to be wealth been dependent on stock prices.

There is no historical precedent for this situation. The only relevant answers to these questions will have to explain who will buy the stocks and where those individuals will get the money to buy them at the time when Social Security needs money to pay beneficiaries. Nothing else matters. If the primary buyers must be workers, then the Social Security problem will be worsened, because the program will have to sell its stocks at the same time that other retirement plans are selling them.

Appendix B provides a sample of a letter that asks the five questions shown here; readers may wish to send such a letter to their senators or representatives.

(Permission is granted to quote, copy, or reproduce the letter if its source, *What If Boomers Can't Retire?* by Thornton Parker, Berrett-Koehler Publishers, is identified.)

Summary

Social Security takes in money from working contributors and pays it out to retired beneficiaries. According to current projections, the number of retirees will increase in relation to the number of workers because Americans are living longer. Something will have to give:

- People who live longer will have to work longer, or
- Workers will have to pay more to provide the current level of benefits to a larger number of retirees, or
- The current level of retirement benefits will have to be reduced, or
- Additional money will have to come from sources other than workers.

Past attempts to make baby boomers pay for their own retirements will not work because their additional payments will have been used to buy securities that will have to be sold when they retire.

It doesn't matter whether the program buys government bonds, other types of securities, baseball cards, or beanie babies. The point is that its assets will have to be sold. The incomes of workers will make up the largest pool of money that can be used to buy the assets.

Social Security is just the tip of the retirement iceberg that millions of baby boomers are sailing toward. Few people understand that nearly all defined benefit pension plans, 401(k) plans, and individual retirement accounts have exactly the same flaw as Social Security does: they depend on buying stocks for gains. But the stocks will have to be sold to convert the gains to retirement incomes, and the largest potential pool of buying power for the stocks must be workers who have discretionary income.

In Chapters 2 and 3, we will get a good look at the iceberg.

The Ballad of Social Security

I wrote the following ditty to relieve an otherwise dreary discussion.

This is to tell
Of what befell
The program called Social Security,
Whose finances were found
To be too unsound
To care for us in maturity.

'Cause poor slobs
Still working at jobs
Couldn't help boomers quit and play,
Without a bigger

Social Security figure
Being deducted from their pay.

There were conservative cries
To privatize
All government programs in sight.
They wanted to let
The free mar-ket
Make all the world just right.

So Clinton began
What seemed like a plan
Discussed in the Union's State,
To dispel the gloom
Of the baby boom
With a scheme that sounded great.

The plan would buy
Stocks already priced high
Hoping prices would go even higher.
He made it seem
It would work like a dream
So the nation went on a flyer.

Brokers said, "Don't squirm
About the long term
When money's to be made right now,
And each higher price
Will do something nice
To the 500 and Dow."

So prices did rise
Near up to the skies
As billions more dollars poured in,
To Microsoft, Intel,
And the Dot-coms as well,
Helping fund managers win.

But nobody told
That the plan so bold
Had a fatal flaw.
There would be no gains
Left in the remains
When boomers needed cash to withdraw.

For stocks to pay
Income some day
They surely had to be sold.
But who would buy
Stocks priced so high?
Was something that never was told.

All went great
Till that fateful date
When selling hit the floor,
And struck with awe
Boomers tried to withdraw
Their savings and head for the door.

The prices of stocks
Fell like boxes of rocks

As boomers told their brokers to sell.
The ensuing crash
Gobbled their cash
In the Great Bear Market from Hell.

'Twas an awful sight
That October night
After the history-making crash,
When the fatal flaw
That nobody saw
Turned millions of plans into hash.

'Cause the poor slobs
Still working in jobs
Were called on to save the day.
But then we learned
After having been burned
They just didn't earn enough pay.

Then Generation X
Put a hex
On hopes they would follow like sheep,
When they decided to try
Their own plan and buy
Boomers' stocks when they were cheap.

Brokers shook in their boots
As tobacco-like suits
Were based on misrepresentation.
And lawyers were earning

Bundles by burning
The financial heads of the nation.

How better it would've
Been had we understood
The eternal lesson most plain,
To follow our hunch
That there's no free lunch
Or retiring on just stocks' gain.

This ends the tale
Of the death of a whale
Of a great American tradition,
And also of how
The stock cash cow
Was just a superstition.

CHAPTER 2

Can Stocks Help Baby Boomers Retire?

Because of the large number of baby boomers and their greater life expectancy, combined with relatively fewer younger adults, the country will soon face questions about aging that it has never faced before. For example, what will all these people do with their later years? How well will they be able to live? Where will they get enough income to live?

The Five Main Sources of Income for People Over 65

Boomers who live past age 65 will need income to survive. There are five primary sources for this income:

- Direct transfer payments from those who are still working
- Sales of assets such as stocks, bonds, and homes
- Current income from assets, such as interest, dividends, rents, and royalties
- Inheritances
- Continuing to work

There are other alternatives, such as cashing in life insurance policies or using some types of annuities or schemes like reverse mortgages, but these are actually different forms of asset sales.

In Chapter 1, we discussed why there is a limit to how much retired boomers can expect to receive as intergenerational transfers from younger people who will still be working. In this chapter we will see that nearly all retirement plans will face the same problem of intergenerational transfers that Social Security faces.

The Stocks-for-Retirement (SFR) Cycle

HIGHLIGHT 5: The stocks-for-retirement (SFR) cycle has a front, or build-up half, and a back, or selling half. Today everybody is concentrating on the front half and ignoring the back half.

Retirees need dependable flows of cash to get through their retirement years. Despite the conventional wisdom that stocks are good retirement investments, with stocks now paying minimal if any dividends the only reason to buy them for retirement accounts is for gains. But stock gains are not cash, and the only way to convert gains into cash is to sell the stocks.

For you to make money from stocks, the money must come from somewhere, and there are only two possible sources. Either it will come directly from the companies as dividends based on their past accom-

plishments or it will come from outside the companies, from whoever buys your stocks when you sell them.

It is helpful to think of securities in retirement accounts as if they were young trees. Putting your money in savings accounts, money market funds, certificates of deposit, bonds, and other securities that pay interest is like planting fruit or nut trees. You expect them to provide crops for years. The same is true for stocks that pay significant dividends—returns come directly from the company.

In contrast, buying no-and low-dividend stocks directly or through intermediaries like pension and mutual funds is like planting timber trees that will have to be harvested. They are onetime crops, and any money you get must come from whoever buys the stocks from you.

To continue with the tree analogy, the timber cycle includes the front or planting and growing half and the back or harvesting half. When it comes to stocks, those who advocate buying them for retirement accounts mention only the front half of what is actually the SFR cycle. They don't explain how the back, or harvesting half, of the cycle can work.

What's the reason for their silence? To answer, here's another analogy. When a stock-based retirement plan is reduced to its simplest terms, it is like a Mom-and-Pop store. The store buys inventory that it expects to sell at a higher price. Then Mom says, "OK, Pop, we know that you can buy. Now, who are you going to sell all this stuff to?" If Pop doesn't have a pretty good answer, he has several pretty big problems.

Promoters and managers of stock-based retirement accounts are just like Pop. They have shown how easy it is to buy lots of stuff, but they haven't offered anything like a good explanation of whom they will sell all the stuff to in the future. There does not seem to be an explanation, because no one knows who will be able to buy the stocks at the prices the baby boomers are being told they can expect to receive.

In addition to the need to provide income, there are important tax reasons why boomers' retirement accounts will sell stocks. Congress intended that all income accumulated in tax-deferred retirement accounts such as 401(k)s and IRAs will eventually be taxed as income.[1]

The tax provisions are complex, but as a general statement these accounts are not intended to be used for accumulating assets to pass on as an estate. A retired person who reaches the age of 70 1 /2 must begin taking money out of tax-deferred retirement accounts in accordance with a formula or pay stiff penalties. The formula, which is based on life expectancies, is designed to shrink a retirement account to zero during the average retiree's (or designated beneficiary's) remaining years.

I am not suggesting that all boomers will run out and dump their stocks when they retire (although some may). But I am saying that under present law, when boomers do reach 70 1/2, they will have to begin selling the stocks they have in tax-deferred retirement accounts to avoid the penalties. Unless the law is changed, it will apply to the oldest boomers by 2017 and its effects will expand each year.

The Critical Flaw in the SFR Cycle

HIGHLIGHT 6: Demographic projections and stock-buying patterns indicate that only about half of the workers who will be contributing to Social Security will have enough income to buy retired boomers' stocks.

The Social Security problem is a warning that all plans that expect to pay retirement incomes to baby boomers by transferring money from workers are likely to run into serious trouble. This includes all stock-based retirement plans such as pension funds, IRAs, 401(k) plans, and annuities, unless it can be shown that these plans do not depend on selling stocks to workers or that the workers of the day will have enough money to buy the stocks at high prices.[2]

In fact, the prospects for stock-based retirement plans are much worse than those of Social Security for two reasons. First, the amount that workers must pay through Social Security is mandated by law. In contrast, when retirees sell stocks to workers, the workers themselves will decide what, if anything, they are willing to pay for them. After it all gets sorted out over the next few decades, workers probably will end up buying most of the retired boomers' stocks. But

Table 2-1
Contributing Workers per OASDI Beneficiary and Peak Earners per Person 65 and Over, 2000–30

Year	Contributing Workers per OASDI Beneficiary	In millions: People 65 and Over	In millions: Peak Earners 40–59	Peak Earners per Person 65 and Over
2000	3.4	34.7	72.8	2.1
2005	3.3	36.2	80.7	2.2
2010	3.1	39.4	82.7	2.1
2015	2.8	45.6	81.1	1.8
2020	2.5	53.2	78.1	1.5
2025	2.2	62.0	76.6	1.2
2030	2.1	69.4	78.7	1.1

Source: Tables 1-1 and 1-2

the prices they pay may not even come close to what the boomers expect to receive.

The second reason why stock-based retirement plans will have problems relates to the number of workers who will have enough income to buy the stocks. Nearly all workers, including those with minimal incomes, are covered by Social Security, so they are included in the program's worker-to-beneficiary ratio. In contrast, most people who buy stocks do so during their twenty years of peak earnings, during the last half of their careers. Successful workers are likely to buy most of the stocks in their retirement accounts between the ages of 40 and 59.[3]

The right-hand column of Table 2-1 compares the number of peak earners to the number of people age 65 and over. It shows that by 2030, there will be only about 1.1 people in their peak earning years per person age 65 and over. That is when there are projected to be about 2.1 contributing workers per Social Security beneficiary, as shown in the left-hand column. This is the part of the stocks-for-retirement cycle that people aren't talking about. To put it bluntly, if you think Social Security has a problem now, you ain't seen nothin' yet.

System-Failure Analysis

> **HIGHLIGHT 7: System-failure analysis shows that the stocks-for-retirement cycle probably can't work for most baby boomers because the most critical requirement of the cycle—adequate buying power—will be missing.**

When advocates of stock-based retirement plans are asked to explain how stocks will be able to support retired baby boomers, they usually respond that there are too many variables to make realistic economic or financial projections. They assume that one can only use conventional economic and financial projection methods.

System-failure analysis, however, is an engineering design technique that is not overpowered by variables. Engineers begin these analyses by identifying which components of the system they are designing must work if the system is going to perform as intended. If just one critical component doesn't work, the system can't work. If any critical component cannot be proven to be reliable, the system must be considered unreliable. It is the same as saying that a chain is only as strong as its weakest link.

There is a big difference between variables and critical requirements. It is indeed hard to predict how a complex system will respond to changes in just a few variables. Even computer simulations can produce multiple if's.

But it is easy to predict with confidence why a system will fail if it lacks a critical requirement. For example, because of winds and other variables it's impossible to say exactly when a properly equipped plane will reach its destination across the ocean. But you know it can't get there if it doesn't have enough fuel to begin with. Adequate fuel is a critical requirement.

Coming back to Pop and his inventory, regardless of how many variables there are, unless he finds enough buyers for his inventory he will not be able to sell it all. Buyers are not a mere variable, they are a critical requirement, and regardless of how many variables there may be, his system can't function if it lacks this critical requirement.

Combining the demographic projections of Table 2-1 with what we have seen in this book so far tells us that during the 2020s, workers who will be in their peak earnings years cannot be expected to share enough of their incomes to provide comfortable retirements to about the same number of boomers by purchasing their stocks at inflated prices.

Thus, system-failure analysis shows the critical flaw in the stocks-for-retirement cycle that is not shown by normal stock portfolio projection methods, which are based on historical performance. It shows that the critical requirement of the cycle—adequate buying power—is missing.

Foreign Buyers

Some advocates of stock-based retirement portfolios believe or hope that as the economies of the world continue to become more integrated, it is a mistake to consider the U.S. stock market in isolation.

That is a valid point. Unfortunately, expanding our view from the U.S. market to the rest of the world doesn't make the picture any brighter. The Organization for Economic Co-operation and Development (OECD) has issued a report titled *Maintaining Prosperity in an Ageing Society.* The report was summarized in an OECD policy brief:

> In the past 25 years, the number of people of pensionable age (65 and over) in OECD countries (excluding Mexico and Turkey) rose by 45 million, but the population of working age rose by 120 million. As a result, population ageing has so far posed no major economic or social problems for our societies. This will change dramatically in the next 25 years when the number of persons of pensionable age will rise by a further 70 million, while the working-age population will rise by only five million.[4]

In *Gray Dawn,* Peter G. Peterson interprets what the OECD numbers will mean. He says,

> I believe that global aging will become the transcendent political and economic issue of the twenty-first century. I will argue that—like it or not, and there's every reason to believe we won't like it—renegotiating the established social contract in response to global aging will soon dominate and daunt the public policy agendas of all the developed countries.[5]

Niall Ferguson and Laurence Kotlikoff expanded on this point in their article "The Degeneration of EMU" in a recent edition of *Foreign Affairs.*[6] They wrote that because most European countries have extensive government-sponsored pension plans, generational accounting paints a bleak long-term picture of unsustainable spending that will either load future generations with mountains of debt or require very deep cuts in other expenditures. If the governments don't reneg on their pension commitments or make other cuts, they will not be able to meet the requirements to stay in the European Monetary Union (EMU).

These are not ideal conditions for stock prices. The stock markets of the United States and other developed countries account for about 90 percent of the capitalized value of the world's public corporations. Of course, it is possible that buyers from other countries may buy many of the boomers' stocks, but that doesn't seem to be a good basis on which to gamble with the future of the baby boomers or the country.

Retirement Investments for Income

Early in this chapter we compared buying securities for retirement accounts with planting trees. So far, we have concentrated on the one-time crop, or the timber analogy. There is, of course, the fruit-and-nut-tree option. Social Security projections show that the current program would not be able to pay more than a fraction of its obligations from the interest it receives from government bonds. Writing in *Barron's,* Donald Lee Rome asked whether the economy as a whole will be able to support many millions of retirees with interest and dividends.[7]

His question involves many variables, but even here system-failure analysis is helpful. Rough calculations indicate that if all the interest produced by the economy in 1998 ($449.3 billion)[8] were distributed evenly to the 34.7 million people who were age 65 and over in 2000, each one would get about $12,950 per year, or $1,080 per month.

To get that interest, people age 65 and over would have to receive all the federal, state, and local bond interest, all the mortgage interest, all the credit card and car payment interest, and all interest that industry pays on bonds and short-term paper. In other words, these older people would have to own all the country's underlying credit instruments, which, of course, they don't and never will.

If we add all the dividends paid by U.S. corporations ($279.2 billion)[9] to all the net interest paid in the economy and distribute the sum evenly to the same people, each would get about $21,000 a year, or $1,750 a month. In other words, they would have to own every dividend-paying share of stock in addition to all credit instruments. Clearly, they don't and won't do that either.

As this chapter is being written, the S&P 500 Index has a dividend yield of less than 1.2 percent. Yet, many retirement accounts are based on the assumption that stocks will earn 8 percent or more for years. For this to happen, the heavy lifting must come from gains, which means selling the stocks.

Before the mid-1970s, there were two classes of large companies: those that were desirable to investors because their revenues and stock prices grew, and those that were desirable because their stock prices were stable and they paid substantial dividends. Investors had a choice.

Many retirees favored the dependable dividend payers as reliable sources of income that would not have to be sold. If there was modest growth, it would be nice for their heirs.

Brokerage houses were less enamored of these stocks because they were not actively traded and did not generate much in the way of commissions. Large institutional investors avoided them because their slow growth would not enhance the performance of their portfolios.

A big—and ironic—change has been the almost total elimination of the stocks that were perfect for retirement accounts just as more people have become concerned about their retirement investments. Many of these were stocks of regulated public utilities. Until its breakup, Ma Bell's $9.00 dividend was taken by retirees as one of life's most solid foundations. But deregulation of utilities has cut power, gas, and telephone companies loose from their geographically based service areas, made their earnings much less predictable, and made their stock prices more volatile, like industrial stocks.

And something even bigger has been the result. In the past, when companies paid significant dividends, the primary return on an investment came directly from the company itself. For years, the market priced these stocks so their dividend yields were higher than government bonds because conventional wisdom held that the stocks and their dividends were less secure. If the company's business was sound and expected to grow so that it could increase its dividends, the yield could fall below the bond rate.

Today, just the opposite is true. Neither Microsoft, the U.S. company with the largest capitalized value when this was written, nor Berkshire Hathaway, the highest-priced stock on the New York Exchange, pay dividends. Not one penny of the returns from the stocks of these companies and thousands of others that pay no dividends comes from the companies themselves. Every penny of the returns comes from outside buyers of the stocks. Owners of these stocks can only convert the returns into cash by selling the stocks.

This brief discussion does not answer completely Donald Lee Rome's question about whether the country produces enough interest and dividends to support retirees. It does show that the question needs careful analysis. Rome appears to have identified a critical requirement that a national financial system must meet if millions of boomers will be able to retire in relative comfort on the real returns from their investments.

Real Returns and Phantom Returns from Stocks

HIGHLIGHT 8: There are just two possible sources of returns from stocks—from within a company and from outside. The difference is critical.

Everybody who buys stocks expects returns. But where do the returns come from? Few of today's traders or the millions of baby boomers and those in the generation that follows them—termed Generation X—who are buying stocks directly or through pension and mutual funds ever ask this simple question.

Virtually none of the thousands of investment articles, books, and advisory letters explain the answer in simple terms. With few exceptions, stock returns that come from within a company are based on what the company has earned or accomplished in the past. Usually, they are paid in real money as dividends. I will call them *real returns.*

As we have seen, if returns don't come from within a company, then they must come from outside it. Nearly all stock price gains come from outside a company, based on what buyers and sellers believe the company, the economy, and other buyers and sellers are going to do in the future. I will call these gains *phantom returns.*

Phantom returns are only numbers on paper until the securities are sold for real money.

Today, most people buy stocks for the phantom returns without ever thinking about their origin. What I am stressing here is the difference between real and phantom returns. Once you understand the difference, you can appreciate how unsound parts of the economy have become.

The Scale Effect Problem

Richard Mahoney of the Center for the Study of American Business has written that more than two-thirds of all listed stocks are held by current retirees and those saving for retirement.[10] Based on my research for this book, I estimated that nearly half of all listed stocks are in retirement accounts. Furthermore, the portion is large and growing. (For more on this, see Figure 7-2 and Table 7-2 in Chapter 7.)

Engineers who design large structures such as bridges, buildings, ships, and other systems must consider what is called the *scale effect problem.* Throughout history, there have been many cases where a formula, a material, or a design technique was used to build ever-larger structures until a scale was reached where factors that had never been considered before came into play. These factors, which were not critical to smaller structures, caused the largest ones to fail.

Examples of the scale effect abound in nature. There are maximum size limits for insects, for example, some of which can walk on water or the ceiling. If you increased the size of an insect, eventually you would hit a point where it could no longer function as an insect does.

Ancient shipbuilders learned after many failures that they could not build ships by just building ever-larger boats without changing the basic designs. This is because wood is a heavy material in relation to its strength. They found that as they increased the size of wooden timbers, the amount of weight that timbers can support decreases in relation to the weight of the timbers themselves.

Much of Henry Petroski's book *Design Paradigms* is devoted to scale effect problems in engineering.[11] He describes how bridge designs and materials that worked well at one size or scale failed when used to build much larger bridges.

The scale effect problem also showed up when designs of nuclear power systems that were originally developed to propel submarines were expanded in an attempt to produce ever-larger amounts of power. Some of the largest utility systems had to be abandoned before they were put into use because of the scale effect.

There is a scale effect problem with the stocks-for-retirement cycle, too. Those who manage and evaluate retirement accounts and who advise baby boomers to buy stocks for their personal accounts use widely accepted investment formulas. But these formulas were created for use on what economists call the *micro level* or scale. They are based on the assumption that for all practical purposes, when someone sells stocks there will always be a nearly infinite number of buyers. These formulas underlie the country's defined benefit pension plans, 401(k) plans, and IRAs.

Most of the retirement planning guides of organizations that sell stock mutual funds contain examples of these formulas. They show how $1,000—or $10,000—invested in their funds would have grown over various time periods. Then they show how this growth may continue into the future, assuming various rates. The projections are based on the logic of compound interest, and they completely ignore what may be the prevailing market conditions when the stocks will be sold.

One more or less typical example provided by a highly regarded mutual fund organization shows the stock portfolio of a person who expects to live for twenty years after retiring. The example is based on stocks growing at 9 percent per year. After the person retires, the growth of the total value of the portfolio will become slower, stop, and then reverse, as the stocks are sold. If the person lives for twenty-five years, the entire portfolio will be depleted.

The conventional formulas, like the one underlying this example, are being used so widely they have become what is, in effect, the single consolidated formula for the national SFR cycle.

At the national scale, the assumption that there will always be a nearly infinite number of stock buyers is simply wrong. Developers of the formulas never intended them to be used so widely that they would lead to a situation where over half the nation's public corporation stocks would be sold to a dwindling pool of buyers during a relatively predictable period of time in order to pay for planned consumption. Yet, that is exactly what must happen for the national SFR cycle to work.

As with most large structures whose weaknesses are hidden by the scale effect problem, the mistakes leading to the national SFR cycle have been and are being made incrementally and unintentionally. The fact remains, however, that the formulas are being used on a far greater scale than they ever were intended for, and no one has explained how the resulting system can work.

Chapter 7 will show how stock purchases for retirement accounts are inflating prices during the front half of the SFR cycle and can be expected to turn around and deflate them during the back or selling half. Conventional formulas and projection techniques ignore the effects of all other retirement plans that will be taking similar actions concurrently. Using them is like figuring out how long it will take to drive through a major city during rush hour by dividing the distance by the speed limit but ignoring the traffic, which will be the controlling factor.

Retirement Plans and Pyramid Schemes

Most pyramid schemes are illegal. The typical pyramid scheme takes in money from an ever-growing base of players that it calls "investors." It uses some of the money to pay "dividends" or "earnings" to the early players. As the base of new players expands, the number of earlier players that can be paid grows, and the scheme takes on the outward appearance of a successful venture. The scheme can continue to work until the pyramid stops adding new players to the base.

Stock-based pension plans have similar characteristics. The plans are working for retirees today for one of two reasons. Either they take in more money from workers than they pay out to retirees, or they are selling stocks from their portfolios at prices much higher than they paid for them. But the demographic projections discussed in this and the previous chapter show that they will not be able to continue to do that when the number of retirees near the top of the pyramid grows too large in relation to the number of workers at the base.

There are three big differences between stock-based retirement plans and conventional pyramid schemes. First, the former are entirely legal, and at least so far, are probably not being used intentionally to defraud investors. Second, retirement plans have long cycles, so it is not obvious that they are merely pyramids. And third, although employers that sponsor pension plans usually make commitments to pay retirees regardless of what happens to stock prices, there are no commitments to support 401(k), IRA, or similar types of plans.

In time, the true nature of retirement plans will be widely understood. It will become obvious that all retirement accounts that are intended to buy stocks and then sell them to the younger workers who will be the newer investors are essentially pyramid arrangements. Yet rather than making them illegal, the government promotes retirement pyramids.

What Else Might Happen?

Most Americans are optimists. We tend to discount warnings when we hear them. When we hear a car alarm, for example, our first reaction is that it is probably a false alarm. And we are usually right.

Similarly, when people first hear about these kinds of retirement issues, it is natural for them to think of reasons why they too may be false alarms. And they may be right. For example:

- Foreign buyers might come forward to acquire the baby boomers' stocks at prices that allow the boomers to retire.
- Younger workers might have different stock-buying patterns than boomers, which will cause them to pay more for stocks than seems likely today.
- The economy might grow enough to support both workers and retirees generously.
- The country might allow many more immigrants to enter and swell the size of the labor force.

However, the key point is that as of today there is neither assurance nor even evidence that any of these developments will occur. I believe that advocates of the stocks-for-retirement cycle should have what lawyers call the "burden of proof" to show not only how those developments *might happen* but why they can be *counted on to happen.*

As it stands now, depending on current retirement plans may be likened to taking an overseas flight on a plane that has too little fuel to make the trip unless it is helped along by unusual winds.

It is important to understand that the United States leads the world in depending on stocks to help pay for retirement. Older people in the most populous countries of the world depend on their children to support them when they can no longer work. This is one reason why populations of less-developed nations have grown so rapidly.

In Europe, most retirement plans are run by the governments and are more generous than Social Security. As already noted, Niall Ferguson and Laurence J. Kotlikoff have written that these plans, in conjunction with aging populations, threaten the European Monetary Union.

Finally, Chile has led South America in adopting a stock-based retirement program. But the program is still in the front half of its cycle. It has not run long enough to show how the back half can work when the ratio of workers to retirees reaches the stage that the United States is approaching.

So unfortunately, the United States can't look to others for advice, examples, or comfort.

Summary

People throughout the developed world are living longer. Like the United States, however, few countries are making adequate arrangements to provide for their older citizens.

Older people must have incomes to buy the goods and services they need, and there are limits to the amount of intergenerational transfer payments that workers are willing to contribute to the support of retirees.

Stocks are being widely promoted as an appealing way to build wealth to support baby boomers when they retire. But the promoters don't mention that the stocks-for-retirement cycle has a front half and a back half. Stocks produce returns primarily in the form of gains that come from the actions of markets outside the companies themselves; this is the front half of the SFR cycle. But the only way to convert stock gains into retirement incomes is to sell the stocks, which is the back half of the cycle. The primary buyers of stocks in this country are workers with discretionary income. Demographic projections show that as the baby boomers move into what are normally thought of as the retirement years, there will not be enough workers with enough income to buy the stocks of the retired boomers at the prices they will need in order to live as they anticipate. Hence, the back half will fail.

Of course, it is impossible to predict what an economy is going to do in the future. But it is easy to show what it can't do if it can't satisfy its critical requirements. The U.S. economy can't use the SFR cycle to support an increasing number of retiring boomers with stock gains unless it can satisfy the critical requirement of adequate buyers for the stocks.

So far, no one has shown how this can be done.

CHAPTER 3

Views from Eight Other Books

When most boomers first hear this book's messages, their normal reaction is to say, "Yes, but..." while they search for reasons why it must be wrong. That is a good reaction and their skepticism is healthy. Regardless of who turns out to be right in the end, an awful lot is at stake.

Some readers will be influenced by other books they have read or by information they have picked up that is in other books. To help you put it all in perspective, in this chapter I summarize and comment on several schools of thought as presented by leading academics and writers. Some of their views differ greatly from mine; some are consistent.

The Optimists

The Roaring 2000s Investor: Strategies for the Life You Want[1] is the latest of Harry S. Dent, Jr.'s three books on investing. In this one, Dent predicts that the Dow Jones Industrial Average will climb to about 41,000 by 2008. He based this prediction primarily on two types of analysis.

First, he plotted the history of the Dow on logarithmic paper to show its upward trend from 1901 through the late 1990s. Then he drew two lines, the first connecting the high points of the plot and the second connecting the low points. He extended these two parallel lines to create a channel that he believes represents the normal growth path for the Dow. (On logarithmic paper, the scale for horizontal lines grows by powers of ten. If the first line is ten, the next up is one hundred, the next one thousand, and so on.)

Dent's second analysis is based on what he calls the *consumer life cycle,* or the spending patterns of different age groups. He shows the typical spending pattern of most people as a bell-shaped curve that builds to its maximum during the 45-to-49 year range and then tapers back down.

He presents population age distribution charts for the United States and other developed countries in 1995. On each chart, he shows how long it will take for the largest cohort to reach the 45to-49 year range. He says that consumption, which drives an economy, is likely to increase until that largest cohort passes 49.

Dent's age analysis shows that the consumption peak will occur in the United States in about 2008. He predicts that consumption will then decline, and there will be a deflation that could reach depression proportions. Stock returns will decline after 2008.

Using this analysis for other countries, he explains that consumption is likely to peak between 2005 and 2020 in most developed countries. Dent's work is generally consistent with the eighty-to-one-hundred-year cycles that are the basis for *The Fourth Turning,* by Strauss and Howe, to which he refers.[2]

Dent suggests several types of investments and industries that are likely to provide the greatest returns as national economies adapt to their changing demographics.

This book is strongly upbeat for the period before 2008, and Dent gives particularly good advice about how people should think about the future in their late forties and early fifties. He says that a midlife crisis can motivate, inspire, or give people a reason to plot where they want to go and how to get there.

Also optimistic is *Retire Rich: The Baby Boomer's Guide to a Secure Future,* by Bambi Holzer.[3] Holzer advises baby boomers to anticipate how much income they will need in later life, depending on their goals. The typical range is from 75 percent to 125 percent of their current spending (not counting debt retirement and children's education expenses).

Holzer presents a series of steps for estimating how much people should save to produce that income. She provides a great deal of information about different types of employer-sponsored and individual retirement plans.

She discusses how to make a retirement fund grow through different types of investments and different types of risk, including market risk (stock prices will go down), business risk (a company may not do well), liquidity risk (you may not be able to get your money out when you want it), and interest risk (interest rate fluctuations will depress the price of long-term bonds, or interest incomes of shorter-term instruments may go down).

The book provides a wealth of information that someone who is going to manage his or her own retirement kitty should know about.

The Historians

What Works on Wall Street: A Guide to the Best-Performing Investment Strategies of All Time, by James P. O'Shaughnessy, is a best-seller.[4] This is a rich compilation and analysis of stock performance data for the 1951 to 1994 period. It includes pages and pages of tables and charts that were compiled by computer from an extensive database.

One of O'Shaughnessy's messages is that it is hard to beat the S&P 500 Index because the Index is emotion-free. He says that when you are committed to the Index, you can't get enthusiastic or depressed about particular companies, possible effects of interest rates, or other considerations and then act on an emotional basis. Emotional reactions, he points out, tend to lead to mistakes.

The last part of the book describes the results of the extensive modeling that used the database to analyze different investment styles or strategies. Based on these results, he explains why different strategies have or have not served specific investment funds well. O'Shaughnessy's conclusion is that although many popular ideas about the market are wrong, the market operates with repetitive patterns that can be understood and used to develop a winning strategy.

Jeremy J. Siegel's *Stocks for the Long Run: The Definitive Guide to Financial Market Returns and Long-Term Investment Strategies* is widely quoted by analysts and financial advisers.[5] The dustcover of the book shows the history of stocks on logarithmic paper as a continuously rising line that began in 1802.

That chart, which is repeated in Chapter 1, presents the main theme of the book. It shows that one dollar invested in stocks in 1802 would have grown to $7.47 million by the late 1990s. Siegel compares this sum with growth to $10,744 if that dollar had been invested in bonds, $3,679 in bills, and $11.17 in gold. He also compares these rates of growth with inflation, showing that in the late 1990s it would take $13.37 to buy what a dollar would have bought in 1802.

These data support Siegel's conclusion that "stocks should constitute the overwhelming proportion of all long-term financial portfolios." He provides detailed advice on how to do this, largely with mutual funds that track several of the leading stock indices.

Siegel presents a wealth of historical and analytical information about different types of investments, business cycles, stock market drops, investing techniques, and various factors that influence stock prices.

It is not entirely fair to label Siegel as just an historian. In a five-page section titled "The Coming Age Wave," he includes information similar to what we discussed in Chapters 1 and 2. We will consider that section later, in our discussion of the Realists.

The Bubblers

At the end of the twentieth century, many people believed there was a huge stock market bubble in this country that would eventually have to burst and collapse.

Edward Chancellor presents a strong case for this view in *Devil Take the Hindmost.*[6] He starts with the origins of financial speculation in the 1600s and carries it down to the collapse of the Long-Term Capital Management hedge fund that was based on the work of Nobel Prize-winning economists. He shows that although optimistic investors were vital contributors to the country's development, speculation-driven markets collapsed several times during the nineteenth and twentieth centuries. He explains how speculation undermined the Japanese economic system.

After this book was published, Chancellor published an article in the the *Wall Street Journal* titled, "When the Bubble Bursts."[7] The last sentence of that article says, "As Daniel Defoe observed after the first British stock market crash of 1696: 'Anyone might have foreseen that ... the raising of stock of all sorts to a value above the Intrinsick must have some fatal issue, and would fall somewhere at last so heavy as to be felt by the whole body of Trade.'"

Chancellor thinks this will happen again in the early 2000s. He bases this conclusion on his analysis of the history of bubbles and the prices of stocks in relation to traditional measures of stock value. He does not include the inflationary and eventual deflationary effects of retirement accounts on stock prices in this analysis.

Money, Greed, and Risk, by Charles R. Morris, is another highly readable study of financial crises.[8] It starts by illustrating the cycle of financial innovation, crisis, and consolidation in America from the early nineteenth century through the market crash of 1929.

The remainder of the book traces the operation of the same cycle in modern markets through six other crises—the S&L crisis of the 1980s, the junk bond crisis, computerized trading and the crash of 1987, derivatives, the mortgage-backed crisis of 1994, and the Mexican and East Asian currency crises. His conclusion is that similar crises are likely in the future and because of rapid communications and interconnected markets, they will probably happen even faster than before.

Morris covers some of the same ground as Chancellor, but he also discusses the role of pension plans. He believes that one of the drivers of the stock price surge of the last quarter of the twentieth century was the Employee Retirement Income Securities Act

(ERISA) of 1974, which "created government insurance for private-sector pensions and set rules for maintaining plan solvency and protecting the rights of employees and retirees." His point is that with this legislation, the government provided legitimacy and protections for the use of stocks in pension plans, thus opening a massive new demand for stocks.

Both of these authors and others like them present a strong note of caution for those who believe that stocks will help millions of boomers enjoy many years of comfortable retirement.

The Realists

The Vanguard Guide to Investing During Retirement is one of the few books that concentrate on managing investments in later life.[9] It says that this phase can be even more difficult than the accumulation phase.

Written by the Vanguard Group that provides Vanguard mutual funds, it is cautious, well balanced, and devoid of anything that could be called promotional. For example, in a section titled "Beware of Averages," it says that during the seventy-year period 1926 to 1996, common stocks returned an average of 10.7 percent. But then it goes on to say:

> It's probably safe to assume that retired investors are not worried about the "risk" that their investment returns will be *better* than the long-term averages suggest. Rather they are concerned that their investments will badly *underperform*

> compared with recent experience. In the 62 rolling 10-year periods from 1926 through 1996 (1926–35, 1927–36, and so on), common stocks provided average annual returns of 8.7% or lower in 24 of those decade-long slices. Thus, in 39% of the decades, stocks underperformed the long-term historical average by more than two percentage points annually. In 14 of the 62 periods—about one in four of the decades—the average annual return from common stocks lagged behind the long-term average by *four percentage points or more.*

This section includes a chart that shows the sixty-two periods in groups, arranged by their stock market returns. The two periods with the lowest total returns—1929 to 1938 and 1930 to 1939—produced returns of −2 percent to 0 percent. The 1939-to-1948 period that followed produced returns of 6 percent to 8 percent while 1940 to 1949 produced returns of 5 percent to 10 percent. Thus, during those twenty-year periods, the total annual returns were 5 percent or less. (Data from other sources show that dividends provided a 5.29 percent average return during those years.)

The book includes a wealth of practical, balanced information for individuals, whether they have reached the retirement stage or are just thinking about the future.

IRAs, 401(k)s, & Other Retirement Plans: Taking Your Money Out, by Twila Slesnick and John C. Suttle, is another realistic book.[10] It concentrates on tax issues related to the removal of funds from retirement accounts. It says:

> Whatever its history, 70 1/2 has become an important milestone; it's the age when most people must crack open their retirement nest eggs, even if they don't want to. Before age 59 1/2, you have to worry about penalties for tapping your retirement money too early. But once you reach 70 1/2, you are required to begin taking distributions.

The book goes on to explain that the intent of the tax laws is to have each retiree withdraw money from retirement accounts and annuities at rates that will reduce the balance to zero by the end of his or her life expectancy. A retiree can designate a beneficiary and extend the withdrawal period to cover the beneficiary's life expectancy.

This book presents two important messages. First, people with retirement accounts that they manage themselves (as opposed to pensions that are managed by employers) must be careful to abide by the rules for withdrawing money from them. Failure to take out all that should be withdrawn in a year can result in a tax penalty of 50 percent of the amount that should have been but was not withdrawn.

This is critical for those who say that they want to pass their stock holdings on to their heirs rather than sell them for income. The tax laws that favor retirement accounts are designed to ensure that the accounts will be liquidated, not passed on through estates. As the laws stand today, they guarantee that massive selling by boomers' retirement accounts will occur.

The second important message is that the laws and tax provisions are very complex. This is a critical point for those who advocate retirement self-sufficiency or believe that they will be able to manage their own retirement investments. Some will be able to do it, but many others will not.

Jeremy Siegel's brief section on "The Coming Age Wave,"[11] is the only discussion that I found in popular books that relates to the first two chapters of this book. This is how he describes the situation:

> The looming problem of the boomer population is reminiscent of an old Wall Street story. A broker recommends that his client buy a small speculative stock with good earning prospects. The investor purchases the stock, accumulating thousands of shares at ever-rising prices. Patting himself on the back, he phones his broker, instructs him to sell all his shares. His broker snaps back, "Sell? Sell to whom? You're the only one who has been buying the stock!"

Siegel says that the problem cannot be resolved by the United States or any country acting alone. The entire world must be involved in a solution that links the economies of the developed countries that have the age-wave problem with developing countries that are producing more young people and ever-more-rapid population growth. In short, Siegel says that boomers will probably have to sell their stocks to China, India, Indonesia, and Latin America.

Some Comparisons

HIGHLIGHT 9: Investment advice varies widely and is often contradictory.

This review of these eight books illustrates the wisdom of someone who said, "The problem with the future is that there are so many of them."

The Optimists don't agree on what to expect after 2008. For example, Holzer suggests that by 2026, a continuing 4 percent inflation rate will raise the price of what is now a 75 cent cup of coffee to $2.43. Dent says that inflation is largely behind us until the next long-term business cycle and that there will be a major deflation before 2026.

Holzer urges boomers to invest for the long term, meaning decades. Dent believes that 2008 is the witching year.

The Historians differ also with each other but much less than do the Optimists. O'Shaughnessy recommends analysis techniques that Siegel (wearing his historian hat) does not believe are practical for most people to use over the long run.

The Bubblers, Chancellor and Morris, agree that bubbles grow until they eventually pop. These authors offer perspective on financial history and public policy more than how-to advice for individuals and financial managers, as the others do.

The Realists (including Siegel wearing his Realist hat) are the only authors in this group to pay much attention to the second half of the stocks-for-retirement cycle, which Holzer explicitly says she does not consider. Siegel alone mentions the problem of millions of boomers having to sell stocks to pay for their retirement.

Putting It All Together

If Dent is correct and another long-cycle depression period is coming by about 2008, the *Vanguard Guide's* presentation of the two twenty-year periods that began in 1929 and 1930 may be an indication of what to expect. Neither Holzer nor the Historians (except for Siegel) suggest such a possibility and thus none tell retirees how they might handle it. Twenty years, however, is about the life expectancy of boomers after they reach age 65.

Both Chancellor and Morris caution that market crashes are likely to occur in the future. These cautions are largely ignored by Holzer, the Historians, and even the Realists (again, except for Siegel).

Dent's predictions for European economies differ widely from the predictions of Peterson and the Organization for Economic Co-operation and Development. As we saw in Chapter 2, Peterson and OECD take into consideration the adjustments that countries will have to make to meet the needs of their aging populations. Dent and O'Shaughnessy include sections on foreign investments, but they pay little attention to the effects of aging populations.

Only Chancellor discusses how the supply and demand for stocks determine their prices. Except for Siegel, none of the advice for individuals, including even that of the *Vanguard Guide,* mentions the effects of boomers shifting from buying stocks to selling them to pay for their retirements. Morris does discuss how boomers' purchases are inflating stock prices, but he does not consider the back half of the cycle.

All the books written for individuals mention risk, and Holzer does a good job of describing five different types of risk. But none of the books explicitly mentions a sixth type: systemic risk. That is when a whole financial system fails for some underlying reason.

The national stocks-for-retirement cycle (discussed in depth in Chapter 2) appears to have that type of systemic risk as a fundamental characteristic. All of the advice from the Optimists, Historians, and Realists is directed toward individuals and portfolio managers. But if too many investors follow the advice, they will invalidate it just because they all follow it.

For example, it is not clear that O'Shaughnessy's and Siegel's technical advice could be used by, let's say, the Fidelity Group, which Peter Lynch said on television may be responsible for 10 percent of the stock trades on any given day. If that volume of trading were based on taking advantage of historical patterns that were widely recognized, it could destroy the patterns. The same goes for the sum of all retirement accounts that follow the advice of the Optimists, Historians, and Realists.

All of the writers use history in their analyses, but they don't explain that history is useless for managing the baby boomers' retirement investments. This is because going as far back as 1802 no generation has ever accumulated stocks and planned to sell them during a predetermined period to a relatively smaller group of workers to pay for consumption. This is unprecedented, and history is not a guide for unprecedented events.

Still, the basic message of *Taking Your Money Out* is that all tax-favored retirement plans must be liquidated. When this is combined with the trend of large companies to allow their defined benefit plans to expire, the result is a guarantee of massive selling. Only Siegel says that the "next millennium reveals factors that are unlike anything we have witnessed for many generations."

Other observers have agreed with Siegel's suggestion that buyers in China, India, Indonesia, and Latin America will come to the boomers' aid. This idea needs more analysis than I can undertake in this volume, other than to suggest a few questions. For example:

- What is most likely to happen in each of the countries Siegel mentions? For example, when can Indonesia be expected to become a developed country socially and politically as well as economically? What can be expected to happen in China as a result of its one-child-per-couple policy? With no system to support older people other than children, the day may be coming when a working Chinese couple must support four older parents. Will these workers also buy stocks from the baby boomers?

- Let us assume that Siegel is correct and these countries do buy the boomers' stocks. Institutional investors have used their voting power to force up stock prices. What objectives might foreign owners have? Might they, for example, use their votes in U.S. companies in order to favor their domestic industries?
- If we think we have a balance of payments problem now, what can happen to the U.S. economy if there is a net transfer of ownership of U.S. corporations to other countries to pay for consumption?
- Under present law, U.S. corporations have many of the rights of citizens, including the right to lobby Congress and the de facto right to influence elections. How will foreign and national security policy be made if these "U.S. citizens" become foreign-owned?

I don't pretend to have answers to any of these questions. I raise them only to show how complex things can get and how much thinking will be needed if the solution to the national stocks-for-retirement cycle problem does involve selling stocks to other countries.

What Difference Does It Make?

HIGHLIGHT 10: Much investment advice for boomers is irrelevant or wrong.

First, to put this section in context, it is important to note that Federal Reserve data show that during the twenty-year period 1979 through 1998, the Gross Domestic Product grew by about 271 percent in current dollars, including inflation. During that period, stock prices increased by about 1,500 percent, which is consistent with the logarithmic presentations of Dent and Siegel. (This is shown in Figure 7-1 and Table 7-1 in Chapter 7.)

So do all the books that discuss stocks, their various risks, and their potential returns really make much difference for boomers and the national SFR cycle?

Not according to some experts who work with government pension plans. They say that the real problem that countries face with aging populations is much larger than just providing incomes to retirees. They explain that the two basic issues are the size of a nation's pie of real goods and services that people consume in their daily lives (the GDP) and how the pie is divided between workers and retirees.

Robert L. Brown of the University of Waterloo in Ontario made this point in a paper he prepared for the Retirement 2000 Conference, a multidisciplinary symposium sponsored by eight associations of actuaries and pension plan professionals in February 2000. His paper, titled *Impacts on Economic Security Programs on Rapidly Shifting Demographics,* says that in Canada and the United States:

> The argument is presented that social security systems, and their participants, can earn a higher rate of return if some of the social security funds are invested in the stock market or in other high-yield private sector assets rather than low-yield government bonds as is the case today. While this is an appealing argument that has wide and growing acceptance, actuaries who work regularly with the financing of social security systems are questioning its long-term validity.[12]

Brown goes on to quote two sources to support this point. The first is Francisco Bayo, a former deputy chief actuary of OASDI:

> For Social Security, you cannot accumulate assets; that is, claims from somebody else's production. If we have a large amount of money in the Social Security trust funds, we have a claim on ourselves, which does not have much meaning. The truth is, whatever is going to be consumed—be it a product that you can get a physical hold of, or services that are very difficult to hold—those products cannot be stockpiled. No matter what kind of financing we are going to have in our Social Security program, you will find that the benefits that will be obtained by the beneficiary in the year 2050 will have to be pro-

> duced by the workers in the year 2050, or just a few years earlier.[13]

Brown then quotes a stronger statement by Nicholas Barr of Britain.

> The widely held (but false) view that funded schemes are inherently "safer" than PAYGO [pay-as-you-go] is an example of the fallacy of composition. For individuals the economic function of a pension scheme is to transfer consumption over time. But (ruling out the case where current output is stored in holes in people's gardens) this is not possible for society as a whole; the consumption of pensioners as a group is produced by the next generation of workers. From an aggregate viewpoint, the economic function of pension systems is to divide total production between workers and pensioners, i.e., to reduce the consumption of workers so that sufficient output remains for pensioners. Once this point is understood, it becomes clear why PAYGO and funded schemes, which are both simply ways of dividing output between workers and pensioners, should not fare very differently in the face of demographic change.[14]

Let's reassemble all this, starting with Barr's point about a "fallacy of composition." As Irving M. Copi explains in *Introduction to LOGIC,* a fallacy of composition is "reasoning fallaciously from the properties of the parts of a whole to the properties of the whole itself. A particularly flagrant example would be to argue that since every part of a certain machine is light in weight, the machine 'as a whole' is light in weight. The error here is manifest when we consider that a very heavy machine may consist of a very large number of lightweight parts."[15]

Thus, Barr is saying is that although providing pension incomes seems like a way to help *individual* retirees buy a share of the pie of real goods and services that they will want, it is fallacious to conclude the *total amount* of the country's goods and services or the pie will increase so that *all* retirees can have more. The problem of how to divide a given-sized pie among workers and retirees will not go away.

Barr uses formal logic to make the point that I made in the previous chapter using the engineering concepts of scale effect and system-failure analysis. They are all different ways of saying that you can't just expand formulas that were developed for individuals into a single formula that applies to everybody. In the real world, things don't work that way.

What Brown, Bayo, and Barr say about pension systems applies to all retirement financing schemes that store up money claims for retirees to use to buy larger slices of the pie. This includes all pension plans, 401(k) plans, IRAs, and other forward-funding schemes. The most that these retirement plans can do is transfer money to retirees to help them consume a larger slice of the pie. Workers who create the pie will get what's left.

Retirement plans that expect to make the transfer to retirees by using stocks are based on the assumption that workers will pay inflated prices for the stocks that retirees sell so that the retirees can buy a larger slice of the pie.

When you put it that way, it doesn't seem like a formula for success.

Summary

All of this leaves us with four problems.

- There is little consistency in the advice to baby boomers about buying stocks for their retirement accounts.
- Few of the advisers mention the market conditions that will set prices when the boomers stop buying stocks and start selling them.
- In order to convert their gains into income, retired boomers will have to sell their stocks to workers. In order to buy the stocks, the workers will have to forgo their own consumption.
- Even if stocks could provide income to retired boomers, the boomers and workers would have to share the national pie that workers will create just before it is consumed.

In conclusion, on a national basis little if any of the advice offered boomers to buy stocks to help pay for their retirement can do them or the country much good. Unless boomers help increase the size of the pie that everybody is going to consume, they will get whatever slice they and the workers determine they will receive. This is not just an economic, financial, or investment issue—it is caused by real-world physical limitations.

CHAPTER 4

How Baby Boomers' Later Years Will Unfold

If the stocks-for-retirement cycle can't be made to work, millions of boomers will learn that they will not be able to retire comfortably when they reach their mid-sixties, as they had hoped. When this happens, at least two major shifts can be expected.

- Many boomers will have to make more complex decisions about their later lives than previous generations, and some boomers will have to work for more years instead of retiring.
- Stocks will lose their aura as retirement investments and the demand for them will shrink. Whether or not stock prices decline severely, less emphasis will be placed on them.

The effects of these shifts will be profound. This chapter discusses some things that could happen if the shifts come as surprises. It goes on to explain how the baby boomers and the country as a whole would benefit from preparing for the shifts in advance. The main point of this chapter is that the country does not have to just wait and see what will happen. By thinking ahead, millions of people and organizations can turn what could be a disaster into a historic opportunity.

I should make two points before discussing how the baby boomers will fare. First, there will certainly be well-to-do boomers with enough wealth to live comfortably on the income from their assets and leave substantial estates to their beneficiaries. I do not include that wealth in this discussion of retirement accounts.

By retirement accounts, I refer to financial assets that have been accumulated specifically to provide income for retirees. That includes defined benefit, defined contribution, and cash balance plans offered by employers, individual retirement accounts that must be liquidated to avoid tax penalties, and other tax-advantaged arrangements that accumulate savings primarily to provide retirement income.

The second point is that there appears to be two groups of baby boomers: those born before 1956 and those born after. Robert Brown (quoted in the previous chapter) calls the baby boomers who were born through 1955 the *Wave Surfers.*[1] According to Brown, these boomers bought houses when they were still relatively cheap, borrowed money at low rates, and joined companies where their superiors were among the small depression-era cohort. Promotions came quickly. By age 30, Surfers were earning one-third more than their fathers.[2]

The *Junior Boomers,* born after 1955, found that all the low-hanging fruit had been picked by the time they got to the orchard. They paid higher prices for houses and mortgages. In large companies, the

Surfers had all the good jobs and promotions were slow. By age 30, the Junior Boomers were earning 10 percent less than their fathers.

Still, regardless of whether they are Wave Surfers or Junior Boomers, all baby boomers are likely to find themselves in one of seven classes as they pass their mid-sixties. They may shift from one class to another if their situation changes.

The Seven Classes of Aging Baby Boomers

1. The wealthy, who will have enough assets to support themselves regardless of what happens to financial markets and the economy
2. The lucky, whose employer-furnished retirement plans will prove to be adequate
3. The surprised, who expect to retire but will find they must work when their retirement plans or assets prove to be inadequate
4. The realistic, who want to work or expect to work because they know they do not have adequate retirement plans
5. The employed, who find appropriate and accessible long-term jobs with adequate benefits
6. The unemployed, who will need appropriate and accessible jobs but will not be able to find them
7. The needy, who will be without adequate retirement plans or assets and will not be able to work even if jobs are available

It should be noted that these classes describe future conditions. This is because few boomers can know in advance what is going to happen to them.

HIGHLIGHT 11: Many boomers are going to findthemselves surprised when they learnthey can't retire as they anticipate.

The Wealthy and the Lucky boomers, who are able to stay in the first two groups, will be OK. But if the SFR cycle fails, many who followed conventional retirement planning advice that they thought would make them wealthy will wind up among the Surprised, who find that they can't retire as they anticipated. In addition, many who expected to be lucky with adequate employer-furnished retirement plans will also find themselves among the Surprised.

The Surprised class will be the most critical. Because these people will have thought they had adequate resources or retirement plans, many will not have prepared for the work they will have to do in their later years. If the explanations given in Chapters 2 and 3 are correct, this class will be very large.

The future of boomers in both the Surprised and the Realistic classes will depend on their being able find appropriate and accessible work and joining the Employed group. If they can't manage that, they will fall back among the Unemployed or Needy. Most of the people in the last two classes will need help from families, communities, or governments.

The majority of the boomers will probably spend many years in the Employed class, either because they want to or because they have to. This class will force communities, employers, and the country as a whole to face issues that are being avoided today. It is not reasonable to expect millions of people in their sixties and above to be as flexible, adaptable, and able to move to other locations as younger people.

Many older couples will eventually include a member with physical or other limitations. As these couples age, security will increasingly be their primary objective. The danger of becoming Unemployed or Needy will always be on their minds.

The Surprised and Realistic boomers are the ones who are most likely to take the country by surprise if they and the country as a whole don't prepare in advance. At minimum, they will need secure jobs that are compatible with their changing capabilities, adequate benefits with particular emphasis on health care, convenient transportation to their jobs, and living arrangements that fit their changing needs and incomes.

The more surprised and realistic boomers there turn out to be, the more the baby boom generation will crush the hopes of industries that expect to sell expensive products and services to millions of wealthy retirees. Many of these boomers will have trouble just maintaining a basic standard of living, much less living as they did when they were younger. The largest market opportunities will be for useful and desirable products and services that older people with modest means will be able to afford.

Riding Down the Escalator

HIGHLIGHT 12: The effects of aging baby boomers may cascade throughout the economy.

It would be foolish to predict that the fates of most boomers will cascade into a national or global depression, but it is important to understand how that could happen. Boomers who own stocks directly or are beneficial owners expect them to contribute to their retirement incomes. If the stocks fail to provide the expected support, the effects on the real-world economy can be large and quick. Here are just a few examples of what might happen.

If stock prices plummet, many employers, including companies and state and local governments, will find that what they thought were fully funded defined benefit retirement plans quickly become seriously underfunded. (A defined benefit plan is a commitment by an employer to pay retirement benefits in accordance with an agreed schedule. Most defined benefit plans depend on stock gains to provide much of the money they will need to pay the benefits.) These employers will have to reneg on their promises to the retired boomers unless they can find the money from other sources to honor their commitments.

State and local governments may have to borrow or raise taxes to honor their commitments. Companies will encounter higher costs and lower profits, which will bite back and depress their stock prices, which will in turn hurt retirement portfolios of individuals and other companies. Because the federal government partly underwrites many company pension plans through the Pension Benefit Guarantee Corporation, that agency's outlays could make the savings-and-loan bailout seem like a warm-up exercise.

It requires investment to create and sustain most jobs. But few employers whose sales are slowing down and retirement plans are suffering portfolio losses will be willing or able to invest in creating appropriate jobs with adequate benefits for aging boomers who will need them.

Meanwhile, boomers with smaller incomes will cut their purchases, and this will cycle back as reduced business for companies and taxes for governments.

When stock prices are high, people who own them feel wealthy and are inclined to buy things they might otherwise do without. This is called the *wealth effect.* If the SFR cycle causes stock prices to collapse, people will watch trillions of dollars that they did not understand was just phantom wealth simply vanish. This will reduce and perhaps reverse the wealth effect, causing purchases to decline. This too will cycle back as reduced sales, profits, and jobs.

Some observers believe that in the 1990s Japan was the first country to show how failing to prepare for an aging population can trigger such a cascade. Population projections show that similar phenomena can happen in Europe in the next ten years, if they have not already started. Americans should watch these developments closely.

The Retirement Self-Sufficiency Problem

HIGHLIGHT 13: The trend toward retirement self-sufficiency will force many boomers to decide how long they expect to live. That is the Impossible Decision.

In addition to the possible failure of the SFR cycle, there is another reason why many boomers may find themselves among the Surprised. An important trend today is for people to assume responsibility for their own retirement accounts. The trend is being supported by the record gains of the stock market, the decisions of many corporations to shift the risks and burdens of paying for retirements to employees, and a wave of antigovernment sentiment.

Today, many retirees who are receiving income for life from defined benefit pension plans are not worried about stretching the sale of their assets. Other retirees are doing well by selling stocks for gains because of the record growth of the stock market in recent years.

In the future, however, many boomers who expect to be among the Wealthy or even the Lucky are being painted into a corner. They are accumulating stocks through 401(k), IRAs, and other plans, which they manage themselves. When they retire, they will have to plan the sale of their stocks for income without having any idea of how long they will need to stretch those sales.

Boomers who have a significant balance in their retirement accounts will be able to buy annuities that will pay specific amounts for the rest of their lives. Insurance companies that sell these annuities fully understand that they are making very longterm commitments, so the payments they offer seem puny compared to stock market gains. There are also often high commission costs that must be paid when annuities are bought. Because of the commissions and modest returns, annuities do not appeal to many retirees today, even though they would eliminate both the Impossible Decision and the need to worry about future stock prices.

Demographers and actuaries routinely make projections of average life expectancies for large groups of people, but no person can arrange to lead an average life. Shifting retirement responsibilities from groups to individuals will force millions of boomers to make a decision that they cannot possibly make but will have serious consequences for themselves and their families. The sum of their decisions will affect their communities and the United States as a whole.

The Vanguard Guide to Investing During Retirement includes a chart that illustrates the problem presented by the Impossible Decision.[3] It shows, for example, that if a person withdraws from a portfolio at a rate of 12 percent per year, the annual return on the portfolio must be 10 percent to make the portfolio last for eighteen years. If the return drops to 6 percent, the portfolio will last for only thirteen years. It is important to keep in mind that, in the previous chapter, we saw that if the history of the 1930s and 1940s were repeated, 6 percent could be high for stocks.

Jonathan Clements wrote a *Wall Street Journal* article titled "Playing the Right Retirement Cards" that explains part of what we call the Impossible Decision.[4] Based on information from T. Rowe Price, another mutual fund company, Clements stresses the risks that historical stock price fluctuations could have on account withdrawal rates if they are repeated in the future. He quotes a company official as saying he "wouldn't adopt a strategy that had less than a 70% chance of success. That means folks who expect a 25-year retirement should probably stick with 5% withdrawal rate, while those looking at a 30-year retirement ought to opt for just 4%."

Clements goes on to say:

> For the legions of wage slaves who dream of early retirement, this isn't good news. To generate $40,000 in annual income, you would need $1 million. And that $40,000 is pretax.
>
> Moreover, a 70% chance of success means there is a 30% chance of failure. The tables were generated by T. Rowe Price as part of a new program, which—for a $500 fee—will help retirees figure out how much income their portfolios can

generate. T. Rowe Price has found that most folks want at least an 85% chance of success.

This article and the tables behind it are based on historical fluctuations in stock prices, which included many long periods of increases. But if the analysis shown in the first three chapters of this book is correct, there is an almost 100 percent probability of a long period of major stock price declines.

Making the Impossible Decision will have serious psychological effects for millions of boomers. Despite their best efforts, many will make decisions that will prove to be wrong. For those who underestimate how long they will live, the penalties include worrying about what will happen when assets run out and finding ways to survive after they do run out. The penalty for overestimating is a lower standard of living than they might have enjoyed. They will lose either way.

In addition to the Impossible Decision, the trend toward self-sufficiency will also require boomers who bought stocks for their retirement plans to predict the gains from their stocks. This is as hard to do as predicting how long you will live. Poor decisions, bad luck, or failure of the SFR cycle will swell the number of Surprised boomers whose hopes for retirement will be dashed to pieces. These people will either have to work, as they would have expected to do had they been Realistic, or join the Unemployed or the Needy, who will need help to survive.

Millions of boomers can be expected to become Needy toward the end of their lives because they will have inadequate income and will be unable to work or retire. They will not be able to care for themselves physically, manage their own affairs, or otherwise be able to cope. Today, there is little on the horizon to prevent millions of those who must be self-sufficient in managing their own retirement finances from ending their lives in despair and tragedy.

It Doesn't Have to Happen

All this doesn't have to happen. Instead of choosing to let events take their course and then picking up the pieces, America can face the situation realistically and act in time to prevent a disaster. This country's history provides examples of both kinds of choices.

> **HIGHLIGHT 14: Before the country increases its dependence on the stocks-for-retirement cycle, it should do and publicize a due-diligence, system-failure analysis that shows how the cycle can work.**

Chapter 2 explains why the SFR cycle appears to be fatally flawed and probably cannot work for most baby boomers. Chapter 3 supports this view with the "error of composition" argument. But it is one thing for a writer like me to assert that the cycle can fail and something entirely different for millions of people to reach the same conclusion. Trillions of dollars in this country are invested in the cycle, and its reliability should be evaluated by asking and answering questions like the following:

- Is it true that stock buyers with adequate purchasing power are a critical requirement for the cycle?
- If it is true, must U.S. workers be the primary buyers or can other buyers with enough purchasing power be realistically expected?
- Is it possible to show how the cycle can work for several generations so that workers and others who buy stocks from the baby boomers can have confidence that stocks will continue to grow for them?
- If the cycle can't work and if boomers can't be assured that they will receive the returns they expect, are there ways to reduce expectations without making the stock market collapse and possibly causing a depression?
- Even if the cycle doesn't fail, won't it just make workers, who produce the national pie, give a larger share of it to retired boomers?

Asking these questions should become a high-priority, national enterprise. Everybody who believes in the SFR cycle should be encouraged to explain how it can work. It is vital to develop a consensus on the cycle's reliability. If good answers cannot be found to these questions and others that follow from them, then the cycle must be treated as fatally flawed and everybody should expect it to fail.

Once it becomes widely understood that the cycle concept is fatally flawed, some people and organizations will try to find ways to prevent the cycle from failing. Others will try to minimize the damage that may occur if or when it fails. Some will look out for their own interests, and others will be concerned about helping communities or the country as a whole. *All these efforts will be important and necessary as long as they lead to solutions that do not just help some at the expense of others.*

In Part II, I discuss the growing concerns about the way large companies are affecting the country and the world. The practices of concern include ignoring and exploiting natural resources, the environment, human and minority rights, cultures, and communities.

An underlying theme for those who raise these concerns is the threat to ecological and societal sustainability. The concept of *sustainability* can be summarized as living in ways that do not reduce the opportunities of future generations to enjoy what people alive today can enjoy.

Those who will want to prevent the SFR cycle from failing, and those who will want to minimize the damage if it does, will find that they have common and overlapping interests with those who are working for sustainability. Solutions to one group's problems can be developed as solutions to the problems of other groups.

There is a very simple reason why this can happen. Since World War II, the views of market economists have dominated the thinking of most Western countries. These economists have advocated maximum competition and reliance on free markets to make as many decisions as possible. They have preached this doctrine as if it were a religion and have made many converts.

But if the failure of the SFR cycle can be predicted, or if it fails with its own Big Bang and leads to a stock market collapse, a basic tenet of the free market doctrine will obviously be wrong. Stock markets, which are among the freest markets on earth, will demonstrate that they are unable to anticipate and accommodate the country's and the world's changing demographics and ecological imperatives. The disillusionment that could result from a major stock market collapse would be comparable with the disillusionment that occurred in the former Soviet Union after the collapse of communism.

For the past twenty-five years, or since the origin of the stockholders' rights movement, America's public companies have increasingly been driven to accomplish one primary goal—increase their stock prices. Chapters 7 and 8 discuss some of the negative effects that concentrating on this goal have had on the economy and society. They explain how retirement accounts have accumulated about half of the country's listed stocks in order to create phantom wealth that is based on the rising prices.

But what if the SFR cycle is destined to fail? The primary goal of the country's most economically and politically powerful organizations will be shown to be linked to a process that is fundamentally flawed. If this is true, stock prices can't continue to be as important as they are thought to be today. As will be discussed in Part III, if stock prices are not very important, then the objectives of investing and the primary goals of companies must change in a big way.

If the SFR cycle is destined to fail, there will also be fundamental changes in what the country considers to be wealth. There will be huge opportunities for those who foresee the need to make those changes to guide the country's shift from phantom wealth to real wealth and sustainability.

So far, advocates of sustainability have had an uphill fight. With the economy seeming to be healthy, few institutional investors or companies see the need to experiment or change. Corporate executives have consistently said that stockholders would not allow them to follow policies that might be costly or reduce their stock's price.

But if it becomes clear that the SFR cycle must fail, and stock prices are seen to have little meaning for the retirement accounts that are inflating them now, the opportunities for those who develop goals that guide companies toward sustainability will be boundless. They may even help avoid a depression.

Summary

Boomers should look realistically at their prospects and plan for their most likely futures. If the SFR cycle fails, some of the saddest cases will be in the large group of Surprised boomers who did not look ahead and find themselves in difficult situations. Not all unpleasant surprises can be avoided, but it is likely that many of them can be.

Employers and insurance companies that sell annuities use projections of how long members of large groups can be expected to live to apportion retirement benefits. But the trend toward retirement self-sufficiency will require millions of individual boomers to make the Impossible Decision of how long they will need to stretch their own retirement assets. The country will become increasingly aware of the magnitude of this problem as more people encounter it.

If the stocks-for-retirement cycle fails, it will affect far more than just the baby boomers. Its effects can cascade through the entire economy and lead to a depression.

The good news is that this doesn't have to happen. The first step toward preventing the cycle from failing is to do an adequate analysis of the cycle to see if it can work. If the analysis does not show that it can work, there is still time to begin guiding investors and companies toward creating a more sustainable economy that does not rest on phantom wealth.

PART II

Phantom Wealth and Its Effects

I introduced Part I with the analogy of the baby boomers living on a volcanic island. In Part II, I will expand the analogy beyond the boomers and their retirement plans to talk about the way in which the country as a whole uses its savings.

Many writers have discussed how large U.S. companies are neglecting the interests of their employees, customers, suppliers, communities—even the planet—in order to reward their stockholders. In this part of the book, we will see how the massive amounts of retirement savings that have been accumulated by large pension and mutual funds provide the financial muscle to force companies to do as they do.

I will carry the discussion farther than most other writers by showing how today's financial processes feed on themselves in self-reinforcing loops and how they distort the economy. The processes are causing weaknesses that could lead to a serious economic collapse even if retirement savings weren't involved.

But retirement savings are not neutral; they are adding to the distortion and hastening the collapse.

This part of the book continues on both the technical or financial level and the mindset or conceptual level. It explains the fallacy of confusing phantom wealth, which is based on stock prices and expectations for the future, with real wealth, which can only be created by actual accomplishments.

CHAPTER 5

Stocks, Wealth, and Phantom Wealth

You are barraged by magazines, books, financial planners, retirement advisers, brokers, TV programs, Internet sites, and newspapers—all trying to tell you how to make money with stocks. Business schools offer courses on subjects ranging from how to start new companies and make a fortune with their stocks to how to manage multibillion-dollar stock portfolios.

As you read this and the next three chapters, however, you will learn that some important aspects of stocks are rarely mentioned. Corporations and their stocks make vital contributions to modern economies but they are mixed blessings, and they are affecting America in ways that few people understand.

Two Analytical Approaches

This chapter explains two unusual ways to look at companies and investing that can help you better understand how stocks really work. We will be concerned only with common stocks (also called equities) of companies. We will not be discussing preferred stocks, bonds, or other instruments that companies also use to raise capital.

Most of what you read or hear about stocks is written for individual investors or portfolio managers. There is an almost universal assumption that because the economy and its financial markets are so broad, nobody needs to think about the combined effects of stocks on the country as a whole. The two approaches I discuss here, however, will show you how millions of people who think they are acting independently can have profound effects on the country when they act in herds.

Productive Versus Parasitic Investing

The first approach distinguishes between productive and parasitic investing. *Productive investing* uses money to buy real-world assets like materials, tools, technologies, and employee skills that companies must have to make the products or services that they sell to earn profits. Productive investors are often actively involved in the business and usually provide more than just money. Most of the country's productive investments are made by large companies using the cash they have produced through their operations.

Parasitic investing uses money to buy financial assets like stocks or mutual fund shares with the sole purpose of making money. Parasitic investors are passive. They don't think of themselves as having any responsibilities as owners. They are rarely aware, much less involved, in the normal operation of a business other than to look out for their interests. If things do not go well, their normal reaction is to sell their stocks rather than find ways to help the company overcome its troubles.

These two types of investing have different effects on companies, investors, and the country.

Stocks by Class of Corporation

The second analytical approach looks at the effects of stocks by classes of corporations. Almost anything that can be said about companies and stocks is true for some of them. But few of the widely used generalizations are true for all of them. Throughout Part II of this book we will use five classes of corporations that are based on their size, rate of growth, and need to raise equity capital. (This book is concerned only with the corporate form of business so, for variety, we will use the terms *company* and *corporation* interchangeably.)

Productive and Parasitic Investing

HIGHLIGHT 15: Productive investors provide money that companies use to create real returns and real wealth. Parasitic investors don't know or care who gets their money, and the returns they seek come primarily from outside the company as phantom wealth.

Productive Investing

It takes money to start a company, develop a product, create a market, and operate for the early period until sales grow and the company becomes self-sustaining. A company needs large amounts of money if it enters a field such as biotech that requires extensive premarket approvals of its product. Similarly, an established company must invest each time it develops a new product or improves its business. If it does not already have the capital it needs, it must obtain money from outside sources.

Almost every worker needs tools of some sort. Money is needed to buy these tools, train workers to use them, and replace the tools when they wear out or become obsolete. In this book, the process of providing money to start new businesses, develop new products, create new markets, upgrade capacities, and provide jobs is called *productive investing.* Those who provide money for these uses are called *productive investors.*

Productive investments involve commitments of both time and risk. Once they have been made, the money cannot normally be recovered until there are sales and the investment begins to provide returns. Figure 5-1, which does not depict any particular company or investment, shows how the relationships between time and cumulative re-

Figure 5-1: Comparison of Returns from Productive vs. Parasitic Investing

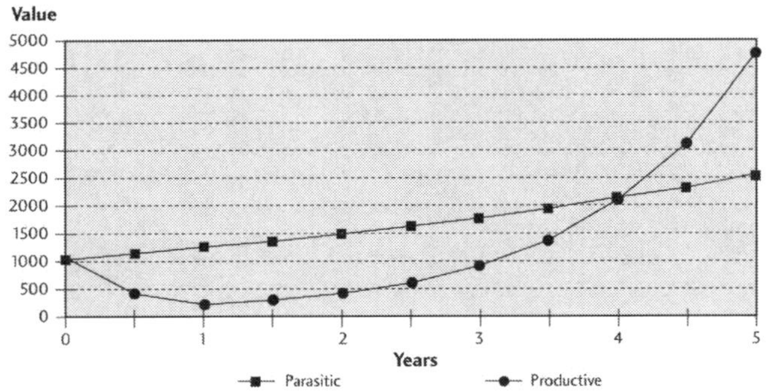

Source: Social Security Administration, Annual Report of the Board of Trustees, 2000.

turns from productive investments differ from those of parasitic investments.

The figure shows the typical "J" curve, or negative sweep, that productive investors must anticipate before they can begin to receive returns. This is a key feature of productive investments.

In this example, more than three years must lapse between the time when a productive investment of $1,000 is made and when that amount is returned. Until then, the investment loses money. The curve shows that it takes about four years for the investment to double or produce a 100 percent return. Nothing guarantees that the investment will be successful, of course, and it may be lost completely.

Productive investments can be made throughout a company's life. They are made when capital is first provided by founders or outside investors. An established company often pays for its productive investments with cash produced by the business.

Successful productive investments are required to create real wealth. They provided the tools and capabilities that the United States needed to become the world's leading economic power. Productive investments are what economists and public leaders have in mind when they urge Americans to save and invest more to make the country grow.

Parasitic Investing

Individuals and financial institutions such as pension and mutual funds do not make productive investments when they buy stocks of public companies from previous shareholders. Instead, their actions are parasitic. The following definition of *parasite* was derived from several sources:

> An organism that lives in or on another living organism and derives its nutriment partly or wholly from its host, often resulting in death or damage to the host; or someone who associates with an organization for the purpose of living at the expense of that organization without contributing anything to its well-being.

Unlike productive investors who want their money to help businesses accomplish real-world goals, parasitic investors buy stocks to make money, regardless of what happens in the real world. Figure 5-1 shows how the typical parasitic investment curve differs from the typical productive investment curve.

Parasitic investors rarely expect the value of their investment to go negative. They would see this as losing money. Instead, they expect it to start providing returns immediately and continue indefinitely. They want it to be liquid so they can withdraw their money at any time if it doesn't perform up to their expectations or if they find a better opportunity. In the view of parasitic investors, buying a stock before the curve starts up would be poor timing.

In fact, economists have received Nobel Prizes for developing modern portfolio theory, which tells financial managers to scan their holdings periodically and replace the underperforming ones with more promising candidates.

The parasitic investment curve in Figure 5-1 shows a compound annual return of 20 percent, or about what the stock market has been doing in recent years. At this rate, an initial investment of $1,000 would double in just under four years. (The productive investment "J" curve was drawn to double in the same time for comparison purposes.) Of course, some parasitic investors want larger and faster gains, such as technology and particularly Internet stocks have shown.

Anyone who wants to make an investment that can be liquidated sooner than a productive investment will allow must go the parasitic route. But parasitic investments are not possible until after productive investments have been made and have started to produce revenue. Somebody has to lead the way through the forest and break the cobwebs—but, of course, not the parasitic investors.

Productive and parasitic investing differ in the types of speculation they involve. Speculation per se is not bad, and real wealth cannot be created without product or business speculation. When a company drills for oil, develops a new product, or makes productive investments to reach any goal for which the results are not assured, it is speculating. But parasitic investors typically limit themselves to financial speculation—or betting on future stock prices. That drives up the stock prices on which phantom wealth is based.

Although the distinctions between parasitic and productive investing are important—particularly when it comes to making economic policy—the line between them can be indistinct. Still, as the judge said of another line that is hard to draw, "I know pornography from art when I see it."

Five Classes of Corporations

Corporations differ in so many ways, we can't discuss or understand their stocks without clustering them. Five classes of corporations were created for the analyses in this book. The lines of demarcation between the classes are not distinct, however. Many companies shift from one class to another and some that hope to shift up find that they are not able to do it.

Not all corporations fit into the five classes. Some that we call *little companies* eventually sell stock to the public without ever being treated as growth companies. Not all mature companies are large. There are also a few very large companies that are privately owned and whose stock does not trade. The United Parcel Service (or UPS), for example, was privately held until it sold stock to the public for the first time in 1999.

- LITTLE companies are privately owned, their stocks are not traded, and they are usually local in scope and with limited growth potential.
- YOUNG GROWTH companies aspire to grow very quickly and are financed by founders and early investors, including angels and venture capitalists, until they sell stock through an initial public offering (IPO).
- RAPID GROWTH companies have progressed beyond the IPO stage and must raise more capital from secondary stock offerings to grow faster than they can with internally generated cash.
- SUSTAINED GROWTH companies are still growing steadily, have enough internal cash flow to finance their needs, and no longer raise capital from outside.
- LARGE MATURE companies are no longer considered growth companies though they may still be growing, have more than enough internal cash flow to meet their needs, and may be buying back their own stock.

Little Companies

You may wonder why we mention little companies in a book about stocks, investors, and retirees. They are not discussed in the mass of information about stocks because the public can't buy shares in them. That, as we will see, is both a problem and a blessing.

Over half of the jobs in the country are provided by little companies, many of which are corporations. Lots of these companies have been doing what they were founded to do for years. A quick look through the Yellow Pages will show that it's full of community-based little companies that are often extensions of the crafts, trades, skills, or professions of their founders and owners.

Although the stocks of incorporated little companies are not traded on stock markets, they can be bought, sold, bequeathed, and otherwise exchanged in direct transactions. This gives the owners more latitude than they would have as individual proprietors or partners. But because the stocks are not traded, they can't be used to create phantom wealth.

All investments in little companies are intended to be productive. Managers of these companies—who are also often their owners—are not concerned with the demands of outside shareholders. But if a little company finds that it needs money to grow more than it had expected to and can make a good case for that, it can sell relatively small amounts of stock to the public.

Despite the vital contributions that little companies make to their communities and the country, they are rarely thought of when corporations are considered by investors, economists, or policy makers. Many of these companies are cash-starved, and they do not have access to the lode of personal savings that are managed by large pension and mutual funds. The little companies that are prospering do so in spite of, rather than because of, the country's "efficient" financial markets.

David L. Birch, the president of Cognetics, Inc., and former faculty member of the Massachusetts Institute of Technology and the Harvard Business School, is one of the country's leading experts on the economic contributions of little companies. In an interview with the *Wall Street Journal,* he explained that very little of the growth in the United States is due to publicly traded companies.[1] He said that even when the economy and most companies are doing very well, only about 30 percent of the companies that are growing significantly are traded on any exchange. Because the smallest companies that are growing don't have access to public investors, the reverse is also true—public investors don't have access to them. We will return to this important point in later chapters.

Young Growth Companies

This class includes high-tech start-ups and other new companies that aspire to grow rapidly. The goal of some of them is to become very large. The goal of others is to develop a business and sell it to a larger company.

During their early days when they are too young and too small to sell stock to the public, these companies usually get capital from their founders, angel investors, venture capitalists, other wealthy individuals, or larger companies. (The term *angel* was originally used to refer to the wealthy patrons who supported theater companies. It is now used for wealthy individuals with strong business experience who provide money, advice, and expertise to start-up companies. Angels often provide the first level of financing after the founders have put in their own capital.) The companies must be constantly aware, however, that they will eventually have to raise capital from outsiders to continue to grow faster than they can with retained earnings.

Often, early investors contribute more than just money. They may provide management and technical advice, access to markets or marketing savvy, introductions, and access to more capital. Frequently, these early investors take a place on the company's board of directors.

There are two reasons for selling stock to the public. One, of course, is to raise capital to finance the company's growth. The second is to create personal fortunes.

The founders and early investors of young growth companies retain large amounts of stock in return for their technologies, management contributions, ideas, energies, and cash. When the companies sell stock to the public through an IPO, the founders' and early investors' shares are automatically *marked to market,* which means they are treated as having the price that the public paid. A successful IPO and subsequent market trading are intended to create millions of dollars of personal wealth (albeit phantom wealth) for the founders and early investors of a young growth company.

Bill Gates, the president of Microsoft, is reputed to be the richest American. There is simply no way he could have become a multibillionaire in such a relatively short time without having retained roughly 20 percent of the company's shares, which increased in value as the market increased the stock price. This is not to detract from his accomplishments, but it shows the power of successful young growth companies' stocks to reward their founders. In the Washington, D.C., area where I live, self-made billionaires who are still in their thirties are constantly in the news.

Thus, stocks are vital for young growth companies. In addition to providing capital to grow, they provide incentives for entrepreneurs and investors to undertake very risky ventures. They enable exit strategies for entrepreneurs and investors who specialize in starting new companies, selling them, and moving on to new ventures. This process was pioneered in California, and it has become a national engine of economic growth.

Stocks are not an unmixed blessing for young growth companies, however, because these companies are in two races—one to establish their businesses and the other to get more capital. A mistake or bad luck in either race can lead to failure. Managing the capital side of these companies competes for time and energies that are also needed to run the business side. These conflicting demands are a negative effect of their capital structure.

The Osborne Computer Corporation is a classic example of how these conflicting demands may interact. Sales grew rapidly in the early 1980s for its pioneering portable computer, which came with extensive software, including a spreadsheet program and a word processor. The company recognized that although its first model was doing well, it needed a newer model to compete with others, such as KayPro, that were coming on the market.

Osborne developed its new model, and needing capital to produce it, held a meeting to demonstrate it to investors. The meeting went well, but news of the new model swept through the industry. Prospective customers who might have bought the original model decided to wait until they could get the new one. This left Osborne with an inventory of computers that had suddenly become obsolete and a factory that was churning out more to meet a demand that had vanished. The company never recovered from that disaster.

In addition to selling stocks through an IPO, founders and early investors may add to their personal wealth by selling the company to larger companies through mergers and buyouts. Young growth companies are significant sources of new technologies and products. Some large companies continuously search for opportunities to invest in promising technologies by buying smaller companies.

This happens almost every day. While I was revising this chapter, the *Wall Street Journal* told of two such companies on March 15, 2000. In one case, Nortel, a maker of optical switches, agreed to buy Xros for $3.25 billion worth of Nortel's stock. Xros, which had been founded in 1996, had yet to ship its first product.[2] In the second example, E.piphany agreed to buy Octane Software for $3.18 billion in stock. E.piphany had had its IPO the year before.[3]

We will refer to both of these examples in the next chapter because they illustrate the power and uses of phantom wealth.

Some IPO buyers of young growth company stocks are called *flippers* because they intend to sell their shares soon after buying them. Over the years, a tendency has been observed for the market price of a company's stock to increase rapidly after an IPO in what is called the bounce. The flippers hope to ride the bounce. Even more than the venture capitalists, the interests of the flippers are definitely short term and may conflict with those of the company's executives.

Rapid Growth Companies

These are usually companies that have gone beyond the young growth stage. They are well on their way toward proving their technologies, developing their initial products, and establishing their markets. They may or may not have reached the stage where they are earning money. From an investment standpoint, their dominant characteristics are their potential for high returns and their need for continuing infusions of capital to gain or keep up momentum.

These companies usually seek funds through one or more secondary offerings. In addition to developing their businesses, they must complete each subsequent round of financing successfully. They may fail, as Osborne did, if they do not acquire capital as they need it to expand and build their market position. Stocks of these companies are listed on local or national markets and they may or may not be widely held or traded.

[The word *secondary* can be confusing. As used in the preceding paragraph, it means public offerings of stocks for sale by the company after the first offering or IPO. The term is also widely used in the context of secondary markets, where outstanding shares are traded without any money going to the company. Most buying and selling of stocks is done through stock exchanges that are secondary markets.]

Rapid growth companies may continue the process of making their founders and early investors immensely wealthy—far beyond what young growth companies can do. By the time companies get to this stage, they usually appear to have good chances of success. These companies provide many new products and services that become available on a nationwide basis. They also provide many new types of jobs.

But rapid growth involves many risks, and few of the companies that enter this stage ever emerge as spectacularly successful. One reason is that, by this stage, they have proven that a market exists for their products or services and the market attracts competitors. This happened in the automobile industry during the 1920s and 1930s. At the end of the twentieth century, many observers expected it to happen to Internet-related companies.

Executives of rapid growth companies are heavily constrained by the need to manage their capital structure while also developing their business. Early investors may have had both philanthropic and substantive interests in helping companies grow during their younger stages, but most investors who come in during the rapid growth stage are primarily concerned with developing and managing their own investment portfolios. To them, a company is a means to an end, not the end itself. If it is not as successful as they anticipated, they often sell their stock to limit their losses rather than help the company resolve its problems.

Sustained Growth Companies

The defining feature of sustained growth companies is that although they are growing rapidly, they produce enough cash through earnings and depreciation to make the productive internal investments that they need to continue to grow. They may occasionally raise capital by selling stock, but when most companies reach this stage they are disconnected from the process of raising equity capital and access to capital is no longer a primary factor in their success.

When a company gets to this stage, its product has a significant impact on some aspect of the national economy. It is large enough for its stocks to be widely traded on national markets, so large financial institutions such as pension and mutual funds often own many of its shares.

In recent years, stocks of some sustained growth companies have created trillions of dollars in phantom wealth for individuals and the retirement plans of millions of Americans. Many executives of these companies, whose compensation is tied to stock performance, have also made substantial fortunes. Bill Gates is once again Exhibit A.

It is important to reemphasize that when personal savings are used to buy outstanding shares of sustained growth companies on secondary markets, the money does not go to the companies—it goes to previous shareholders. When these companies make productive investments internally, they use the money they have already produced from operations. Outsiders who buy their stocks are not making productive investments. There is no positive direct link between purchases of these companies' stocks and their internal productive investments.

Stocks of these companies are held by individuals and institutional investors whose goal is appreciation. As long as the stock prices grow fast enough to satisfy the large shareholders, executives have wide latitude to run their companies as they see best.

Large Mature Companies

These are America's largest companies. Many of them are growing to some degree, but they are no longer thought of as growth companies. Because they usually generate more cash from profits and depreciation than they need for internal productive investments, they may use their excess cash to increase dividends, buy other companies, or buy back their own stock.

If a sustained growth company stumbles, or its growth slows, it can quickly graduate to the large mature company class. This is not an honor. An example of this is Coca-Cola Company, which celebrated its elevation to maturity by watching its stock fall from a high of 70[3]/[8] to 47[5]/[16] in 1999.

When the graduation occurs, large shareholders force a company's executives to concentrate on increasing stock prices. These shareholders may, for example, discourage a company from making productive internal investments in new products or markets unless it can be shown that they will increase stock prices quickly. The large shareholders may also use their votes to force the replacement of board members and executives in order to promote policies that will lead to higher stock prices.

Because most of these companies are very large, they are major components of many individual and most institutional stock portfolios. They are also important components of major market indexes such as the Dow Jones Averages and the S&P 500 Index. But as with sustained growth companies, the purchase of the outstanding shares of large mature companies by individuals and financial institutions doesn't provide them with additional capital.

Summary

This chapter has explained that although all corporations issue stock, and hundreds of millions of shares are traded every market day, the effects of stocks on the issuing companies vary by class of company.

Stocks help little companies raise small amounts of capital, make productive investments, and operate. Their stocks are bought and sold through direct, person-to-person transactions rather than through exchanges. The stocks are not listed on stock markets where large financial institutions do most of their trading, and almost none of the country's lode of personal savings that are managed by those institutions ever gets to these companies.

Stocks allow a young growth company either to acquire more capital as it advances to the next stage or to be acquired, if that is what the founders want to do.

There would not be many young and rapid growth companies around if it were not for stocks. For all classes of growth companies, stocks offer a unique path to great personal wealth.

Even though many people believe otherwise, public financial markets actually perform their function of raising capital almost exclusively for rapid growth companies. The conventional idea that millions of people can help the economy by saving and buying stocks is only correct when it refers to buying the stocks offered by these companies when they raise capital.

When companies reach the sustained growth and large mature stages, they no longer need outside capital—they may not even know what to do with the capital they already have. Although the stocks of these companies are the most widely held and traded, the trading brings no capital to them, and the buyers of these stocks cannot be considered to be productive investors.

Thus, stocks play an important role in this country's economy, but the role is not nearly as simple or as direct as most people believe. In the next chapter, we will see how stocks can also have important negative effects.

CHAPTER 6

The Drive to Create Phantom Wealth

America's "efficient" equity market seems like a perpetual motion machine that just goes on cranking out wealth. Few people who benefit from it understand how the machine works, much less care about its economic, social, political, and environmental costs. But sooner or later its defects—including that much of the wealth it creates is just phantom wealth—will become obvious to everybody.

Real and Phantom Returns

First let's look at the difference between real and phantom returns.

Real Returns

A little company must sell its product or services and produce revenue before it can pass anything on to its owners. The returns that owners receive from a little company are *real returns* because they are produced by the company itself and are a reward for helping it accomplish something in the real world. Investors can receive real returns from companies of all sizes, usually in the form of dividends.

HIGHLIGHT 16: Phantom returns can make a few people appear very rich—at least for a while.

Phantom Returns

Probably the best way to show how *phantom returns* are created is to trace what happens to an imaginary young growth company that we will call Azwilbe, Inc. Its founding president invests $100,000 in the venture, and each of the three vice presidents adds $50,000. The company issues stock to the founders—10 million shares to the president and 5 million to each of the vice presidents in return for their combined $250,000. Their stock costs them a penny a share.

As the company gets under way, angel investors add $2.5 million, for which they receive 10 million shares. Their stock costs them 25 cents a share.

Early developments go well and the company is able to attract $25 million from venture capitalists, who receive 25 million shares (at $1.00 a share). At this stage, 60 million Azwilbe shares are outstanding and the four founders control 40 percent of them.

Then the company sells 10 million shares through a successful initial public offering for $10 a share and receives $100 million.

This is how things stand right after the IPO when every one of the 60 million shares held by the early investors is *marked to market,* or treated as if it were worth the market price of $10. (In the following section, Ph$ means phantom wealth dollars.)

- The president's initial $100,000 has become $100 million, including Ph$99.9 million (10 million shares × $10.00 per share).
- Each of the vice presidents' $50,000 investments is now worth $50 million, including Ph$49.95 million (5 million shares × $10).
- The angels' $2.5 million is now worth $100 million, including Ph$97.5 million (10 million shares × $10).
- The venture capitalists' $25 million has jumped to $250 million, including Ph$225 million (25 million shares × $10).
- Azwilbe, which received $27.75 million from its founders and early investors plus $100 million from the IPO is now treated like a $700 million company, including Ph$572.25 million (70 million shares × $10 per share).

Then comes the *bounce* (the price spurt that newly issued shares often enjoy shortly after an IPO). Half of the publicly owned shares (or just 5 million shares) change hands on the secondary market, and the price doubles to $20. Azwilbe is now treated like a $1.4 billion company, and the accepted value of each of the early investors' shares also doubles.

Where did the money come from to turn the $127.75 million that the company actually received into what everybody treats like $1.4 billion?

Nobody knows! Or cares!

Let's look particularly at the bounce. Assume that as the price doubled from $10 a share to $20, the average trade price was $15. By paying an average of $5 more than the IPO, those who bought the 5 million shares on the secondary market created Ph$700 million for all shareholders by adding at most $25 million to the pot. All of the $25 million went to the IPO buyers, who sold their shares for a quick profit. Azwilbe didn't get a penny of that money.

Or did it? The company's charter authorizes it to issue 200 million shares, but it has only 70 million shares outstanding. If it handles the unissued shares well, it can use each of them like a $20 bill (or whatever the market says a share is worth) to buy things that it wants or needs. The unissued shares become a kind of money that just came from the sky. (I am ignoring dilution because it doesn't seem to work for these companies as it used to.)

Azwilbe prospers and decides to expand in order to become a national (maybe even international) player. To get the capital it needs, it has several secondary offerings that put it in the rapid growth company class. The offerings are successful, and the follow-on trading carries the stock up to $100 a share. We won't do all the extensions, but the president, who put in $100,000 and held on to his shares, is now accorded all the respect due to a billionaire (10 million shares × $100 per share).

Having sold out their holdings, many of the early investors are substantially richer and have gone on to new ventures. They recycle the money that came to them as if from the sky to feed the process all over again, and the perpetual motion equity machine keeps chugging along as phantom wealth begets more phantom wealth.

After its earnings become adequate to support its continuing need for capital, Azwilbe moves to the sustained growth class. Its stock is now more widely traded, so large institutional investors acquire significant blocks of the stock, which is split four for one. Trading brings the price of the new shares to $50 (equivalent to $200 per original share), and the president picks up another Ph$1 billion.

Azwilbe, Inc. is a completely fictitious company and any similarity with a real company of that name is accidental. For every company that prospers as it did, hundreds of others either fail or peak out at lower levels of operations and market value. The numbers were made up to be easy to follow, but they are realistic enough to show how the perpetual motion equity machine works.

So, where do phantom returns come from? They come from outside of companies. Instead of being produced by what companies have actually accomplished through operations, they are created in two ways:

- *By trading that sets stock prices,* which is really betting on what a company (plus its industry, the economy, interest rates, and other stock traders) will do in the future, and

- *By marking to market,* or treating all of a company's outstanding shares as if they are worth the most recent traded price.

The perpetual motion equity machine is like a gasoline engine. The trading that sets stock prices is like the spark that the machine could not run without. But the power comes from the fuel, which is treating all of a company's shares as being worth the most recent trade price. Marking to market is the multiplier.

The president of Azwilbe retained 10 million shares for an initial $100,000 investment or a penny a share. When the company sold stock through its IPO for $10 a share, the president acquired a $100 million fortune because of the marking-to-market convention. Follow-on trading carried him up to the multibillionaire level the same way.

You might read through the Azwilbe story again and see how each time its share price went up, everybody's shares went up. This is truly the tide that lifts all boats. Both the spark and the fuel will be discussed in Chapter 8. At this point, we need only to add that unlike the double-entry books that are used to account for a company's operations, there are no offsetting entries for the gains in stock prices. Nothing goes up or down in the company's accounts or its financial statements to counterbalance the stock price gains. The phantom numbers just float out there.

Similarly, at the national level, there are no offsets or payments to match stock price gains in the statistical accounts that are used to track the economy.

But like Azwilbe's unissued stocks that became like $20 bills (and later $200 bills), the process of driving companies to produce phantom returns is like printing money. Unlike counterfeiting, however, creating money with phantom returns is legal, accepted, encouraged by the government—and widely practiced.

Let's break for an actual example. On January 10, 2000, America Online agreed to buy Time Warner by absorbing Time Warner's debts of $17 billion and exchanging 1[1]/[2] shares of AOL stock for each share of TWX. When AOL offered to issue new shares for the transaction based on its closing stock price that day, in effect it simply printed $156 billion in stock certificates to make the purchase.[1]

Note the compounding or pyramiding effect. Before the offer, the owners of TWX stock already had significant amounts of phantom wealth based on its price. AOL treated that phantom wealth as if it were real wealth when it made its offer. Thus, the offer had the effect of building phantom wealth on top of phantom wealth.

Here's another example. The cover story in the March 20, 2000 *Fortune* is titled "New Ethics or No Ethics?"[2] The cover of the magazine shows a cartoon of an entrepreneur offering a toast, "Here's to the Internet! It's made me wealthy beyond my *wildest* dreams!" A list pinned to the wall behind him reads:

To Do
Inflate revenues

Dole out friends—and—family shares
Hand-pick analysts
Dump stock

The article, by Jerry Useem, tells how the same process that was explained here for Azwilbe runs in fast forward for Internet companies that appear to be producing instantaneous riches. But time will probably show that many of the riches are phantom wealth.

When stock prices fall they make phantom wealth vanish as quickly as rising prices multiply it. Very few people have thought through how this accordion-like process, which is most dramatic with Internet stocks, is affecting the economy or the retirement investments of baby boomers now or how it will affect them in the future.

Large Parasitic Investors and Phantom Returns

HIGHLIGHT 17: The drive to create phantom wealth hurts people, companies, communities, and society.

Managing Stock Prices

When Azwilbe was founded and as it grew through the rapid growth stage, investors who provided capital directly to it expected that most of their money would be used to make productive investments. As the company progressed toward the sustained growth stage, however, its stockholders increasingly bought their shares from previous stockholders in trades that did not affect the company's cash position. Gradually but steadily, large institutional investors acquired much of its stock and they were parasitic investors.

Everybody was happy as the company grew until...

Azwilbe stumbled!

It failed to meet the profit projections of Wall Street's industry analysts. Even worse, it warned that for the next several quarters, its earnings might actually decline.

All of a sudden, Azwilbe became a large mature company and its world changed. The institutional investors began to look closely at its operations and found things they didn't like. They criticized some of its business ventures that were not growing as quickly or were not as profitable as they wanted. They pointed to R&D expenditures and overhead costs that were too high. They even got personal and insisted on replacing the chief financial officer, who was one of the original vice presidents.

The institutional investors, who had done nothing to help build the company, assumed that it existed solely to enhance their portfolios. They decided that because it had probably reached the end of its growth trajectory, they wanted it to be run in ways that would continue to increase the price of its stock even though its business was no longer growing as fast.

That meant cutting costs.

In order to keep their jobs, the president and the two remaining vice presidents were forced to rank all of the company's operations and opportunities to make productive internal investments by their effect on the stock price and lop off from the bottom. This is what happened:

- Aziz, a wholly owned subsidiary, was identified as a slow starter and sold to a competitor. This reduced competition in that industry, and because they were the "mergees," many Aziz employees were laid off.
- The R&D program was cut back, and only projects that were expected to lead quickly to new products in Azwilbe's primary lines of business were retained.
- Several divisions were downsized and layoffs were threatened if enough older employees did not retire early.
- Azwilbe outsourced some of its operations to companies with plants around the world that had lower labor costs so it could lay off domestic workers.
- It reduced its contribution to the community in which it was born but maintained its headquarters there. Then it forced the community to compete to retain it against offers of tax breaks and benefits made by other communities that tried to induce it to move.
- It even replaced its customer service people with recorded telephone-answering tree mes-

sages. ("To hear a dial tone, please press nine, followed by the pound sign.")

The squeeze was on. Everything that was not expected to increase the stock price was eliminated.

Stories about this kind of activity appear almost every day in your local paper and in financial publications. The point is that as long as a large public company grows at rates that satisfy its large parasitic investors, its executives can do pretty much as they think best. But eventually, when continued growth is no longer possible, the parasitic investors force it to shift into a costcutting mode.

The negative effects of stocks and parasitic investing are greatest for large mature companies. To illustrate the situation by deliberately overstating it, after companies have raised all the capital they need by selling stocks to the public, the stocks become like used containers. They have outlived their capital-raising purpose, but the companies can't dispose of them. For as long as the companies exist, they have to take care of the containers.

Obviously, that is not a fair explanation, but it is not entirely wrong. When a public company no longer needs to raise capital, Wall Street shifts from serving the company to serving those who trade the outstanding shares like commodities. The company is then forced to shift from obtaining capital to influencing the price at which its shares trade. That is a different game.

Today, large amounts of baby boomers' retirement savings are flowing into stocks through intermediaries such as pension funds and mutual funds. There are thousands of these intermediaries, including more mutual funds than stocks listed on the New York Stock Exchange. But a small number of the largest pension fund and mutual fund firms have enough power to force companies to concentrate on their stock prices over all other considerations.

Much of the downsizing, outsourcing, cost cutting, laying off of employees, limiting employees' benefits, avoiding long-term investments needed for environmental sustainability, and reducing corporate citizenship for their communities is due to shareholder demands that large mature companies increase their stock prices.

The fate of most sustained growth companies is to become large mature companies. It may take years or even decades, but it eventually happens. It too is part of the economy's perpetual motion equity machine that runs on phantom returns.

A magazine article about Ben & Jerry's, the ice cream maker, provides a classic example of the Wall Street view and how parasitic investors think. The company has been widely praised for its dedication to community service. Paul Hawken used the company as an example of corporate citizenship in *The Ecology of Commerce*[3] and, as Joseph Abe wrote in *Business Ecology,*[4] Ralph Estes (author of *Tyranny of the Bottom Line)* helped the company develop its multistakeholder accounting system.

With that as background, here is an excerpt from Matthew M. Stichnoth's article "Just Deserts: An Acquirer Could Unfreeze Ben & Jerry's Value for Neglected Shareholders," which appeared in *Bloomberg Personal Finance* in March 2000.[5]

> If Wall Street handed out citations for reckless indifference to shareholders, Ben & Jerry's Homemade, Inc. (BJICA) of South Burlington, Vermont, would get a ticket every quarter. On the one hand, the company has a terrific niche in the ice cream business, turning out ultrarich, ultra-delicious products with names like "Phish Food." On the other, it spends wads of cash on social causes that don't help shareholders much. The result: returns you wouldn't wish on your worst enemy. So despite its big consumer following, the stock's a perennial oinker.
>
> Things are looking up for investors, though, thanks to unsolicited buyout interest the company has received from three (count 'em, three) potential suitors. And while a deal is far from certain, the potential for costcutting at Ben & Jerry's is so vast that a buyer might be willing to pay a lot more for the company than the market realizes.
>
> Fully 7.5% of the company's pretax earnings, for instance, go to the Ben & Jerry's Foundation, which funds "grassroots social

> change organizations" mainly in the Vermont area. Last year's contribution came to nearly $800,000 or 12 cents per share, pretax. That, according to Jeff Kanter of Prudential Securities, shaved 3 percentage points off return on equity (ROE)—a measure of how profitably management deploys shareholders' investment in the company, derived by dividing shareholders' equity into net income.
>
> The company also supports family farmers in Vermont by paying them above-market rates for milk and butterfat, key raw materials for making ice-cream. It may be a noble gesture, but it squeezes gross profit (net sales minus cost of goods sold) by 20 percent.
>
> This kind of behavior is a big-time fiduciary no-no. *The coldhearted fact is that the first, last, and only job of management of a public company is to maximize the value for shareholders.* [Emphasis added]

Subsequently, Ben & Jerry's was bought by the Dutch conglomerate Unilever in a friendly acquisition. Unilever has promised to continue the company's commitments to all of its stakeholders. The magazine article is quoted here because it shows how parasitic investors, who are concerned only with making money for stockholders, press companies to concentrate on their stock prices.

Some companies are profitable enough to follow enlightened policies and keep their stockholders content. But once they get into a tight profit situation, their stockholders' tolerance for those policies can vanish quickly.

EVA, MVA, and the Cost-of-Equity Paradox

EVA (for Economic Value Added) and MVA (for Market Value Added) are the smoking guns of parasitic investing.

In the past, companies traditionally paid to use other people's money through interest and dividends. These payments were seen as borrowing costs and equity costs to the company. Phantom returns have changed the traditional idea of equity costs.

Most people with training in economics believe that rising stock prices reduce the cost of obtaining equity for companies. Few of them understand that this benefit is almost entirely restricted to rapid growth companies and smaller companies that aspire to join that select group. The paradox is that rising stock prices actually increase what is now treated as the equity costs of sustained growth and large mature companies.

It works this way. Sustained growth and large mature companies typically produce significant amounts of cash from profits and depreciation, which they must somehow use. The consulting firm Stern Stewart and *Fortune* magazine are recommending a concept that they call Economic Value Added. According to this idea, public companies should set their hurdle rates (the rates of return that companies use to analyze their investment opportunities) high enough so that each operation or investment will increase the companies' share prices.[6] In other words, every investment that a company makes with the money it already has is expected to earn enough to increase profits and the stock price.

Any investment that a company made in the past that is not earning enough to increase the stock price should be eliminated. Hence downsizing.

EVA turns the future stock price growth that shareholders have come to expect into a requirement that each of a company's internal investments must meet. That requirement is then built into the decision criteria that the company uses to evaluate its existing businesses and to reinvest cash that is being produced by operations.

Because of EVA, the cost of equity of sustained growth and large mature companies is being increased by past and expected future stock appreciation. This is just the reverse of what many economists and business school professors believe and teach.

The resulting high hurdle rates permit only internal investments that offer the highest returns or most rapid paybacks. Shareholders' expectations of future stock appreciation are thus being treated like the capital cost for using money that the company already has. This is not what conventional economics teaches.

The concept of value added was developed by the Japanese after World War II. They were a vanquished people with a devastated homeland, few natural resources, little fuel, and almost no friends. The only thing they were rich in was poor people. By all conventional measures, they were an economic basket case with no choice other than to take whatever place competitive world markets determined for them.

They decided that to accept that fate would be like losing the war all over again. So they took a lesson from the history of the British Empire and developed a new theory that would guide their emergence as the world's second largest economy. Their theory was to import as little material and fuel as possible, use knowledge such as technology and workforce skills to add value, and make products that they could sell to the rest of the world for high prices. Everything that could be retained in Japan was part of the value added. This included employee pay and benefits, profits, interest, and taxes. Value added was a national concept. Japan's present troubles notwithstanding, the concept worked so well that it became a model for developing countries and even for improving U.S. manufacturing processes.

EVA is a corruption of the original value-added concept. It treats all returns from a corporation as if they were the rightful property of the stockholders—not the whole country (or as some put it, all the stakeholders). It is a formula for sucking as much wealth as possible out of anyone who becomes involved with a corporation, including employees, suppliers, customers, communities, and even the country.

The formula is consistent with the definition of parasitic practice.

According to *Fortune* and Stern Stewart, the reason for using the EVA concept is to build Market Value Added, or MVA. Regardless of how it is described, MVA really just means inflated stock prices. Each year, *Fortune* publishes a list of the country's leading corporations ranked by their MVA, which is the amount that their capitalized value (their stock price multiplied by the number of shares outstanding) exceeds their invested capital. (In our Azwilbe, Inc. example, when the $127.75 million that investors put into the company grew to $700 million after the IPO, its MVA was Ph$572.25 million.) According to this measure, the primary purpose of a corporation is to inflate its stock price.

EVA has many effects, as a few examples will illustrate. The ranking of businesses by profitability has made the country's largest companies organize their components as profit centers and get rid of the less profitable ones. This has turned what were formerly strong integrated producers that were largely self-sufficient into highly specialized producers. It has forced large mature companies to reduce their practice of using cash generated by mature divisions to subsidize the long-term development costs of new divisions.

Another effect of EVA has been to make large companies buy things and services that they formerly provided for themselves from suppliers. The suppliers' lower prices are usually attributed to their greater efficiency or productivity. When this is so, the results may be good business for both the large companies and the suppliers.

Often, however, the suppliers are little and young growth companies that, along with their employees, are forced to subsidize a large company's customers and stockholders by earning less from their work and their capital than the large mature company requires of its own operations. When this happens, part of the cost of increasing stock prices is paid by smaller companies and their employees. The two-tiered earnings and profitability structure that results is fine from the standpoint of institutional investors who don't own stocks of the smaller companies.

Large mature companies that cannot find enough ways to invest their cash internally at high hurdle rates are forced to buy back their own stock or to buy other companies. Much of the merger and acquisitions business is being driven by large mature companies spinning off divisions and combining with other companies to reduce costs of what then become redundant operations. For example, when banks merge, they usually reduce their combined costs and their competition by closing and consolidating adjacent branches.

This process may have to run to completion before its effects will be fully understood. There are reasons to fear that turning large mature companies into overspecialized instruments for increasing stock prices will leave them vulnerable to long-term competition and business cycle fluctuations, but that is conjecture.

It is clear, however, that EVA and all other types of investment analysis that are based on discounting or the logic of compound interest make the time horizon of a company a function of the interest or hurdle rate that the company uses. The higher the hurdle rate, the faster an investment must double in value. This is particularly significant for a large mature company with large amounts of cash. Unless its management is unusually astute or lucky, its hurdle rate will not let it invest in creating new businesses to replace its present lines as they become obsolete. This leaves the company the choice of either buying other established businesses or retiring capital through stock buybacks. Many large mature companies are doing both. In announcing its decision to lay off fourteen thousand employees, Exxon Mobil's chairman, Lee Raymond, said that through its acquisition of Mobil, the company "hadn't solved its primary problem: a lack of high-yielding investments for its considerable cash flow."[7]

According to Stern Stewart, EVA works. Their September 22, 1999, advertisement in *Fortune* was headlined, "What's an Extra 51% of Total Return to Your Shareholders? For Our EVA Clients, It's Worth $79,608,525,070."[8] The body of the ad goes on to say: "From health care to car parts, a new stock market survey shows that those companies using Stern Stewart EVA programs for financial management and incentive compensation are beating their 10 closest competitors by 8.6 percentage points each year—or 51 percentage points of extra total return over five years."

But the use of MVA and inflated stock prices may be a misleading way to evaluate companies. During most of the 1970s and 1980s, IBM was *the* stock that all large portfolios had to have. In 1988, it ranked first in Stern Stewart's ranking of one thousand companies by MVA. But then the company stumbled, and by 1992 it ranked one-thousandth.[9] In other words, it dropped from the top of the list to the bottom in four years. This might suggest that the stock of IBM was way overpriced in 1988, and the company's place on the list, which was based on phantom wealth, was meaningless. But the drop wasn't really justified, because in terms of total sales, IBM ended 1999 among the top ten on the *Fortune* 500 list.

Free market advocates argue that the discipline imposed by measures such as EVA and MVA is part of the normal healthy process of capitalism. They say that the downsizing of companies releases capital to be reinvested in other companies that can make better use of it.

To some degree that is true. But when companies buy back their own stock, the capital that they release to the former shareholders is only recycled if the sellers then provide it to companies that need it rather than use it for parasitic buying of other outstanding stocks. This means that to keep the investment process healthy among today's financial institutions, most of the capital that is released by large mature companies must go to rapid growth companies when they sell stock. In aggregate, however, Federal Reserve Board data show that U.S. companies have been retiring more stock than they were issuing for more than twenty years.

Summary

Companies create real worth by producing things or services that they sell at a profit. Real returns that investors receive from companies are normally in the form of dividends.

Phantom wealth is created by treating all shares of a company's stock as if they were worth the most recent market price. It is created most dramatically by companies that progress through the young, rapid, and sustained growth stages.

If these companies are successful, the phantom wealth creation process allows their founders and executives to create personal fortunes very rapidly. The process also provides very low-cost equity capital to these companies, particularly when they use unissued shares of their stock to compensate their executives and employees or to buy assets and other businesses.

But as sustained growth companies approach the end of their growth cycle and become large mature companies, the institutional investors that own many of their shares want the stock prices to keep on growing. When this happens, companies are faced with what are treated as much higher capital costs. The main ways that companies can respond are by reducing their operating costs and by investing only in activities that will produce high returns.

Company managers use the concepts of Earned Value Added and Market Value Added to allocate the capital at their disposal in ways that will increase their stock prices the most. These concepts, which are based on phantom wealth creation, actually increase what companies treat as their cost of capital.

The shift in the cost of equity capital from being very low to being very high as companies mature is not recognized by many economists. Its effects will be considered in the next two chapters.

CHAPTER 7

Why Stock Prices Don't CreateReal Wealth

Figure 7-1: Growth of Gross Domestic Product, Corporate Profits and Value of All Stocks 1978–98

(In percent increase)

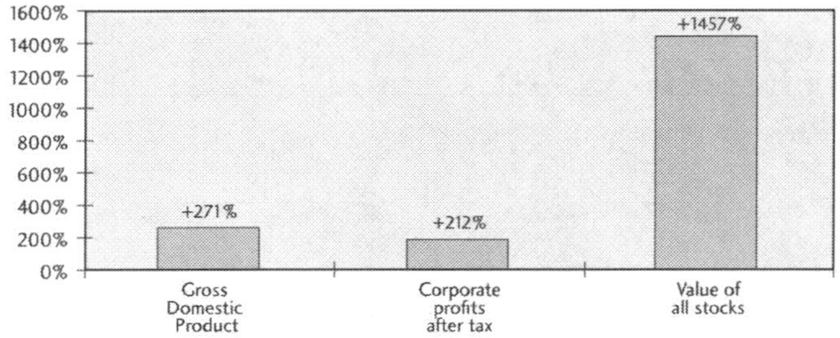

Source: Federal Reserve, Flow of Funds Accounts.

With everybody paying so much attention to stock prices, we need to understand how they are set and what they really mean. In this chapter we will look at some forces that influence prices and why they don't deserve nearly the prominence they receive for measuring the wealth of individuals, retirement portfolios, and the economy. Stock prices are like props that hold up a set for a Western movie. Knock out a few critical ones and the whole streetfront will collapse, saloon and all.

Obviously, what is said in this chapter conflicts with much conventional financial theory and nearly all of the widely available advice on how to make money with stocks. It is a bit more detailed than other chapters in this volume, but details are often the price you must pay for understanding. Figure 7-1 sets the stage for the discussion.

Figure 7-1 is based on Table 7-1, which makes two main points.

- The upper section of the table shows that during the twenty years through 1998, the GDP grew by 271 percent, corporate profits grew by 212 percent, and the capitalized value of all the stocks in the country grew by 1,457 percent.
- The lower section shows that during the same period, corporations actually reduced their outstanding shares by $381 billion, so the increase in their capitalized value due to market action was $14,827.8 billion, or a hair under 1,500 percent.

Table 7-1: Indications of Phantom Wealth, 1978–98 (In billions of current dollars)

	1978	1998	Change	
Gross Domestic Product	2,291.4	8,510.6	6,219.2	271%
Corporate profits after tax	154.6	483.1	328.5	212%
Value of all stocks (Dec. 31)	991.2	15,437.7	14,446.5	1457%
Value of all stocks (Dec. 31, 1978)	991.2			
Net stock issues (retirements)	(381.3)			
Increase due to market action	14,827.8			
Value of all stocks (Dec. 31, 1998)	15,437.7			
Increase due to market action	1496%			

Source: Federal Reserve, Flow of Funds Accounts.

Where did the $14.8 trillion increase in twenty years come from? How reliable are the processes that produced it? How *real* is it? Because the increase is based entirely on stock prices, we need to discuss some of the factors that helped set those prices.

One way of looking at the increase is to examine the price/earnings ratio, or p/e ratio, which compares a stock's price with its earnings. If a stock price is $75 and it earns $5, its p/e ratio is 15. The same measure can be applied to indices that measure the price level of the whole market. At the end of 1978, the value of all stocks divided by their earnings indicated a p/e ratio of 6.4. At the end of 1998, the p/e ratio was almost 32. How did the stock market drive the p/e ratio up five times?

HIGHLIGHT 18: Only shares of a public corporation's stock thattrade set the price, but all shares are treated asbeing worth the price of the last trade.

That highlighted sentence is deceptively simple and a bit repetitive of what we have already discussed. But it is so fundamental to everything in this chapter that it's worth repeating. In this discussion, "stock" refers to all outstanding shares of a company's common stock, and sometimes even unissued shares.

Capitalized Value

Conventional practice treats all of a company's shares as being worth the price of the last trade; that is, they are marked to market. When all of a company's outstanding shares are marked to market, the result is a measure of a company's size that is termed its *capitalized value, market valuation, market capitalization,* or *market cap.*

Similarly, the value of a stock portfolio is normally considered to be the sum of all the shares it contains multiplied by their respective market prices. And the sum of the capitalized value of all companies in the country (shown as $15.4 trillion in Table 7-1) is treated as a measure of the country's wealth and productive might.

Strong logic, good data, simple arithmetic, but bad conclusions.

Recall the tale of Azwilbe, Inc., recounted in Chapter 6. Although its sales were minimal and it was not yet earning money at the time of its IPO, it had a promising product and a good story. The IPO made its founders wealthy (on paper) overnight when the shares that had cost them a penny were treated as worth the $10 IPO price. At the same time, the company's capitalized value jumped to more than five times the amount that all investors, including the IPO buyers, had paid into it.

Many of the IPO buyers were "flippers" who sold their shares quickly and profitably, receiving up to twice what they had paid. These trades doubled the wealth of the original owners and the capitalized value of the company without contributing a single dollar to it. The IPO buyers who kept their shares instead of selling them also enjoyed watching them double in value.

In this more or less typical case, the difference between what was actually invested in the company and its capitalized value was based entirely on the hopes and speculation of a relatively small number of outside traders about what would happen to the stock price—not on what the company had accomplished through its operations or retained as earnings. If Azwilbe were an Internet company, the flippers may not have known or cared what the company did. The returns to stockholders were entirely phantom.

The spread between Azwilbe's capitalized value and its contribution to the GDP was too great to mean anything. Because nobody knew whether it would succeed or fail, little significance should have been inferred from its capitalized value for the portfolios that held the stock or for the country.

Instead, Azwilbe's capitalized value was treated as part of the nation's store of capital. As time went on, any of its shares that were in pension and mutual fund portfolios were valued at the most recent market price. Back on the farm, that would have been called counting chickens before they've hatched.

It is a mistake to overgeneralize, but it appears that companies whose businesses are related to the Internet can be used as medical researchers use little creatures with short life spans to accelerate the effects of treatments they are testing. For example, as I was revising this chapter, Greg Schneider wrote an article titled "A New Economy Nightmare" in the *Washington Post.*[1] The article told about Value America, a merchandising company that sells products on-line with no inventory. They send customer orders to manufacturers for direct shipment.

In 1997, the company had a total revenue of $134,000. In 1998, that jumped to $41.5 million, but its losses were $53.6 million. Nevertheless, the company sold stock for $23 a share during its IPO in April 1999. On the first day of trading, it rose to $55 a share. Value America's market capitalization reached more than $3 billion. For a time, its founder, Craig Winn, was a billionaire because he retained 35 percent of the outstanding stock. (Does this sound like Azwilbe?)

The tale continues. Unfortunately, during the first nine months of 1999, the company lost $129.8 million. Then, during the peak Christmas ordering season, it couldn't deliver as promised all the merchandise it sold. On December 29, Glenda Dourchak, the new chief executive, told the company's six hundred employees that nearly half of them would be out of a job by the end of the day.

Value America's tale shows how meaningless its $3 billion market capitalization was. When the stock price had dropped to four dollars and change, the market cap had shrunk more than 90 percent. About Ph$2.75 billion had just vanished.

Value America is not alone. Another article in the *Washington Post* about the so-called e-retailers showed that between December 31, 1999 and March 3, 2000, Etoys lost 45 percent, Cybershop.com lost

42 percent, Beyond.com lost 33 percent, Amazon.com lost 18 percent, Ashford.com lost 16 percent, and Value America lost 14 percent of their market capitalizations.[2]

The Azwilbe tale helps explain why Silicon Valley and hightech industries thrive. They are the result of vast amounts of new knowledge and an investment process that offers huge rewards to entrepreneurs and investors who can create a believable picture of a bright future.

All smoke and mirrors? Of course not.

Could it work without smoke and mirrors? Of course not.

Does the process create durable wealth? Look at the e-retailers.

The corporation is intended to be a particularly effective type of business organization, so in the aggregate corporations should be expected to grow faster than the economy. Their stockholders should expect to do better than investors in less effective types of organizations. That said, however, Figure 7-1 and Table 7-1 show that between 1978 and 1998 stockholders enjoyed much larger returns than could be justified by corporate earnings or the economy as measured by the GDP. Thus, it's important to look at the way stock prices are set that create the returns.

Nearly all trading is done in the listed stocks of rapid growth, sustained growth, and large mature companies. Trades are constantly changing stock prices, which are the most current and accurate numbers available about any aspect of the economy.

A typical trade transfers a tiny fraction of a company's stock from one shareholder to another. It neither provides cash to the company nor changes the value of the company's assets. It just changes paper ownership and sets the stock's most recent trade price. Period.

The country's stocks are increasingly owned by large financial institutions that are solely concerned with portfolio growth. Except for index funds, portfolio theory dictates that fund managers must continuously evaluate their portfolios, buy stocks with the best prospects for growth, influence lagging corporations to increase their stock prices, and sell those that don't respond. The high volume of trades caused by this process, along with trading by individuals and computer-driven programmed trading, sets stock prices.

Managers of the largest funds would insist that the previous paragraph overgeneralizes. For example, Dale Hanson, the former head of the California Public Employees Retirement System, said that because CALPERS is so big, it has to be a long-term owner of the stocks of the country's largest companies just because the companies exist. The largest funds can't just buy and sell their holdings with reckless abandon without affecting stock prices.

His explanation is valid up to a point, but it doesn't change the fact that the large blocks of shares that lie dormant in their portfolios without being traded have little effect on prices in the short run, whereas large funds' short-term trades, often with other shares of the same company's stock, do help set prices.

Even the efficient markets of Wall Street—to which all things are supposedly known—don't always accept the conventional idea of capitalized value.

Jerry Knight discussed this subject in his article "What Michael Saylor Is *Really* Worth" in the *Washington Business* section of the *Washington Post.*[3] One example he gave was Palm, Inc., which sold 6 percent of its stock through an IPO after it was spun off by 3Com Corp. By the end of the first day of trading, the number of public shares of Palm, Inc. multiplied by the market price indicated that the public shares were worth $53 billion.

According to the logic of capitalized value, Palm, Inc. should have been an $883 billion company and the remaining 94 percent should have been worth $830 billion. But the market capitalization of 3Com Corp., the owner of the remaining shares, was only $28 billion. Something happened to the phantom!

Supply and Demand

HIGHLIGHT 19: Stock prices result from the balance between supply and demand, but the balance is not as freely determined as market theorists say it is.

Many books and articles use techniques such as value analysis, technical analysis, price momentum, interest rate projections, industry and economic forecasts, and other approaches to explain stock prices, but there is little discussion of the supply of and the demand for stocks. In *Devil Take the Hindmost,* however, Edward Chancellor says that as long as three hundred years ago it was obvious to the Scottish investor John Law that stock prices are simply the result of the supply of stocks offered for sale in relation to the demand for them.[4]

Thus it is important to examine why stocks are traded by looking at supply and demand. Let's consider the buying side first. The total demand for stocks can be divided into *synthetic* demand, *systemic* demand, and *true* demand.

Synthetic Demand

Most trades occur when a buyer expects a stock to do better than the seller expects it to. (The exceptions are when an investor has cash that must be used to buy stocks, a seller needs cash, or a seller wants to use the money for a different investment.) Because of commissions and other transaction costs, buyers pay more than sellers actually receive. For this reason, the market has a natural stability that resists trading when potential buyers don't expect a stock to do better than the potential sellers expect by more than the transaction costs.

For example, if both the buyer and the seller must pay a dime to trade a share, the buyer must expect the stock to do more than twenty cents better than the seller expects it to. If transaction costs are reduced to a penny for the buyer and the seller, the buyer need only expect the stock to do two cents better than the seller does. Lower transaction costs have reduced the market's natural resistance to trading in recent years, and the volume of trading has increased accordingly.

Despite lower transaction costs, the market still has a natural resistance to trading because, in aggregate, few buyers should have reason to believe that their expectations will be consistently more correct than sellers' expectations. Of those who have similar objectives, half of them will turn out to be wrong just as half the people who call coin tosses lose. Potential buyers of an outstanding (read "used") stock must think they know more about its prospects than the current owners who want to sell—which, as with used cars, is often questionable.

Members of the financial services industry create synthetic demand when they provide advice on which stocks to buy. They may be in the business of selling advice, or they may want to receive the transaction fees or even increase the market price. The industry prospers when it can overcome the market's natural stability by creating a bias in favor of trading that increases prices.

Another example from the *Washington Post* shows how artificial demand can be created. Fred Barbash writes about an experiment he did using the *Gilder Technology Report* market advisory service.[5] From time to time, this report, which is distributed monthly on-line and then by mail, adds a new stock to its list of ones to buy. At 11:00A.M. on February 17, 2000, when the on-line version of the advisory was published, Barbash found that its Web site was jammed and he couldn't get in for several minutes. When he did get in, he learned that Xcelera.com (XLA) had just been added to the list. It had closed the previous day at $129 a share on a trading volume of 79,900 shares.

Barbash immediately used a second computer to order one hundred shares at the market price through his on-line broker. But by then, the jam had moved to the American Stock Ex-change, which had temporarily halted XLA trading because there were so many orders. When trading resumed and Barbash's order was executed, he paid $200 a share at 11:57A.M. It closed the day at $190 on a volume of 928,300 shares. On February 18, it closed at $240 and on February 19, at $325. (Barbash, who insists that he did this only as a matter of reportorial curiosity, sold his shares at $240.)

This is synthetic demand in action and it goes on all the time.

Because advice to sell can hurt a stock's price, perhaps lead to litigation, and certainly hurt an analyst's standing with a company, there is relatively little advice to sell stocks. Most advice is on the buy side of the trades.

Systemic Demand

Unlike synthetic demand, which tends to increase stock prices, systemic demand can reinforce price movements up or down. An example of systemic demand is the self-reinforcing loop of a stock that is included in an index like the S&P 500. Today, the flow of savings into pension and mutual funds that are tied to an index maintains a demand for those particular stocks that has nothing to do with the underlying value of the companies themselves. They are being bought, often for retirement portfolios, just because they are in the index. If, however, a continuing outflow of savings were to begin, the self-reinforcement would reverse and reduce systemic demand for these stocks.

Momentum investing is another example of systemic demand. This technique creates demands for stocks just because they are rising. It is based on the theory that there is always a greater fool to whom inflated stocks can be sold at an even higher price. If enough fools don't show up some day, however, the momentum can stop and prices can drop because they are no longer expected to rise.

True Demand

True demand is caused by the sum of desires to buy stocks as investments. The best examples are the managers of pension and mutual fund portfolios who often find themselves trapped. Each day, bags of money are dumped on their desks and they have to do something with it. They are expected to make it grow and can lose their jobs if they don't. It doesn't matter how they may feel about the current market, if they manage stock funds, they have to buy stocks. Theirs is true demand.

Most theoretical explanations of how stock prices are set concentrate on the underlying value of stocks or on technical characteristics of price movements and trading volume. In a way, however, those analyses are like jumping contests in an elevator when the most important question is whether the elevator is going up or down. Today, retirement savings are like the morning rush of office workers who want the elevators to go up. Like those who work on the upper floors, pension and mutual funds have no alternative but to take an elevator by using much of the influx to buy stocks. This contributes to the true demand for stocks.

Cascading Demands

Often, more than one type of demand can interact to affect a particular stock or the market as a whole. The initial demand for the XLA that Barbash had fun with was obviously synthetic. But it is highly likely that after the price started to move up, some of the demand was systemic due to momentum investing by traders who did not know of the *Gilder Technology Report* recommendation.

As Chapter 2 suggested, in the long run the true demand for stocks by retirement accounts may turn out to be a form of long-term momentum investing. If people who are saving for retirement eventually decide that stock growth is not a safe bet, the process can reverse. As this was being written, however, synthetic, systemic, and true demand all tended to foster price increases. In addition, nearly everybody who has any connection with stocks wants prices to increase. Never before has there been such a strong confluence of all types of demand for America's stocks.

The Supply of Stocks

Trading requires a supply of stocks offered for sale as well as a demand for them. Other than the few financial services that advise which stocks to sell and the weeding operations of portfolios, there aren't many examples of what could be called synthetic supply, so we will only consider *true* supply and *systemic* supply.

True Supply

There haven't been many additions to the total number of shares outstanding for years. When young and rapid growth companies stage their IPOs, the total supply of stocks increases. Secondary offerings of larger companies also increase the true supply.

Figure 7-2: Shifting Stock Ownership, Year-End Holdings, 1968–98

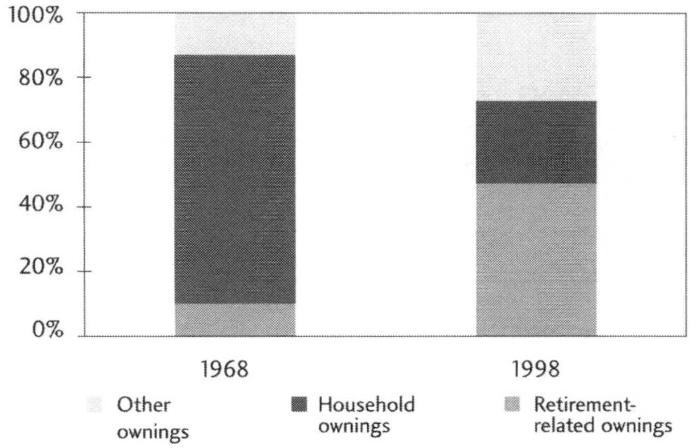

Source: Federal Reserve Flow of Funds Accounts.

But when companies buy back their stock, retire the stocks of an acquired company, go private, or go out of business, they remove stocks from the market and reduce the true supply. Primarily because of buybacks and mergers, the true supply of stocks outstanding declined by $381.3 billion (as shown in Table 7-1) during the twenty years ending December 31, 1998.

Systemic Supply

The effects that long-term stock portfolios have on prices are not widely recognized. The large and continuing trend to buy and hold large blocks of stocks in retirement accounts takes these shares off the market for long periods of time, thus reducing the effective supply available for trading.

Table 7-2
Shifting Stock Ownership Year-End Holdings, 1968–98
(In billions of current dollars)

	1968	%	1998	%
Issues at market value[a]	996.1		15,437.7	
Less private holdings at 20%[b]	199.2		3,087.5	
Listed stocks	796.9	100.0	12,350.2	100.0
Private pension funds	61.5	7.7	2,232.3	18.1
State and local govt. ret. funds	5.8	0.7	1,592.8	12.9
Life insurance companies	13.0	1.6	746.1	6.0
Mutual fund shares in ret. accts.[c]	0.0	0.0	1,263.2	10.2
Retirement-related stockholders	80.3	***10.1***	5,834.4	***47.2***
Other mutual fund shares[c]	46.1	5.8	1,263.2	10.2
All other[d]	54.4	6.8	2,063.3	16.7
Other net buyers	100.5	12.6	3,326.5	26.9
Net sellers—households[e]	815.3		6,279.8	
Less private holdings	199.2		3,087.5	
Household ownings of listed stocks	616.1	***77.3***	3,192.3	***25.8***

Notes:

[a] Includes U.S.-owned foreign stocks and American depository receipts (ADRs).

[b] Federal Reserve staff estimates that about 20% of all stocks were in privately held corporations in 1998.

[c] About half of stock mutual fund shares are now held in retirement accounts.

[d] Primarily foreign owners, bank personal trusts and estates, and other insurance companies

[e] Some of the stocks owned by households are in tax-favored retirement accounts like IRAs.

Source: Federal Reserve, Flow of Funds Accounts.

Figure 7-2 tracks shifting stock ownership for thirty years—from 1968 to 1998. It shows that the holdings of retirement-related funds increased from 10.1 percent to 47.2 percent of all stocks outstanding. Households were the primary source of the stocks available for trading as their holdings shrank from 77.3 percent to 25.8 percent of stocks outstanding.

Table 7-2 summarizes the data behind the chart and needs a few explanations.

- By comparing the two sets of year-end holdings, the table shows the net of all the buying and selling activity that occurred during the thirty-year period. Many net sellers also bought some stocks and many net buyers also sold some.
- Mutual funds increased their share of all listed stocks from 5.8 percent to 20.4 percent. In 1968, virtually no mutual fund shares were held in retirement accounts, but by 1998 retirement accounts held about half of them.
- The table understates retirement-related holdings because IRAs are included in the household category and some of the stocks in the "all other" category are also retirement-related.

Some of the sales by households were made to liquidate IRAs, pay income, and move to investments that pay interest to current retirees. We don't know how much of this is going on, but it may help to explain why personal savings are so low. When the baby boomers start to sell significant amounts of their stocks, one of the effects will be to reduce national net savings, and they may become negative for years.

It is useful to think of all retirement-related accounts as if they were a single national account. At any given time, this account is either taking in savings and using them to buy stocks or it is selling stocks and raising money to pay retirees. Within this large, seemingly placid lake, a lot of buying and selling is going on that nets itself out. For example, if a retirement-related fund sells a stock to another retirement-related fund, the net effect on the total holdings of retirement accounts is zero. One reason why the California Public Employees Retirement System shifted to index investing was that it found that some of its independently managed portfolios were selling stocks that other portfolios were buying and it was paying both the buying and selling commissions.

In the main, stocks of the country's largest corporations that are acquired by retirement-related accounts tend to become dormant and relatively unavailable for trading. This is particularly true of stocks in indexed portfolios and portfolios whose managers retain shares of the relatively few, large companies that drive the major indexes. Thus, the systemic supply of stocks, or the supply available for trading, has declined for thirty years and the process is still going on.

There has been little notice of the fact that retirement account purchases increase the demand for stocks, and to the degree the stocks then become dormant, retirement accounts also reduce the supply of them available for trading. This is not the way that markets, with supposedly infinitely large numbers of buyers and sellers, are supposed to work.

The Net Effect of Supply and Demand

Acting in concert, the growth of all three types of demand and the shrinking of the two primary types of supply have led to record high prices. The inflation can be seen in traditional valuation measures like price-to-earnings, price-to-dividends, and price-to-book value ratios.

Trading

Because trades set prices, it is important to understand why traders trade. Some market observers insist that trades are based on all the information about a company, its industry, the market, the economy, and the world that is available at the time. This belief is supported by the continuing flow of predictions (often contradictory) of how the market and individual stocks are going to perform.

There are, however, several reasons to question the market's efficiency in considering all available information when it sets prices. For example:

- As the Xcelera.com example showed, the financial services industry provides advice on which stocks to buy. If those who sold before noon didn't know of the *Gilder Technology Report* recommendation, the market didn't reflect all the information available. If the sellers as well as the buyers don't routinely have the same information, prices do not reflect mutual knowledge, so the theory of market efficiency is flawed.

- Buyers and sellers may be concerned with different time frames. Many advisers concentrate on intermediate or long-term periods because of the time needed to communicate their advice and for their clients to act. Traders who act more swiftly often concentrate on the short term—in some cases, hours or even minutes. Buyers and sellers may know everything that the advisers say and still act on the basis of other factors that they think will affect prices in the time frames they are considering.
- The objectives of buyers and sellers often don't match. It is not at all clear what a stock price means if it was set by a value investor who sold because the price appeared too high and was bought by a momentum player who hoped it would keep going up. The buyer's and seller's reasons are often a bit like the two parts of a non sequitur—they just aren't related.
- Behind most trades, there was a buyer who thought the stock was worth the trade price and a seller who didn't. In addition, there were all the other owners who kept their stock because they thought it was worth more, and all the other potential buyers who did not buy because they thought the price was too high. Thus, because only a small fraction of a company's stock trades in a normal day, the market sets prices that most potential

traders and even those who sell think is wrong! Over any period of time, either those who don't buy or those who don't sell are proven wrong. (This explanation does not apply to sellers like retirees who have to sell stocks for income, and some would argue that it does not apply to those who must buy to provide for future retirements.)

- The volume of trading that is done for short-term reasons is greater than the buying and selling done for long-term reasons. There have been days when the total number of some Internet company shares traded was several times greater than the total number of shares that were available for trading. Average holding periods were several hours. These are extreme cases, but because of this general tendency, the market doesn't reflect long-term considerations when it sets stock prices. The information may be there, but the short-term traders just don't care.
- The best explanation of trading is that most traders simply try to outguess what other traders are going to do over some period of time. Driving the process are informed guesses about what the companies and the economy are going to do, how other traders will act on their own guesses, and, most important, how other traders will react to news about what companies and the economy actually do.

The preceding paragraphs do not attempt to explain all buying and selling, but they do explain a large volume of each day's trades. And they show that there is virtually no relationship between the way prices are set and the way they are used to determine wealth or the future value of retirement portfolios.

Managing Stock Prices

Nearly all executives of public corporations will acknowledge that one of their main duties is to manage their stock prices. "How to Fix GM" in *Barron's* offers a revealing road map for one way to do it.[6] Starting from the premise that General Motors stock is underpriced, the article explains how the company could increase its stock price by more than 200 percent in five years without significantly increasing sales and even by reducing its net income.

The logic goes like this. GM should cut its roughly 648 million shares outstanding to about 200 million over five years through stock buybacks. Part of the money to do this would come from selling its interest in Hughes Electronics (which GM executives apparently want to keep for long-term reasons). The rest of the money would come from using about 80 percent of the company's earnings to repurchase stock.

The proposal assumes that although total earnings would decline slightly because of the sale of Hughes, earnings per share would increase greatly. This would justify a higher stock price, which the proposal assumes, probably for conservative purposes, would stay at a nearly constant price/earnings ratio. I offer several comments.

- The proposal doesn't mention dividends. With 80 percent of the earnings used for buybacks, a significant payout ratio would be impossible. The returns to stockholders that don't sell could only be phantom, not real.
- It doesn't mention that because the buybacks would simultaneously increase the demand for the stock while reducing the supply available for trading, the process could increase prices more than the proposal suggests.
- Portfolios that are linked to either the Dow Jones Industrial Average or the S&P 500 Index would have to continue to buy GM as they receive more cash, and they could not sell shares to GM unless they were reducing their entire portfolios. This would create even more demand and further reduce the supply available for trading. (I'm ignoring the technical point about selling shares to rebalance the Index.)
- The proposal might increase the valuation of portfolios that hold GM stock more that the article suggests, and it would pay increasing prices to those who want to sell their stock over the next five years. But except for the wealth effect (which might help sell cars and trucks) it would cause almost no change in the real-world economy where cars and trucks are built.

This is how things look in the world of "financial engineering," where phantom returns are all that count.

Company Valuations

HIGHLIGHT 20: Stock prices aren't a realistic basis for evaluating either companies or retirement portfolios.

When assessors are asked to determine the value of a corporation, they always ask why the client wants to know. This is because the valuation process and the result will depend on whether the client is interested in buying the company to operate as a going concern, buying it for its assets or its markets, selling it as a going concern, liquidating it to get out of the business quickly, suing it for damages, determining the fair value of a partial owner's shares of a private company, settling an estate and transferring partial ownership without interrupting operations, settling tax claims, or some other reason. A company never has just one value.

Capitalized value based on stock price is merely one of the values that can be placed on a corporation. Of all the possible values, it is both *the easiest to calculate and the least useful.* It is almost never the price at which a company can actually be bought or sold. Institutional investors know they cannot sell a large number of a company's shares quickly without depressing the price. Conversely, a serious offer to buy a large number of shares quickly or to acquire a company must be higher than the market price.

The capitalized value of a company has little relationship to the value of the company as an operating entity. Stock prices that are determined by the supply and demand for the stocks as commodities have no direct relationship to the underlying value of companies, the sum of all corporate values of the economy, or the value of investment portfolios. Capitalized value is about as far as you can get from a rational determination of what a company is worth in the context of the economy.

Stock prices are basically unstable for each company and for the country as a whole. They fluctuate far more widely than the economy does throughout the business cycle.

Of course, long-term considerations influence long-term investors, but the current volume of trading indicates that most trades have nothing to do with the long term. Traders are just trying to outguess what other traders will do in the short run. Because relatively few trades are made on the basis of long-term economic considerations, there is little reason to read long-term significance into market prices. And most trades represent basic disagreements between the parties. So it is a mistake to treat current stock prices as if they were a basis for projecting the future value of retirement portfolios.

It is also a mistake to infer too much about the long-term future of specific companies from their stock prices. As we discussed in the previous chapter, in 1988 in their annual ranking of companies by Market Value Added (MVA), Stern Stewart and *Fortune* magazine ranked IBM Number 1 on their list of a thousand companies. After its stock price fell, IBM was moved to the bottom of the list by 1992. Nevertheless, the company has continued to be a strong operation. In retrospect, it was neither as good nor as bad an investment as its fluctuating stock prices indicated. Its stock just went from being a wildly popular to an unpopular commodity.

In her *Fortune* article "Mr. Buffett on the Stock Market," Carol Loomis wrote about how Warren Buffett compared the Internet industry with the auto and aircraft industries.[7] Buffett pointed out that, historically, few people got rich from either. Loomis quoted him as follows:

> All told, there appear to have been at least 2,000 car makes in an industry that had an incredible impact on people's lives. If you had foreseen in the early days of cars how this industry would develop, you would have said, "Here is the road to riches." So what did we progress to by the 1990s? After corporate carnage that never let up, we came down to three U.S. car companies—themselves no lollapaloozas for investors. So here is an industry that had an enormous impact on America—and also an enormous impact, though not the anticipated one, on investors.

The article goes on to quote Buffett's observations about the aircraft industry, which has included about 300 manufacturers, only a handful of which are still breathing today, and 129 airlines that filed for bankruptcy. He sums up this industry by saying, "As of 1992, in fact—though the picture has improved since then—the money that has been made since the dawn of aviation by all of this country's airline companies was zero. Absolutely zero."

Multiply the example of Azwilbe, Inc. by hundreds of rapid and sustained growth companies, factor in what happened to automobile and aircraft manufacturers, airlines, and IBM, and you have examples of what is treated as value stored in America's retirement investment portfolios. The time is coming when the country will ask why it depends so much on stock prices, and why it sacrifices so much to inflate them.

Measurement Error

As this was being written, the S&P 500 Index was helping to inflate stock prices. The Index was created to be a measuring instrument, like a thermometer, to show the general price level of the market.

But it also became an investment instrument in its own right when large pension and mutual funds began to assemble portfolios of stocks that replicate the Index or are designed to perform as it does. Indexed funds have many appeals, including their low trading volume that allows minimal administrative costs. According to Standard & Poor's, by April 2000 more than $1 trillion worth of stocks in institutional stock portfolios were indexed to the S&P 500. (An indexed fund contains the same stocks in the same proportions as the index on which it is based.)

The multiple functions of the Index interact as a self-reinforcing, positive feedback loop. The success of indexed funds encourages money to flow into them. When they buy, they exert a continuing, systemic demand for the particular stocks in the Index. Most shares acquired by indexed funds then become dormant and are no longer available for trading. In addition, many actively managed funds retain stocks that are in the Index as a defensive measure.

Thus, indexed funds are adding to the upward pressure caused by retirement-related buyers. They simultaneously increase the demand for and reduce the effective supply of particular stocks. This is one reason why stocks of many successful companies that are not in the Index have not performed as well as comparable stocks that are.

What is called the *S&P Effect* was illustrated dramatically in late 1999 when the price of Yahoo! Inc. surged more than 60 percent the week after the announcement that it would be added to the Index.[8] This happened because indexed portfolios bought the shares they needed to keep their holdings aligned with the Index. At the same time, prices of other stocks in the Index declined as the portfolios sold them to balance their portfolios with the Index. In other fields, this kind of reaction is called *measurement error.*

As indexing has grown, the market has done spectacularly well as measured by—you guessed it—the Index. Those who work in physical and life sciences must be careful to use measurement techniques that have minimal effects on what they are measuring. Using the Index as both an investment instrument and a measurement instrument, however, makes it drive what it is supposed to be measuring.

During the 1980s, large indexed funds began to increase their performance by ranking the stocks that the Index required them to own and pressing executives of the lagging companies to increase stock prices. Other large fund managers also do this and the pressure is a primary cause of downsizing, cost-cutting, outsourcing, exporting jobs, laying off employees, limiting employee pay and benefits, and buying back stock all to increase stock prices. Some of the effects of this activity on the nation will be discussed in the next chapter, but as the Red Queen might have explained it to Alice, "Here, my dear, the doctor shakes down the patients to care for the thermometer."

Summary

Nearly everyone concerned with stocks is acting to inflate them. The compounding effects of household net sellers, retirement-related net buyers, indexing, and corporations themselves are in a world apart from conventional explanations of how the stock market sets prices. But they help explain why conventional measures of stock value such as price/earnings, price/dividend, and price/book ratios, particularly of stocks in the S&P 500 Index, appear to have no upper limits. Those measures are simply not germane to the process of shifting stocks from the declining pool held by the net selling households to the largely dormant portfolios of the net buying retirement-related accounts.

If this explanation is valid, then it is a warning that stock prices, which are the basis for phantom wealth, are not a sound foundation for individual retirement plans, the country's retirement plans in aggregate, or the whole economy.

CHAPTER 8

How Phantom Wealth Hurts the Economy

HIGHLIGHT 21: The drive to create phantom wealth has many hidden costs.

Some negative effects of the drive to produce phantom wealth primarily affect specific companies, their employees, customers, suppliers, consumers, or communities. But other important effects cut across all classes of companies and have an impact on the country as a whole. These effects can be summarized as follows:

- The productive investment gap
- Dangers of unsustainable growth
- Economic distortion
- National costs of stock price gains
- Market and wealth concentration
- Economic regulation
- The leak

All of these effects are related, but we will discuss each one separately.

The Productive Investment Gap

Stocks are like the dog that Sherlock Holmes said didn't bark. One reason they are important is because of what doesn't happen. In recent years, anybody could have doubled his or her money in four years or less with a mutual fund that tracks the S&P 500. That index has become a parasitic investment in its own right, and it has set a standard for all equity investments. As a result, very little capital is available for productive investments in companies or projects that are not expected to do as well or better than it does.

Each idea, company, product, or project in which you can invest money is an investment opportunity. As shown in Figure 8-1, the investment opportunities of the country (or a company) are like a pyramid. The few that can double in four years or less are at the pinnacle. The economy, which doubles in ten or more years (not adjusted for inflation) is at the base.

Figure 8-1: The Productive Investment Pyramid

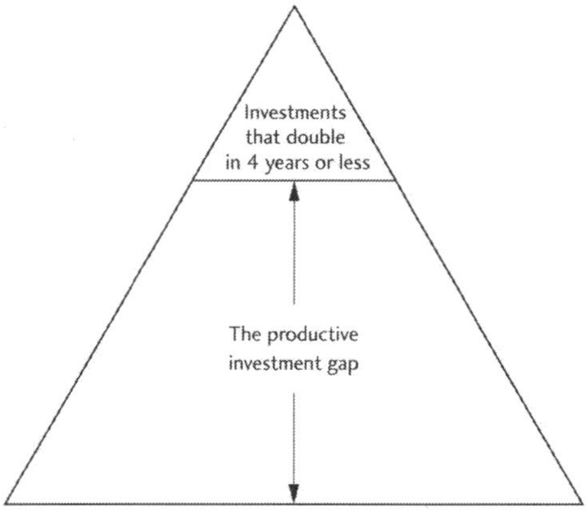

The economy: doubles in more than ten years (in current dollars)

Most of the country's productive investment opportunities fall into the wide gap between the pinnacle and the base. They include investments that are needed to provide jobs for people with marginal skills, expand thousands of local businesses, restore vibrant life to communities, and convert the country to more sustainable processes. All of these investments would help the country, but they are being avoided as the country's savings are attracted to the pinnacle.

A typical investor who looks at the pyramid is drawn to the stock market opportunities at the top. The choice between a productive investment in the gap or a parasitic investment in the pinnacle is usually a no-brainer. To make the productive investment with its operational risks, higher administrative costs, and lower returns would be to incur what economists call an *opportunity cost,* referring to what would be given up by not taking the most rewarding opportunity.

Just as large institutional parasitic investors are driving capital away from important but unspectacular internal investment opportunities in corporations, the stock market and mutual funds are driving capital away from little companies and community opportunities. The reasons are different, but the root cause is the same. They can't compete with what appear to be more rewarding alternatives.

As Chapter 9 will explain, by 2030 the country will need affordable homes for 34 million more people over age 65, along with adequate transportation and secure appropriate jobs for many of them. Few of the productive investments that will be needed to meet those massive requirements can possibly double in four years or less. Unless investment practices and priorities are changed, the private sector will not make those investments.

Dangers of Unsustainable Growth

Three of the five classes of companies we have used in our analysis are growth companies because growth increases stock prices. As the pinnacle of the investment pyramid has become ever more obvious and attractive, it has attracted ever more savings in a self-reinforcing cycle.

Executives, investors, and, increasingly, the employees of growth companies want to share in the stock gains. The sooner a person associates with a successful growth company, the greater his or her personal gains. A *Wall Street Journal* article said that an estimated eighty thousand employees of companies that went public in the San Francisco Bay Area between 1979 and 1999 gained an average $700,000 each on stock options.[1]

But overconcentration on the stocks of growth companies can lead to a problem that has hurt regions of this country many times in the past.

If the sales of a stable business stop growing or even decline for a while, the company and its employees carry on from day to day with minimal dislocation. If the economy stops growing, most stable businesses just hunker down and continue much as before until things pick back up.

High-growth companies, however, are often concentrated in industries where markets are driven by growth of major sectors of the broad economy. If the broad economy slows down, growth industries stop growing. They stop buying things needed to continue their growth, and the business of companies that supplied those things can just vanish. If these supplier companies are publicly owned, they become former growth companies and their stocks "tank." This was part of the chain reaction that hit Asia in the late 1990s.

Another example occurred in Texas, Oklahoma, and Louisiana in the 1980s. When oil prices soared after the embargoes of the 1970s, drilling became a growth industry. Some companies grew even faster by providing equipment and services that the drillers needed to grow. Their business depended on the growth of the drillers. When oil prices declined and the active drill rig count leveled off, the business of companies that made new rigs tumbled. When drilling activity declined, the business of the service companies dropped precipitously.

Today, growth company stocks are in demand and have very high prices in relation to their underlying businesses because of optimistic projections of future business growth. From the standpoint of parasitic investors, they are doing just fine. But economies and companies can be vulnerable if they depend too heavily on the process of growth. The cyclical pattern of the construction industry is well understood, and there are reasons to fear that some high-tech fields may experience even more serious reversals if their markets merely stabilize, much less decline.

Growth stocks have led to a popular investment technique called momentum investing, which calls for buying the shares of public companies just because their stock prices are rising rapidly. Today, momentum investing, which is entirely parasitic, is concentrated on stocks of rapid and sustained growth companies. Many experienced observers believe that momentum investing is unsound and can lead to bubbles that eventually burst.

The appeal of anticipated growth is based almost entirely on phantom returns from stocks. These returns, as we have seen, are caused by treating all shares of a company's stock as being worth the most recent trade price.

But phantom returns go negative when the market price of a stock declines. A cascading effect may occur if baby boom retirement portfolios sell stocks, if the sales cause the economy to slow down, if that slowdown causes the businesses of growth companies to drop, and if that drop hits their stock prices.

Economic Distortion

In theory, markets are supposed to be an efficient way to help people make choices. You may or may not have reservations about the principle, but you know that in your daily life you consider prices when you're deciding what to buy. So, presumably, does everybody else, and so the economy putts along on the sum of all the freely made choices.

This leads us to the combined effects of the productive investment gap and the dangers of unsustainable growth. The cost of capital is very important to companies. Without getting too technical, if they have to pay high interest rates to borrow money they will borrow as little as possible.

That also applies to equity capital. Because many people think it's possible to double money with a mutual fund linked to the S&P 500 Index in four years or less, companies have come to believe that they must make productive investments that will do better. This means they must concentrate on opportunities that they expect to double quickly and go on to produce large profits.

High-tech, fast-growth industries with short product cycles fit this model perfectly. The large public investments in science and education that produced an unprecedented body of knowledge and people who know how to use it have combined with the chance to get wealthy quickly with stocks. The combination has fostered the fastest growing part of the country's economy. California's Silicon Valley, Boston's Route 128, and other high-tech concentrations are due as much to phantom returns from stocks as they are to leading universities and technology.

Few economists recognize this self-reinforcing distortion when they extol the virtues of free markets. It is not shown by the statistics they use to analyze the economy. But if you doubt that it exists, just ask the executive of any high-tech company about the relationship between product cycles and investment returns. Read any growth company's annual report or read the financial pages for a week and you will see that this is exactly how those who are running high-tech companies think. For them, phantom returns are the name of the game.

The causes of the productive investment gap and the country's emphasis on unsustainable growth are the same: the drive for phantom returns from stocks.

National Costs of Stock Price Gains

We have discussed how institutional investor pressure on large mature companies to concentrate on their stock prices has affected the companies. But we should also look at the effects on communities, society, and even the economy.

Ranking operations and investment opportunities by profitability and lopping off from the bottom is the primary cause of downsizing, outsourcing, merging, exporting jobs, reducing contributions to communities, and avoiding long-term investments to protect the environment. It is also a primary cause of economic, social, political, and even racial tensions. It is not just a coincidence that white backlash to affirmative action grew as the country's major corporations laid off semiskilled people from what they had thought were secure, high-paying jobs.

In "There's a Minor Upside to Corporate Downsizing" in the November 8, 1999, *Barron's,* Gene Epstein wrote, "The folklore on Wall Street about corporate downsizing is that firms are far more willing to apply the ax than ever before. The other generally held belief is that when a company announces the intention to lay off workers, the market rewards it by boosting the price of its shares." He included a chart showing that from 1982 through 1997, *Fortune* 500 companies had layoff rates that ranged from 2.6 percent to 4.6 percent. The average layoff rate was 3.7 percent.[2]

Corporate executives often explain they must take these actions to compete in global markets where capital, knowledge, jobs, and products can flow across national boundaries. In specific situations they may be right, but that is only part of the story. The same executives often promote treaties that encourage global markets. Then they use markets in their Flip Wilson-style defense, "The Devil made me do it!" But they helped create the Devil by promoting more global trade.

The combination of the concentration of personal savings in large institutional portfolios, portfolio managers' drive for higher stock prices, corporate actions to increase stock prices, many types of deregulation, and political demands for reduced government expenditures is causing society's business increasingly to become nobody's business.

Many examples may be found in the electric utility industry as a result of deregulation. Low-cost producers are being encouraged to sell power beyond their former geographic limits. Higher-cost producers have become defensive and are primarily concerned with retaining their largest customers. Deregulation has made the earnings of power companies less predictable, so the market now treats their stocks like trading commodities, similar to industrial company stocks. Institutional investors that used to avoid them because they were too sluggish are now trading them for price gains. This has forced power companies to reduce their costs, increase their profits, and shift from paying high dividends to repurchasing their stock—all to increase their stock prices.

Changes of this type are in the wrong direction for two reasons. First, many retired people need the safe and predictable dividend flow with opportunities for modest growth that utility stocks used to provide. Retirement investments should pay incomes from then-current earning streams, not from stock sales. They should provide real, not phantom returns.

Second, planning was fundamental to the success of regulated utility companies because they had to make large, long-term investments. Their future was linked directly to the future of the areas they served. After government assistance programs that had helped communities plan their orderly development were curtailed, utility companies were ideally positioned to help the communities and small industrial customers in their service areas. But now that utilities are being decoupled from their geographic boundaries, that help has been reduced or eliminated in waves of cost-cutting. So far, nothing is filling the void.

Market and Wealth Concentration

In another ironic development, the emphasis on increasing the prices of large mature company stocks has reduced the benefits of competition for customers. As these companies narrowed their operations to their most profitable businesses, they followed the General Electric example and sold divisions that were not the first, second, or perhaps third largest competitor in their respective markets.

Other companies already in those other markets bought the cast-off divisions to expand their positions. The consolidation process is still going on in this country and is accelerating around the world. Companies are using what are called *killer marketing* strategies in their drive to dominate their consolidated markets quickly.

These sales, mergers, and acquisitions are having two big effects. The first is that consumers get fewer choices. An example of this is the soft drink business, where at the national level, Coke and Pepsi compete fiercely. But they are competing by forcing large restaurant chains and sports facilities to buy from only one of them. As a result, competition occurs at a mezzanine level, but the end effect is to deny customers their freedom of choice and the value of competition. Airline hubs are another example.

Whether they can't find shoe sizes they need, are "slammed" into long distance telephone carriers with which they don't want to do business, wait in airports they didn't want to visit, or are forced to answer telemarketing calls that they don't want but can't eliminate, millions of Americans are increasingly realizing that from the corporate viewpoint, their main reason for being is to provide cash. Customers are not people to be served, they are just resources to be mined.

The second effect of these consolidations has been massive layoffs of people. From managers to workers at the lowest levels, millions of people who had been told they were doing a good job found that they were no longer wanted—or redundant—when their company or division was taken over by another. In fact, one of the main justifications for mergers is that reducing the total labor cost required to continue the combined level of sales is good for profits and stock prices. For example, on December 15, 1999, Exxon Mobil announced that as a result of the merger, it would cut 14,000 jobs or about 12 percent of its workforce to save $3.8 billion over the next three years.[3] Many years will pass before the country realizes the full cost of the loss of trust that has resulted from mergers like this one.

Wealth and power are being concentrated because of the drive to create phantom wealth in the following interacting sequence:

- The first level of concentration occurs as private savings are turned over to large financial institutions like pension and mutual funds.
- The second level is the power that managers of these institutions obtain through the voting rights of the stocks in the portfolios they manage.
- The third level results from portfolio managers exercising this power to force companies to increase their stock prices by cutting costs and concentrating on their most profitable lines of business to attain market dominance.
- The fourth level is the income and wealth concentration that successful company executives, the financial services industry, and wealthy individuals can amass as the result of the first three levels of concentration.
- The fifth level is the political power that those who control vast amounts of financial wealth use to perpetuate the system of wealth concentration.

This entire sequence is achieved primarily by using other peoples'—and often the baby boomers'—money to produce phantom returns from stocks. It is no accident that for the last twenty-five years, since the beginning of the shareholders' rights movement, personal wealth has grown much faster for the few at the top of the national income distribution pyramid than for those in the middle or at the base.

David Korten says that money is purchasing power, which is really a claim on real wealth.[4] When stocks, which are heavily concentrated among the wealthiest members of society, go up faster than the economy as a whole, the claims of the stockholders also go up faster than the economy. He makes an important point that we can expand upon.

It is obvious that at any particular time, the economy can provide only so many goods and services. A market economy rations the available goods and services by putting a price on each of them. The more money you have, the more you can buy. The less money you have, the more you must be careful in your purchases. People who counterfeit money are just trying to increase their buying ability the easy way.

Those who rely on phantom returns from stocks to increase their ability to buy are not very different from counterfeiters. The more stocks they have and the faster their phantom wealth grows, the greater the claim they have on the limited amount of goods and services available. But as their claim increases, the claim of those who do not have access to the phantom wealth production process must decrease. Thus phantom wealth provides a highly efficient way to transfer purchasing power from the poor, who must live on the real returns from their work, to the wealthy, who can enjoy the phantom returns from stocks. The rich get richer, and relatively speaking, the poor get poorer.

We discussed this point in Chapter 3 in the context of the effect of retirement plans and how they would transfer a larger slice of the country's total pie from workers to retirees.

Economic Regulation

There are not many ways to guide a market economy in order to smooth what used to be catastrophic cyclical fluctuations. In this country today, the guiding is done primarily by the Federal Reserve Board, whose main tool is short-term interest rates. Simply put, the idea is that by raising or lowering these rates, the Fed can change the total amount of money (mostly credit) that is in circulation by changing the cost of borrowing from banks. This influences the level of business and increases or decreases general price levels. In practice, the link between interest rates and the economy is very indirect; the process is somewhat like backing a tractor-and-two-trailer rig. You can control what the tractor and the first trailer do, but the second trailer has a will of its own. By the time you see what it's doing, it's too late to change it.

In recent years, the huge amount of phantom wealth that is attributed to stock prices has become a major concern for the Fed. Because stock prices are driven by trades that are based on guesses about what other traders will do in the future, they react more quickly than any other aspect of the economy. Chairman Greenspan can tell Congress that he believes the economy should slow down, or speed up, or just stay the same during the next twelve months, and by the time he gets back to his office, the stock markets around the world will have reacted.

On top of this, the Fed must consider how the perpetual motion equity machine creates a form of currency that nobody controls. There are frequent articles in the financial press about how companies use stocks to compensate executives, reward employees, and buy other companies. From a national standpoint, these companies might just as well be printing their own money, which in a sense, they are. The *Wall Street Journal* article mentioned earlier that discussed the $Ph56 billion created by the options of eighty thousand employees in the San Francisco Bay Area is an example. Thus, although one of the Federal Reserve Board's primary jobs is to control the nation's money supply, phantom wealth is a form of money over which it has little if any control.

But the Fed must now take stock prices and the aggregate capitalized value of all companies seriously, so it is caught between the quick reaction of stock markets and the more sedate responses of the economy as a whole when it changes interest rates. Stock prices have added another trailer to the rig that it's trying to back up.

Chairman Greenspan's "irrational exuberance" comment has been widely quoted, but he offered a more complete explanation in his speech at a symposium at Jackson Hole, Wyoming, in August 1999.[5] The following are two paragraphs from that speech.

> History tells us that sharp reversals in confidence happen abruptly, most often with little advance notice. These reversals can be self-reinforcing processes that can compress sizable adjustments into a very short time period. Panic market reactions are characterized by dramatic shifts in behavior to minimize short-term losses. Claims on far-distant future values are discounted to insignificance. What is so intriguing is that this type of behavior has characterized human interaction with little appreciable difference over the generations. Whether Dutch tulip bulbs or Russian equities, the market price patterns remain much the same.
>
> We can readily describe this process, but, to date, economists have been unable to anticipate sharp reversals in confidence. Collapsing confidence is generally described as a bursting bubble, an event incontrovertibly evident only in retrospect. To anticipate a bubble about to burst requires the forecast of a plunge in the prices of assets previously set by the judgments of millions of investors, many of whom are highly knowledgeable about the prospects for the specific companies that make up our broad stock prices.

To put that in other words, Dr. Greenspan and the Fed have a problem.

In recent years, many companies have used the high market valuation of their stocks as a form of purchasing power to acquire or merge with other companies. For example, in April 1999 AOL's stock reached $167.50, but by August 5 it had declined to $83.94. An AOL executive was quoted the following day in the *Washington Post:* "The currency we use for acquisitions is our stock. The price clearly impacts how we do those deals."[6] This was demonstrated when AOL agreed to buy Time Warner by exchanging one and a half shares of its stock for each share of Time Warner. In other words, AOL simply printed about Ph$156 billion.

The Leak

This and the previous three chapters have made the distinction between two types of investment—productive and parasitic. Productive investment, which increases the power of humanity to feed, house, nourish, and provide for itself, is one of mankind's most powerful tools. In contrast, parasitic investment just uses money to make money without regard to the real world.

Anybody can see that buying a horse to work is different from betting on a horse to win. But for some reason, few people see (or care) that buying a truck, a machine, or a computer to use in a company is fundamentally different from just buying the outstanding stock of that company from a previous stockholder. Yet buying the outstanding stock is just betting on the company as if it were a horse.

To use another analogy, accumulating capital is like damming up a river to turn a waterwheel. The water that flows over the wheel can do useful work. But if water leaks around the wheel, the opportunity to use its energy is lost forever. Productive investing is like sending the water to the wheel to do work. Parasitic investing is like letting it leak around the wheel.

A leak around the waterwheel is obvious. But by concentrating on just the monetary returns that investments produce and not the work that they do, the country has allowed parasitic investing to develop to the point where there are huge losses that are not even seen.

Other Discussions of the Effects of Parasitic Investing for Phantom Returns

Many books have been written about the way large corporations are hurting society. The four noted here take different approaches in describing the problems caused by corporate actions and ways to solve them. These books don't use the terms *phantom wealth* or *parasitic investing.* But if you read them, you will see how these two concepts underlie the pictures their authors paint.

In *The Ecology of Commerce,* Paul Hawken argues that we need to create profitable, expandable companies that don't degrade the environment around them.[7]

In *Tyranny of the Bottom Line,* Ralph Estes describes how companies are forced to increase profits because conventional accounting systems do not show the full costs of their actions. He advocates a new form of stakeholder accounting that shows costs and benefits to all those that have an interest in corporations, including employees, customers, communities, and the environment, as well as the shareholders.[8]

In *The Emperor's Nightingale,* Robert A.G. Monks explains how corporations have drawn away from their original purpose and become amoral entities. He believes the pension plans that own much of their stock should become more involved in looking out for the well-being of their communities and society.[9]

In *The Post-Corporate World,* David C. Korten details how corporations have become highly efficient in using anything they touch for their own purposes. He proposes reducing the role of large corporations and replacing them with more locally based, stakeholder-owned companies.[10]

Summary

Trillions of dollars of the country's wealth that are attributed to equities are based on phantom returns that result from treating all stocks as if they are worth the price of the last trade. This is like printing money. And this practice is causing or contributing to several other undesirable side effects:

- Overemphasis on growth, novelty, change, and knowledge-based value added, with little provision for those left behind, who must pay the costs of change
- The drive for corporate growth that overrides communities and ordinary people
- The business attitude that people aren't important—just getting their money is
- Concentration of financial, corporate, economic, and market power
- Short-term materialistic focus and lack of concern for the needs of future generations or the environment
- Externalized costs of change
- Inflated capital costs
- Concentration of personal wealth
- Unrealistic investment and retirement expectations
- Financial domination of democratic institutions
- Deception

Not a pretty list.

The perpetual motion equity machine is like a leak around a waterwheel. Much of the country today, including the financial industry, is devoted to worsening the leak while making it look as if all the water is doing something useful. Our country and its people are paying a price for this deception.

If retirement investments, which are helping to create the leak, eventually cause the stock market to collapse, the result will be like destroying the dam. No more capital. Nothing to turn the wheel.

Let's look back on what we've discussed in Parts I and II.

The Introduction listed the five main messages of this book. So far, we have discussed the first four of them, which are as follows:

1. Much of the country's economy and many of its retirement plans are built on a structure of phantom wealth that depends on stock prices.
2. Stock prices are based on projected future events or what people hope will happen, not on actual corporate accomplishments. Using stock prices to measure wealth is like counting chickens before they've hatched.
3. The drive to create phantom wealth by inflating stock prices helps some people, but it distorts the economy and hurts society as a whole.
4. Demographic trends and retirement plans are helping to build the phantom wealth structure. But unless the structure is replaced with one that is more sustainable, those same trends will eventually make it fail, and that in turn will drag down the retirement plans and the economy.

Our discussion of these four messages can be summarized as follows:

- Baby boomers and others put their retirement savings into pension and mutual funds for growth.

- The funds buy outstanding stocks of public companies from previous owners in transactions that do not provide money to the companies.
- Managers of these funds press companies to make their stocks grow.
- Large companies respond by cutting costs to increase profits, which will increase stock prices.
- The cost cutting and pressure to increase stock prices have serious social, economic, environmental, and political costs.
- Large companies inflate their internal cost of capital and avoid many needed productive investments in order to provide the phantom returns that parasitic investors demand.
- Stock prices, which are set by short-term traders, are used to determine the value of companies and to project the long-term condition of retirement accounts—uses that are not considered by the traders who set the prices.
- Retirement investments now exert a strong inflationary bias in both the demand for and the supply of stocks available for trading. These biases can be expected to reverse when the baby boomers retire.
- When the boomers retire, they will have to sell stocks to produce income, but the number of buyers in relation to sellers will be shrinking.
- Because most buyers are likely to be workers in their peak earning years, there will be only about one worker-buyer for each retiree-seller.

- If this is the case, then stock prices will fall to the level that the buyers can afford.
- The massive loss of phantom wealth could destroy the retirement hopes of millions of boomers and even lead to a depression.

And nearly everybody acts as if this makes sense!

At a more fundamental level, the economy can only produce a limited quantity of goods and services for current consumption. All retirement accounts of any kind can do is provide money to help retirees consume a larger share of the national pie that has been created by workers.

Retirement accounts are simply a way to increase the retirees' share of the pie while reducing the workers' share. Retirement accounts that depend on stocks to provide the money run the risk of destroying trillions of dollars of phantom wealth and triggering a depression.

PART III

Guiding the Future—Yours and Society's

In Part III, our concentration shifts from the problems to what individuals and organizations can do to provide for a sustainable future. We concentrate on the fifth message of the book: Individuals and organizations can help prevent retirement plans and the economy as a whole from collapsing—or protect themselves in case there is a collapse—by creating real wealth based on work, earnings, and solid accomplishments instead of just hopes. But doing this requires a different mindset that includes new values, goals, and ways of thinking about living, aging, investing, and running companies.

Our emphasis changes, also. We examine some technical ideas and how they might work, but they are not mere lists of how-to's. Instead, the discussion is designed to make individuals, organizations, and the country as a whole think more deeply about values and goals than they usually do.

If my analysis is correct, the country is sailing into uncharted waters. We will have to think and feel our way through. This will force us to test concepts that many of us have accepted without asking enough critical questions.

Chapter 9 starts by discussing what the people who founded this country thought and did, and how they could be our model and our inspiration today.

CHAPTER 9

How We Can Meet Our Real Needs

In this chapter we will consider five approaches for escaping from the absurd financial trap described in the first two parts of the book. The five approaches are these:

- Changing our ways of thinking
- Projecting our needs and the resources available to meet them
- Replacing the phantom wealth structure
- Reviewing our lifestyles and consumption patterns
- Preparing for active aging

This chapter sets the stage for the next two chapters, which consider first what individuals and then what organizations can do to help avoid a fiscal crisis.

Changing Our Ways of Thinking

America may be approaching a period resembling that of the last third of the eighteenth century. The more I read about what people did at that time to form the United States politically, socially, and economically, as well as militarily, the more I respect them. In addition to their bravery and commitment, they did huge amounts of clear and deep thinking about the future while living their daily lives.

But for years, none of the explanations I read about what happened seemed to explain adequately *how* or *why* it happened. Then I found *The Creation of the American Republic 1776–1787* by Gordon S. Wood.[1] For those who are interested in that period, I can't recommend this book highly enough.

It's not easy to read. First published in 1969 and then republished in 1998, it has sentences that contain two or more quotes from different sources, paragraphs that run for more than a page, and some pages that are one-third footnotes. Yet much of the subject matter applies directly to what we are discussing. Here are two lessons I take from it.

Historical Lesson No.1: It Took Many Minds and Many Experiments to Create This Country

Every year we celebrate July 4, the date when the Continental Congress enacted the Declaration of Independence. But Wood shows that May 15, 1776, was an even more important date because that is when the Congress advised all the colonies to develop their own governments to replace the British colonial governments.

That action handed the thirteen colonies the task of developing new ways to govern themselves. Each colony had to figure out how to become a state on its own. There followed years of discussion, debate, and exchange of ideas locally and up and down the Atlantic Coast. There was a remarkable amount of writing, reading, listening, and understanding of other points of view. The colonists considered questions such as these:

- Is a legislature adequate to run a state or is something more needed?
- Do individual legislators represent all of a state or factions within a state?
- What role should property ownership play as a qualification for voting?
- If a constitution is needed, can the legislature adopt it or must the voters adopt it by some other means in order to make it permanent?
- Can sovereign power be shared by separate branches of government?
- What is sovereignty? Must it reside in the government, with some rights granted to the people as in England, or can it reside with the people, who transfer some responsibilities to their governments?

These were not academic issues for philosophical discussion; they were critical and pioneering explorations into unfamiliar realms to develop a better way for people to live together in peace. Wood uses primary sources to trace the development of answers to dozens of questions like these. Learned thinkers from the ancient Greeks down had pondered some of these questions, but never before had they been considered by the ordinary people who had to live with the answers.

I believe there is a lesson in this for us today because it shows that all the heavy lifting was not done by a few delegates in Philadelphia. It was done by the people themselves—thousands of them. In western Massachusetts, it was done in town meetings. In some colonies, it was done in conventions. Some state constitutions required ratification by direct votes of citizens, which were preceded by long public discussions.

This period also presents a lesson for us today because it shows that nobody had a corner on the best ideas. The colonists were primarily angry at King George III and the English Parliament, where they had no representatives. So, many Whigs believed the states needed only elected legislatures to govern themselves.

But the early experience of some states showed that if legislatures were not counterbalanced by other branches of government, they could be as bad as the King and Parliament were. As needs and weaknesses were recognized, early state constitutions were revised.

The founders of the United States concentrated primarily on how people should relate to their governments. Today, I believe, the debate has shifted to how people should relate to their business and economic institutions. As the new debate expands, some of what we now take to be laws of economics may prove to be no more durable than the divine right of kings or primogeniture.

Indeed, this is why the most that I (or anyone) can possibly do is to suggest ideas to be considered, improved, tested, and adopted or discarded. Some of the very astute readers who reviewed early drafts of this book felt that my recommendations were not strong enough or adequately detailed. They said that my descriptions of the problems were more specific than the solutions I proposed. My respectful answer to them is that what they asked for is simply not possible for me or anybody else to do. It is a job for all of us to do, over time.

Historical Lesson No. 2: The American Revolution Was an Anticipatory Act

The people of the United States have become so used to reacting after problems occur that we are inclined to think this was always how it was done. Wood's book shows how things were different back in Revolutionary times. He and other writers have explained that the Stamp Act really wasn't so onerous that it hurt business much; besides, it was to pay for the British costs of defending the colonies during the French and Indian Wars. The issue was blown up to gain popular support, but as a cause for rebellion it was pretty small beer.

In fact, during the 1774–75 period the Whigs were not reacting to what had been done but to what the

Stamp Act suggested *could be done* in future. Their point was that if the colonies submitted to taxation without representation, there was no limit to how their freedoms could be restricted.

According to Wood, the American Revolution was an anticipatory action by the colonists to deal with what they perceived as a potential danger.

Let's bring these lessons up to the present. If, after reading the first two parts of this book, you find yourself tentatively agreeing that the ideas presented in them may be right (and I can't ask for more) and if you then begin to think along these lines and ask questions on your own, you will be following in the footsteps of the people in the thirteen colonies after May 15, 1776. And if you see a potential danger, you can begin to consider actions to deal with that danger.

Part III of this book is for those who wish to keep that American tradition alive. It's an old process—only the subject matter is new. With care and luck, this revolution will be peaceful.

A Few Different Ways of Thinking

It's time to start asking fundamental questions about this country's economic beliefs and their power over us. We have been sold a bill of goods by economists that almost all things that matter can be equated with money. But we know this isn't true. For example, we are told that the primary goal of the economy is to satisfy consumers and minimize their costs. But what about the needs of the same people as producers? What about the satisfaction of doing a job well—as a life experience—rather than just doing something fast and cheap? What about the millions of people for whom predictability, stability, and security is more important than novelty and quantity of purchases? How are consumers satisfied when producers use advertising to create demand for products that they never wanted before?

Unlike most sciences, economics rests heavily on assumptions rather than verifiable facts. It is time to question some of those assumptions, as we began doing in Parts I and II when we examined conventional ideas about how stocks work. If the underlying assumptions are not correct, then some of what economics teaches may be as limited or incorrect as Newtonian physics.

Projecting Our Needs and theResources Available to Meet Them

Americans have mixed feelings about planning. We are told that this country emerged as the world's only superpower because free capitalism is superior to central planning. Yet many of those who are the strongest opponents of planning by the federal government expect the armed services always to be ready for whatever may need to be done and also are quick to criticize the government if it seems slow in providing relief services after disasters. Yet both military preparedness and disaster relief preparedness require extensive planning.

Americans often overlook the results of the country's many successful plans. Here are just two of countless examples.

- In the 1780s, even before the Constitution was written, Congress enacted the Northwest Ordinances, which provided for settling the territories west of the original thirteen states. The Ordinance of 1787 became the basic plan under which the nation expanded to forty-eight states.
- After World War I, research work that was pioneered by the National Advisory Committee for Aeronautics (a predecessor of NASA) laid the foundation for the U.S. lead in military and civilian aviation that continues to this day.

As with all successful plans, both of these started with projections of future needs. But neither the Northwest Ordinances nor the aeronautical research plan told individuals what to do. They just made it easier for people to do what they would probably want to do. If they wanted to organize a new state, a plan told how to do it. If they wanted to design a new wing, tested formulas were provided to help.

It is time to follow these kinds of examples and project the needs of this country's aging population. A good place to start is with demographic projections like those shown in Table 1-1 in Chapter 1. Of course, the data will be revised based on the 2000 census, but the fact that more people are going to live longer will not change.

Absorbing those older people into states and communities will require actions that can be anticipated much as the Northwest Ordinances anticipated the process of organizing communities, economies, and governments. Providing for these people will require new knowledge, much like what the fledgling aircraft industry needed.

Both the real-world and financial needs of older Americans should be projected. The seven classes of baby boomers discussed in Chapter 2 (the Wealthy, the Lucky, the Surprised, the Realistic, the Employed, the Unemployed, and the Needy) provide points of departure for this kind of practical planning.

We can consider their real-world needs by asking the types of questions that regional and county planners all around the country ask when they are given the opportunity. Here are a few:

- How does the size, location, and configuration of present housing compare with what older people will need and be able to afford?
- How accessible is the housing to appropriate work, shopping, health care, and other services?
- What types of transportation will be needed to move older people from where they live to where they work, shop, and receive services?

The least expensive place to house people is where land is cheap. But many older people who will have to work will need to live near their jobs or have adequate transportation. There are linkages and tradeoffs among income levels, job locations, housing locations and costs, and transportation modes and costs. The linkages and tradeoffs are affected by physical limits, such as land above flood plains and available water. They are also affected by popular wishes, such as limiting urban sprawl, protecting agricultural lands and open spaces, and coping with automobiles.

An example of the consequences of a lack of planning can be found in the plight of older women in rural British villages. Many of them live alone on small pensions and have no car. They are too dispersed for public transportation to take them to the large shopping areas near large towns and cities that are replacing their village shops. The free market is letting these people down just as it is letting people down in rural parts of the United States.

Once the real-world needs have been considered, questions will have to be asked about jobs. For example:

- How many of these older people will probably need to work?
- Can the private sector, and particularly large companies, be expected to provide appropriate jobs?
- If not, who will provide the jobs?

Older people who must work will need stable jobs that can be adjusted to their changing capabilities. Today's trend toward transient and temporary workers will not meet the need for security that becomes increasingly important for many people as they grow older. If adequate national medical insurance is not available, they will need health benefits from their employers.

If the global economy continues to expand, the effects of comparative labor costs must be considered. If multinational corporations can have their products made anywhere in the world, will they make their products here in order to provide jobs? So far, the answer has been a resounding "No!"

Before large corporations can provide the needed jobs and benefits, they will have to reverse their present policies of cutting costs that encourage older employees to retire or accept part-time jobs. Instead, they will have to return to the principles of corporate citizenship and responsibility to their communities.

Few corporations that decide to meet their community's real needs will be as profitable as investors expect them to be today. The experience of Ben & Jerry's (discussed in Chapter 6)—a company that has always held community responsibility as one of its standards but was reviled by the business press for not returning enough to shareholders—is a good example, and there are countless others. But if companies don't meet the country's real needs, then savings may have to be channeled to other types of organizations that will—perhaps new types of financial institutions and business organizations or nonprofit and governmental organizations.

There are other questions to ask about incomes.

- How much income will the 75 million people who are projected to be over 65 by 2030 need to live in minimal comfort? (A possible test of adequacy at the local level might be the minimum incomes that states or communities use today in attracting new residents who will pay at least as much in taxes as they cost in services.)
- How does this level of income compare with projected Social Security benefits?
- How does it compare with the amount of interest and dividends paid in the country today?
- How much additional income would have to come from other sources?
- If some of the older people have assets that they expect to sell, such as homes and securities, who will be able to buy them?

Most of the data that state and local governments need to approximate answers to these questions are readily available. If just a few states and communities ask them and publish their preliminary findings, others across the country will see the need to ask these questions too. I believe that most of the analyses will show huge gaps between what older people and their communities will want and need, and what industry can be expected to provide based on today's investment practices.

The analyses will show the shortfall when it comes to working and retirement incomes, affordable homes, access to work and services, and of course, health care. They will also show that most of the private sector investments required to make up the difference will fall into the productive investment gap that was discussed in Chapter 8, which means that, under present conditions, they will not be made. As the picture emerges, the need to stop the leak and channel savings away from parasitic speculation into productive investments will become obvious.

A lot can be learned from simple "back-of-the-envelope" arithmetic. For example, the Census Bureau projects that from 2000 to 2030, the number of people over age 65 will double from 34.7 million to 69.4 million. This indicates that almost 35 million more people over age 65 will need affordable housing, food, transportation, medical care, and other services.

That will be like providing the housing, jobs, services, and transportation for triple the combined populations of New York City, Chicago, and Houston—in thirty years. That is the equivalent of creating nine huge new cities. The first set of the three-city equivalents will be needed by about 2016, or about five years after the boomers begin to turn 65. All of these people have homes today, but many will find that their homes no longer meet their needs or that they can't afford to stay where they raised their families.

State and local governments don't have to let this wave of needs take them by surprise.

Replacing the Phantom Wealth Structure

HIGHLIGHT 22: The phantom wealth structure is based on false expectations. The way to replace the structure is to remove the expectations.

The last part of the summary in Chapter 8, which reviewed what we discussed in Parts I and II, outlined the self-reinforcing cycle that is expanding the phantom wealth structure. If this country is going to solve the problems that the structure is helping to create, it will have to break the cycle. Because the structure is based on false expectations, the easiest way to do that is to remove the expectations. That suggests a sequence of six steps—none of which necessarily involves action by the federal government.

1. Help people understand why stock prices can't keep rising once the baby boomers stop buying and start selling.
2. When people understand that, they will make more realistic evaluations of their retirement accounts by considering what market conditions will be like when the boomers' accounts must be sold.
3. More realistic evaluations will discourage the flow of retirement savings into stocks in search of phantom returns, so prices will not continue to rise as a result of retirement-driven momentum.

4. Boomers and other investors will then look for alternative investments that can protect rather than destroy their capital while helping to meet the country's real needs. It will also encourage boomers to think about having to work into their later years.
5. The foregoing will reduce the demand for stocks and make it futile for pension and mutual funds to press companies for stock price gains. The financial services industry will then have an incentive to develop other, more sustainable financial products that meet the country's and society's real needs.
6. Communities and other jurisdictions will be able to consider how to meet their real needs by using the money, including the baby boomers' savings, that will no longer be flowing into stocks.

In the next section of the chapter, we will discuss how to take these steps.

Investment Quality

Nearly everybody knows that as the world's economies become integrated and global competition expands, economic efficiency becomes more important. People differ over how fast globalization should proceed, but there is no reason to expect it to stop in the foreseeable future. So it's time to think about what investments should do and how they should be measured in relation to regional and community needs.

Many economists and investors believe that because the United States has the most efficient capital markets the world has ever seen it must also have an efficient economy. They point to the buying and selling of stocks and other securities almost instantaneously with minuscule transaction costs as evidence of how well the markets match those who have capital with those who need it.

Transaction costs and market efficiency, however, are poor indicators of economic efficiency because they measure inputs and outputs in the same units—money. Using them is like determining the efficiency of an engine by how little energy it uses in the process of burning fuel.

But the efficiency of most engines and other machines is measured by how much work they do in relation to the fuel they consume—as with miles per gallon. The inputs (in gallons) produce outputs (vehicle miles) and the ratios of the different units are used, for example, to compare the efficiency of cars or engines.

Parasitic investors rarely use real-world units to measure the work that their stocks help perform. Because they are just interested in making money with money, they are content to measure phantom returns in relation to purchase prices and transaction costs. They don't know or care if buying outstanding shares of a large mature company's stock will lead to appropriate, accessible, and dependable jobs with adequate benefits for older people. Indeed, as we have discussed, buying these shares often leads to the opposite results.

What Investment Should Mean

Economists and other advisers urge Americans to save more and invest their savings to provide for their retirements and to help the economy grow. They assume that efficient capital markets will match the savings with the country's needs because the greatest needs offer the highest returns. According to this reasoning, investors, who are assumed to make wise choices when they seek the highest returns, will automatically serve the needs of society. But as we have seen, it ain't necessarily so.

There will always be a productive investment pyramid (see again Figure 8-1) with the opportunities that promise the largest and fastest returns near the top. But the country does not have to allow (much less encourage) phantom returns from parasitic investments to compete with and displace productive investments by allowing them to set the standard for all returns. The best way to encourage investors to provide capital for the important productive investments that are farther down the pyramid is to reduce competition from parasitic investments. This comes back to the fourth main message of this book: Demographic trends and retirement plans are helping to build the phantom wealth structure. But unless the structure is replaced with one that is more sustainable, those trends will eventually make it fail, and that in turn will drag down the retirement plans and the economy.

It is obvious that the structure is going to be replaced anyway. The question is whether the country will manage the replacement process or be managed by it.

In the remainder of this book, we will concentrate on productive investments that are intended to

- Accomplish real-world purposes, and
- Provide real returns to investors on the basis of what they actually help to accomplish.

To get back to the waterwheel analogy, we want investments that are like the flow of water over a wheel that provides power to do work. We want to reduce the leaks of water around the wheel that waste power, accomplish no useful purpose, and even do damage.

Investments and Sustainability

The cost of making and administering productive investments will always be higher than the cost of parasitic investments because of the due diligence and constant monitoring that they require. At a minimum, a productive investor must understand the company's business, how it will use additional capital, what the investment is expected to accomplish in real terms, and the risks that must be faced. That investor must know about conventional ratios and dollar projections but also go far beyond that and be able to make judgments about a company's managers and other information that is often proprietary and not available to the public. The cost of obtaining this knowledge will always be higher than the cost of buying and selling stocks.

In addition, a productive investor must watch the operation of the company. If it has trouble, the investor must look for ways to help it overcome the trouble. Productive investors are owners in the fullest sense of the word. Although millions of individuals cannot possibly monitor and help companies, they can turn their savings over to intermediaries who provide that function as their agents.

All this leads to a very simple conclusion. To be responsible, Americans should use their savings to meet the needs of society, pay a fair share to workers, provide incomes for those who cannot work from then-current earnings, and not reduce the ability of future generations to enjoy what we enjoy today. The word that describes this process is *sustainable.*

There will probably always be different opinions about what is or isn't sustainable as more is learned about the earth's processes. But it should be obvious that parasitic investments that lead to consuming critical resources like fresh water faster than they can be replenished are not sustainable. There are some examples of sustainable investments, particularly in Northern Europe, but it is a relatively new concept and there are not many precedents.

Although individuals and some types of financial institutions should be free to do as much parasitic, financial speculation as they wish, their activities should not be confused with, treated like, or even called investing for retirement accounts. Nor should they be allowed to dominate the country's equity investment structure as they do today.

Changing Financial Institutions in Time

Economists assert that people should be encouraged to save and that financial institutions should channel their savings to companies that need capital. The economists are right—that is exactly what people and institutions should do.

But except for high-pressure IPOs and secondary offerings by growth companies, today's equity investment practices are not what the economists advocate. Instead, parasitic investing and the quest for phantom returns hurts some parts of the economy while it overstimulates others. Again, the key word is sustainable. If the eventual baby boom retirement sales of stocks are the threat they appear to be, then today's investment practices are among the least sustainable things around.

Practical investment alternatives should be developed *before* demand for them grows. If the demand for alternatives comes too quickly before they are available, it could trigger a financial disaster instead of preventing one. This could happen, for example, if too many people sell their stocks in anticipation of a decline before there are enough alternative productive investments. The process of developing productive investment alternatives to today's stock-based retirement and mutual funds may be likened to the testing of ideas at the state level that occurred before they were adopted by the U.S. Constitution. In addition, ways will probably have to be developed to ease the orderly transfer of money from stocks to the new alternatives.

We will discuss these points further in Chapters 10 and 11.

Financial System Objectives

Without repeating all the problems and needs, let's translate them into objectives that could be used to improve the financial system.

- New financial institutions and instruments should allow individuals to put their savings into productive investments that are sustainable in business, social, and environmental terms by aligning the interests of workers, customers, suppliers, communities, managers, and investors, not keeping them in opposition.
- Some of the new financial institutions and instruments should channel savings to smaller, often community-based companies that need equity capital but do not have the growth potential that attracts venture capitalists. The institutions should be active partners that help the companies succeed.

- Retirement investors and portfolio managers should be able to choose from a wide array of sound, productive investments.
- The soundness and financial condition of retirement accounts should be evaluated on the basis of their safety and ability to produce reliable income for retirees from the current earnings of companies.
- Any stock held in a retirement portfolio for eventual sale should be valued at a conservative price. Gains should not be anticipated and they should only be recorded when the stocks are sold.
- New arrangements should allow individuals to pool their retirement accounts for consolidated management, thus eliminating the need for each of them to manage their own funds as they age and make the Impossible Decision.
- To the degree possible, government should set and enforce the rules of the game, and when necessary, guide the economy rather than fight it or try to offset its effects (as with tax incentives and assistance programs).
- The best way to reach these objectives is to inform people and organizations of what is at stake so they can act in their own best interests.

Reviewing Our Lifestyles and Consumption Patterns

As more and more people have moved to large cities, we have become less and less self-reliant in a physical sense. We are like cogs in a machine. We work to get money and then use the money to meet our wants and needs. Most of us neither make the things we use nor fix them when they break. We just buy more new things. (Think of nearly everything we buy as a "thing.")

In order to sell more things, companies use advertising to make us anticipate the pleasure we will get from things we don't have. Advertising and widely available credit leads us efficiently from spurts of anticipation to purchases, just as companies intend for them to do.

Millions of people are on a treadmill where they must run as fast as they can just to keep up. Parents work to earn money, and then spend large amounts of it to buy the toys their children have seen advertised on TV. But, guess what? The anticipation is greater than the fulfillment. The toys accumulate, largely unused. "But the next toy will really make me happy!"

Children carry this lesson into adulthood. As the bumper sticker on the six-wheel pickup says, "The Bigger the Boys, the Bigger Their Toys." But the toys cost more than money. More pickups require more fuel, more roads, and more parking spaces. Working couples, who have to own two vehicles to get to their jobs, spend hours locked in traffic. Around major cities, the question at any time is, "What's jammed now?" For years, environmental writers have pointed to the ecological costs of the ever-increasing spiral of consumption.

Feelings about consumption will be particularly important for retired boomers and the communities where they live. The amount of income that they will want will be directly related to their consumption desires.

Turning that around and putting it more positively, the more boomers learn how to find joy and fulfillment with minimal consumption, the more they are likely to be truly happy if they retire on limited means.

Preparing for Active Aging

The Organization for Economic Co-operation and Development (OECD) discusses active aging in its publication *Maintaining Prosperity in an Ageing Society.*[2] It explains that peoples' disabilities are often concentrated in the last two years of their life; productive life spans vary from individual to individual; educational limitations are often more important than the availability of jobs for people of all ages, including older people who can still work; and work and leisure should be distributed more evenly over a person's life rather than concentrated in phases as they tend to be today.

The new economy, which uses technology, information, and the Internet and is fueled by stock options and phantom wealth, is forcing people in just the opposite direction from active aging. Young people are driving themselves up to sixteen hours and more a day in order to produce things, particularly software, in return for stock and options that are just forms of phantom wealth. In the view of some observers, these people lead nothing even close to a balanced life. Can such lives be sustainable?

We will discuss active aging in the context of what individuals and organizations can do in the next two chapters. *But if somebody were to ask me what is the single most important thing for boomers and younger people to do to prepare for their later years, I would say without hesitation that they should prepare for active aging.*

Summary

We can take five approaches to escape from the absurd financial trap that our nation finds itself in today. They are:

1. Changing our ways of thinking
2. Projecting our needs and the resources available to meet them
3. Replacing the phantom wealth structure
4. Reviewing our lifestyles and consumption patterns
5. Preparing for active aging

This country's founders provided a strong precedent by doing in their time the type of deep thinking that millions of busy Americans will probably have to do now.

Much of the thinking must involve projecting the real-world needs of the country and its citizens, particularly its older citizens. This must be matched with thinking about how these needs can be met.

The phantom wealth structure must be replaced. It will not be able to survive after the false expectations on which it is based are removed. When that happens, more capital will become available for making sustainable, productive investments that meet real needs instead of just using money to make money. The country's financial system will need to be upgraded, and new objectives for the system will be needed to guide millions of interested parties toward making their best long-term decisions.

The magnitude of the problem of providing adequate income to older boomers will be influenced greatly by how much they think they must consume in order to be happy. The less that is, the easier the financial problem will be to solve.

As people live longer, they must change their life strategy. Learning, working hard until your mid-sixties, and then retiring can't be the formula when there are too many people of retirement age. Active aging appears to be one of the best ideas so far behind a practical new strategy.

CHAPTER 10

What Individuals Can Do

In the Preface I explained that this book was written primarily for ten groups of readers. Let's now get specific in this chapter, and see how members of each group can use what the book says.

HIGHLIGHT 23: Millions of individuals can help change the course of history by looking ahead and acting in their own interests and the interests of the country.

Baby Boomers

Baby boomers and others who are buying (or are being urged to buy) stocks directly and indirectly through pension and mutual funds to help pay for their retirement have the greatest interest in replacing the phantom wealth structure. Their savings are being used to expand the structure, and much of their savings will be lost if it collapses. Here are nine actions that boomers can take to help both themselves and the country.

Eliminate Debts

Some advisers say it's a good idea for boomers to retain their mortgages and use what they borrow to invest more in stocks. Others suggest that it is OK to borrow for trips or other pleasures while there is time to enjoy them.

But if retirement accounts are prey to the investment and economic threats that we have discussed, most boomers should aim to be debt-free as they approach their mid-sixties for at least two reasons.

- Boomers may have to absorb losses in both their investment accounts and the value of their homes or other property at the same time. That is what to expect if there is a depression. It is important to keep in mind that a depression shrinks most asset values but doesn't shrink debts, and it is easy to wind up owing more than what the original purchases are worth.
- If boomers own their own homes and things get tight, they may want to get a reverse mortgage, a scheme by which the owners sell their homes to a lender but continue to live there and receive monthly payments, perhaps for life. To do this, however, the owner needs substantial equity in the home.

Don't Wait for Government Help

Regardless of how you may feel about government, it will not take the lead in changing the way the country manages capital until it has no choice but to do so, for two simple reasons.

- All the elected federal officials and candidates who would like to be bearers of the messages in this book could meet in a phone booth. In other words, people don't get elected or stay in office by predicting big problems.
- Organizations that have vested interests in maintaining the status quo make large campaign contributions. Ideas and pressures for change will have to come first from individuals. This means you, the reader.

Review the Seven Classes of Aging Baby Boomers

Going back to Chapter 4, reviewing the seven classes of boomers, and thinking about which class or classes you may belong to is the second step to take. Think particularly about whether you may be one of the Surprised, who expect to retire but will find you must work when your retirement plans prove inadequate. Those who think they may fall into this class must learn more. The best way to do this is to take the next steps shown here.

Ask Questions and Insist on Good Answers

When this book was written, few pension plan and mutual fund managers or financial and estate planning specialists would discuss the SFR cycle. Many had never heard of it or thought about it. That will change as the back half of the cycle approaches.

Boomers who expect stocks to help finance their retirements should ask their advisers or those who manage their accounts about how the cycle can affect them. These individuals can ask very simple questions based on the system-failure analysis technique.

Two sets of questions that can be used as a guide are included as Appendixes C and D of this book. Readers are encouraged to quote them, use them as a guide for asking their own questions, or send photocopies of them to those whom they want to ask. Indeed, it is important to do so. Here's why.

- Asking these questions can shift what lawyers call the *burden of proof* from those who question today's investment practices to those who advocate them and have the greatest interest in continuing them.
- If enough people ask their advisers, retirement plan managers, brokers, and other financial services professionals about the SFR cycle, those professionals will have to take the questions seriously. (A later section in this chapter addresses those professionals specifically and explains why this is so.)
- If the financial services professionals can provide a sound explanation for how the cycle can work, the baby boomers will be able to trust their retirement plans.

- If the financial services industry does not provide a good explanation, then millions of boomers and others will want to shift from buying stocks for phantom returns to sounder investments.
- If the financial services industry continues to avoid questions about the cycle, the avoidance will be obvious and it will become a national issue.
- Eventually, the industry will realize that the questions and their answers form a *public record.* If the industry misleads the public and the cycle fails, this record would be like the records that are so important in the liability litigation of other industries, like asbestos, automobiles, tobacco, and guns.

A letter written with Appendixes C and D as guidelines might read, in part, as follows (see the Appendixes for the actual guidelines):

> The main reason to invest retirement savings in stocks or funds that buy them is to receive gains. The stocks must be sold to realize the gains. I expect to begin selling my stocks for retirement income or to convert them to securities that pay interest in about _____ [give the year].
>
> Because any gains or losses that I may receive will be determined by the supply of and demand for stocks when they will be sold, what do you anticipate will be the market conditions when I expect to begin selling my stocks and for the following _____ [insert a number] years?

> Based on demographic projections, how many working Americans are expected to be in their peak earning years and buying stocks for retirement accounts, and how many baby boomers are expected to be selling stocks for retirement incomes when I expect to be selling?
>
> Can you provide or refer me to studies of the supply and demand conditions that are expected to prevail when baby boomers sell their stocks for retirement income and the anticipated effects of these conditions on market prices?
>
> Can you provide or refer me to studies that show, from the national standpoint, how baby boomers will be able to retire without imposing the cost of their consumption on workers?

Answers based on the history of the stock market will not be valid unless they are linked to a specific period when waves of planned selling—like what can be expected when boomers' retirement accounts do their planned selling—occurred.

If boomers ask these questions and get weak or unresponsive answers, they would be wise to base their actions on the cold logic of system-failure analysis. It is very simple. If the SFR cycle depends on buyers and nobody can explain who the buyers may be, then boomers can't depend on the cycle to support them.

Prepare to Work If You Can

Chapter 4's discussion of the seven classes of baby boomers explained why work will be an important source of income for millions of them. If at all possible, readers should try to be among the Realistic.

A quick look at different parts of the country today shows vastly different employment patterns for older people. In Florida, retirees are welcome, but aging professionals in many fields are not encouraged to hang up their shingles. In rural parts of the northern states, so many young people have moved away that despite the strong national economy, many communities are left with mostly older people who are having trouble providing for themselves.

Until there are statewide and national strategies for helping older people provide for themselves, aging boomers should plan to be as self-supporting as they can, even considering the work opportunities that different areas offer when deciding where to live.

Integrate Work and Lifestyle

People today have the opportunity to enjoy far more rewarding lives. The conventional pattern is to learn and prepare for a career, work hard, postpone pleasure, and save for retirement. It may be that, for many, a more balanced alternative includes a lifetime of learning, some pleasure along the way, and enjoyable work. Some people of all ages are doing this now, and it may become a normal pattern for everyone.

This leads directly into active aging.

Start or Join Active Aging Clubs or Retirement Clubs

The term *active aging* was used by the Organization for Economic and Co-operative Development (OECD) to describe "the capacity of people, as they grow older, to lead productive lives in the society and economy. This means that people can make flexible choices in the way they spend time over life—in learning, in work, in leisure, and in care-giving."[1]

Thousands of community-based organizations offer people help, ideas, and advice on a wide range of subjects. Some are associated with churches or synagogues; others are nonprofit community service centers. Some concentrate on helping senior citizens.

So far, few of these organizations are focused on helping boomers prepare for their later years. The sooner they begin to do so, the more good they will be able to do.

These organizations could investigate a wide range of issues, including finances, housing, employment, transportation, and of course, health care. Their members could brainstorm problems and develop ways to solve them, guide elected officials at federal and state levels, exert pressure on employers and the financial services industry, and form self-help teams to meet local needs. They could also help aging Americans find creative ways to make more money or negotiate as a group for better deals than they could obtain as individuals.

Thousands of investment clubs provide education, information, social interaction, and opportunities to make money. Most concentrate on stock gains. If the stocks-for-retirement cycle is flawed, the appeal of stocks will eventually decline. But the investment club model and perhaps even existing clubs can adapt and provide comparable services for active aging and retirement. There is probably a need for networks of active aging and retirement clubs, complete with educational organizations and journals to support them. The Internet is a natural tool for these networks. You may want to become involved with an existing organization and help it meet the needs of boomers, or you may want to help start a new one.

Demand New Types of Sustainable Investments

It is unlikely that investments to build the facilities needed by the growing number of people over age 65 could double in four years or less. These investments fall into the productive investment gap, and thus they will not be made by the private sector as long as the costs of capital are inflated by expectations of stock gains.

The country should not only end the investment competition from stock speculation but also find ways to channel savings into productive investments that are intended to provide real returns for years. Instead of being like one-time crops that must be harvested, these investments must protect capital and pay retirement incomes from then-current earnings.

For decades, the stocks of some large companies—particularly utilities—met the need for large, dependable dividends. Those stocks are now few and far between. But if stock prices are destined to become much less important, that kind of investment will have to return—brought back "by popular demand."

Find Ways to Avoid the Impossible Decision

Unless they are in an unusual situation, people can't predict how long they will live. For years, people have bought life insurance to protect against the risk that they might die too soon (or in order to build estates). But now, millions of people face the opposite risk: living longer than their capabilities and assets will sustain them.

Life expectancies, illnesses, and disabilities can be projected for groups of people but not for individuals. Today, it is hard for older people to spread their individual risks by joining a group at reasonable costs. For example, the premiums for long-term care insurance increase rapidly as the age at which one purchases them increases.

When 401(k) plans kick people out to face an uncertain future, they can buy annuities to join a group. But annuities can bring two problems: high commission costs and dependence on the SFR cycle. To promise high-income payments, annuity issuers must project portfolio earnings. Unfortunately, in many cases these projected earnings assume the continuation of historic stock gains—exactly what we have seen may not be in the cards.

Unfortunately, there are not many good solutions to the Impossible Decision problem right now, largely because not many people are demanding them. You can help create demand for them by taking the steps already mentioned: joining or forming active aging or retirement clubs; working through your union; dealing directly with financial services professionals; and contacting your local, state, and federal officials.

Work with Your Employer

Employers face uncertainties every bit as great as do baby boomers. For example, state and local governments that depend on stocks to help pay the cost of defined benefit pension plans will have to look to other sources if stocks don't do the job. This could mean reduced services or higher taxes for their jurisdictions. Similarly, if stocks fail, companies with defined benefit plans will have to pay the cost of pensions out of their earnings and assets. The next chapter discusses some alternatives for employers to today's retirement plans.

Employees must understand that this is a serious issue for employers. Poor decisions could lead to bankruptcy, which of course, would affect the employees. Conversely, employers must work with their employees and avoid even the appearance of trickery. There is no substitute for open, honest, and constructive exchange of ideas to develop plans for aging employees that will stand the test of time.

Younger Workers

People born after 1964 have different considerations from those of the baby boomers. (Although they do have more in common with the Junior Boomers, who were born after 1955.) Many of these younger people already believe that they are on their own and will have to provide for their own later years. They may be right.

Many also believe that stocks offer their best path to future comfort, but that may not be right. No book written today can project what will happen when 60 million Generation Xers start turning 65 around the year 2030. The best we can do now is to suggest some things for them to keep in mind.

Whether or not the analysis of the SFR cycle in this book is correct, the drive to inflate stock prices must end sometime. In the best of all worlds, the prices will level off and stay relatively stable for years while the country's investment systems are being upgraded. The sixteen years from 1965 to 1980 might offer a precedent of a best-case scenario. During that period, when many Generation Xers were born, the stock market as measured by the Dow Jones Industrial Average rose less than a single point. Of course, that wasn't exactly the best of times, because the market lost nearly half of its value in 1973–74. As stock advocates are quick to point out, however, it did come back up.

But if the best case is stock price stagnation while improvements are being made to the financial system, other possibilities such as a sustained bear market are far worse. To understand why a bear market might happen, Gen Xers need only consider that if their peak earnings years follow the historical pattern of those of people ages 40 to 60, they will do most of their stock buying between about 2005 and 2035. This will probably coincide pretty closely with the time when retired boomers will be selling many of their stocks. If there turns out to be only about one Gen Xer to buy each boomer's stocks, even stagnant stock prices will be hard to achieve.

Here are a few points for Generation Xers to consider.

- *Consider life over the long term.* The world, the country, and local communities will have many needs. Look for fulfilling work and investment opportunities that help meet those needs.

- *Watch how the boomers' SFR cycle evolves.* This will probably be the single most important factor to consider when Gen Xers make their own investment plans.
- *If it becomes clear that the cycle won't work for boomers, then there's no hurry to buy stocks for retirement accounts.* It could be a big mistake to buy the boomers' stocks for the long term before the market reacts to their sales. It should be noted that this conflicts directly with the most prevalent advice to buy stocks early so their gains can compound for decades.
- *Plan to work well beyond the age of 65.* The younger people following Generation X will be to them as they are to the boomers. There are limits to how much any generation can support its predecessors.
- *Study the history of former growth industries.* Those Gen Xers who are doing well in today's fastest-growing industries should study the history of the auto industry and the aircraft, radio, consumer electronics, and even large computer industries. Many people did well professionally, but investors often did not.

Finally, there are three reasons why Generation Xers should think about how they can help the country recover if the boomers' SFR cycle fails. First, there is duty, obligation, and service—ideas that helped build the country for everyone to enjoy and pass on.

Second, it will be their problem to live with. The sooner it is cleaned up, the better things will be for them.

Third, there is self-interest. If the SFR cycle does lead to serious problems, those who help provide the best solutions will probably be those who do the best as well.

Parents of Baby Boomers

The beginning of the twenty-first century offers a unique opportunity—not just in rhetoric but in the lives of real people. Millions of Americans are parents of baby boomers and Gen Xers and grandparents of the children of both. Many of these mature people have the financial independence, time, education, experience, wisdom, historical perspective, and (I believe) the obligation to help the next generation make wise preparations. It would be a tragic mistake for the country not to use these resources while they are available.

The basic premise of William Strauss and Neil Howe is that the lessons of the past are always lost rather than used to prevent disasters from recurring.[2] But millions of people are alive today who remember the Great Depression or remember hearing their parents describe it. These people are ideally placed to use their understanding to help anticipate how a similar disaster might happen in the future and to take actions to prevent it.

Older people who understand a region—be it a rural area, a suburb, a city, or a state—and its past can be particularly valuable in helping to anticipate its future needs. It would be a tragic mistake to make each generation solve its own problems, particularly when some of the problems appear to be so predictable and even repetitive. As my grandfather used to say, "Who can even guess at what is lost when a learned person dies?" I recently came across the same thought in a book, expressed this way: "When an older person dies, a library is lost." Let's save and use as much as we can while we can.

Today's older generation can try to help their descendants think realistically about the future. They can use their contacts, influence, and other resources to get leaders of companies, financial organizations, communities, states, and the federal government to consider the stocks-for-retirement cycle and its ramifications. Many parents of boomers also have a direct interest in what boomers do, because their own financial futures are on the line. Those who live into the time when boomers start selling their stocks may have their own situations affected by any financial upheavals that result.

Wealthy People

By wealthy individuals, I refer to those who have enough assets to provide for their needs and comfort, regardless of what happens to stock and real estate prices, and who expect to leave assets to their heirs or to causes. I also refer to individuals who are considered to be qualified investors by securities laws.

Wealthy people usually have three main concerns: to protect their wealth, use it effectively while they are alive, and pass it on when they die. Because stocks now represent such a large accumulation of what the country treats as wealth, the SFR cycle is vitally important to most wealthy people regardless of their age.

Protecting Wealth

If the SFR cycle poses a threat to stock prices, stocks are obviously not safe places to store wealth for the long term. Just as most baby boomers who have pension plans or retirement accounts should ask about the cycle, wealthy people (some of whom are boomers) should ask their investment advisers about how the cycle can affect them. If it can't work, they need to consider other ways to protect the wealth they have in stocks.

It may be wise to rank assets by relative safety and compare them with alternative investments. There are two aspects to this ranking: nominal value and purchasing power value. Although business setbacks or a sustained bear market and a depression would destroy the nominal value of stocks, it is impossible to predict purchasing power or inflation. Falling stock prices would be deflationary. But if the government tries to offset falling stock prices and stimulate the economy by injecting more purchasing power, its actions would tend to be inflationary. No one can know in advance which of these opposing forces would prevail.

Although stocks have generally been considered to be a good hedge against inflation, they might not provide protection if their prices are being driven down by liquidation of retirement savings. Thus, regardless of what the history of stock prices suggests, today's stocks may not be secure, long-term investments.

Some wealthy people have put significant amounts of money into hedge funds that use derivatives and formulas to offset market risk. No matter that developers of some of these formulas received Nobel Prices for their work, it is important to consider the scale-effect problem that was discussed in Chapter 2. Unless the formulas that are used to manage today's investments take into consideration the total supply of and demand for securities in the entire market, those formulas are unreliable.

This discussion boils down to the simple point that the more you depend on parasitic investments to provide phantom returns, the greater the risk you run, because phantom returns come entirely from market actions and can vanish without a trace.

What to Do with Wealth

If the SFR cycle can't work, stocks will not provide the broad road to wealth for as long into the future as they have in the past. If that is the case, one of the surest ways to create wealth may be by making productive investments and nurturing them for the real returns that they produce.

There are not many good ways to do this today. Most large companies do not want more capital, and except for angel and venture funds, the financial system is not efficient in channeling equity capital to small companies that need it. This is particularly true of community-based little companies that have sound prospects but nowhere near the potential for rapid growth that angels and venture capitalists seek.

Little companies usually need more than just money, including advice, contacts, and sometimes a bit of clout. Wealthy individuals could experiment by putting small amounts of money into pools run by experienced operational managers. These managers would work with the companies in their portfolios and help them prosper in the long run in exchange for a portion of the results.

There are few such pools today, for a variety of reasons. The main one is that with stocks doing so well, there is no demand for them. But wealthy individuals who see the need to find alternatives for protecting their wealth for decades or longer could provide the necessary demand, and at the same time create opportunities for themselves and help meet national needs. Those who pioneer this type of investing may do very well by it.

Passing on Wealth

Today, stock portfolios are the preferred way to build wealth and pass it on to beneficiaries. Tax laws encourage this strategy. But the farther into the future a person plans to use the approach, the more unreliable it appears. We cannot predict when market prices will start to be affected by the impending baby boom sales, but the strategy may not be very good from that point on.

In the past some wealthy families built companies and buildings that they could leave to heirs as long-term, operating entities that were intended to provide real returns for years or generations. A few examples of this are Corning, Du Pont, Ford, Eastman Kodak, Motorola, and Pittsburgh Plate Glass. The Chrysler Building in New York was built for this purpose.[3] The time may be coming for wealthy individuals to reconsider strategies of this type to help communities and the country as a whole while preserving their estates and providing for their heirs.

Visionary Leaders

A large group of people in the United States today are trying to reduce the emphasis on materialism and find a better balance of values and goals. This group includes those who are working for more socially, ethically, politically, and environmentally sustainable business practices. Hazel Henderson, the internationally published futurist, lecturer, and organizational consultant who wrote the Foreword to this book, is an outstanding example.

These people are working under a tremendous hardship. Even when they advise corporate executives, government officials, and others who are of like minds, their proposals are often resisted for fear of hurting corporate profits and stock prices. The earlier discussion of Ben & Jerry's showed just how poorly financial analysts can view corporate attempts to consider more than just stockholder returns.

In spite of their uphill struggle, many visionary leaders are proving that idealism and realism are compatible. Their case is easiest to make when the costs of their proposals are low or can be recovered quickly. Actions that require significant expenditures or costs that can only be recovered slowly are a tougher sell.

Until recently there have not been many reasons why a company should change its practices if the cost of change would be high or the recovery period long. But, now, a visionary leader who understands the SFR cycle and its implications can explain the costs of not changing, and what may happen if a company does not start planning to do so in time.

To put it simply, the story could go like this. Company X does not want to rock the boat. What it is doing seems to be working, and although it could treat its employees better, be a better corporate citizen, or do more to protect the environment, its executives don't want to risk hurting earnings or upsetting shareholders. The executives may not like it, but they are convinced that their jobs, their careers, and their financial welfare depend on increasing share prices. And after all, what good will it do if they lose their jobs? Will their replacements be any better?

Understanding the flaw in the SFR cycle gives a visionary leader a three-part approach to stand this kind of reluctance on its ear. The first part includes explaining how the SFR cycle will greatly reduce stock prices and hence their importance. If baby boom sales dominate the stock market, prices can drop like a box of rocks and there will be little that any company can do to fight that national trend.

The second part involves asking how the company will function when its stock price becomes less important. Who will be its most powerful constituents then and what will be its goals? If stock prices fall and lose their significance abruptly, how will the company identify its new reasons for being and convert to them? Are there any practical steps the company can take to prepare for its metamorphosis from a caterpillar to a butterfly, or will it just have to "wing it" when the time comes? For as the mature butterfly said to the youngster just emerging from its chrysalis, "You can forget most of that stuff you learned as a caterpillar; it isn't relevant anymore."

There are good answers to these questions. The corporation will best be able to prosper if society needs it. Its main constituents will be those who depend on it the most: the stakeholders that have been identified by critics of today's stockholder domination, including employees, retirees, customers, suppliers, communities, and the environment, in addition to the investors.

The third part of a visionary leader's approach can be modeled on that of companies with large research and development programs. Frequently, ideas emerge in R&D facilities that may be important if they can be made to work but initially are shrouded in unknowns. Such ideas go through an awkward stage, when their continued development would be too expensive to hide or absorb in the overhead budget but there is just not enough information to justify full-fledged development efforts.

Some companies that know their future depends on a continuing stream of new product ideas have a budget for exploring these ideas that treats them like options.[4] If further exploration shows the results will be negative, well, that's the breaks. But if the results are positive, the return can be very satisfactory. And if several options work out, the resulting opportunities in combination may be huge.

There are strong reasons why a successful corporation should establish this kind of options budget to help it make the transition. The principle is sound. Some experiments could be financed from the options budget that would be useful whether or not they will be needed for the metamorphosis. The point is that important, low-cost experiments can be undertaken quietly that may produce very important knowledge for when it is needed.

If visionary leaders and consultants explain why today's wasteful investment processes must change when stock prices no longer drive corporate America, and couple that with the options approach to experimentation, they will have a stronger argument. Furthermore, variations of this push-pull approach to change can be used to help communities, local and state governments, and eventually the federal government prepare for the changes that are coming.

Financial Services Professionals

Brokers, mutual and pension fund managers, investment advisers, financial and estate planners, and other financial services professionals may find themselves in a sticky situation. They can expect an increasing stream of questions about the SFR cycle from baby boomers and others until a consensus emerges on how it will work.

Many of these professionals will not want to admit, even to themselves, that the cycle is flawed. But they have fiduciary responsibilities and are accountable for their actions and advice. That can put them in a double-bind.

Consider the managers of portfolios who conclude that the cycle involves serious risks and that their funds should be shifted out of stocks in time to prevent losses. If they do it too soon and the market continues to rise they may lose their jobs; this happened to several managers of large mutual funds during the late 1990s. They may even be sued for failing to meet their fiduciary responsibilities to produce market returns, which also happened. But if the cycle does fail, a whole new body of law may be written when portfolio managers are sued because they didn't see it coming.

Financial advisers may be in a similar position. If they brush off or answer questions about the cycle incorrectly and it eventually does fail, they may find themselves in legal trouble. If they acknowledge that it is a serious problem but don't have good answers to the next predictable questions from their clients about alternative investments, they may lose the clients. They can hurt their own business by just being honest.

The tobacco industry found that warning labels on cigarette packages didn't provide much legal protection. Similarly, financial services professionals may find that if they provide smallprint, boilerplate cautions it will not protect them from complaints about the strong messages and bold graphs they use to promote their products.

In sum, financial services professionals have particularly strong reasons to learn more about the SFR cycle as soon as they can. If they become satisfied that they can explain how it can work as everybody hopes it will, they will be able to proceed with confidence. But if they don't see how it can work, the sooner they understand that, the better they will be able to serve their clients and protect themselves. In addition, they will see why they must find or develop alternative investment products to recommend to their clients.

Financial professionals should have their associations analyze the SFR cycle and its implications. How to do this will be discussed in the next chapter. Probably the worst thing they can do is ignore the cycle and hope it will just go away. It probably won't.

Corporate Directors, Executives, and Managers

This is another group of individuals who are in a difficult spot. Today, those who run large public corporations that have institutional shareholders know who's the boss. Regardless of what they may believe personally, unless they meet the demands of these shareholders, they can't expect to keep their jobs. In addition, their compensation is often tied to the price performance of their stock.

They are not powerless, however, and at least three paths are open to them.

- They can do their own examination of the SFR cycle and project how it may affect their companies.
- They can analyze the retirement plans of their employees to see how large drops in stock prices might affect the plans, the future profits of their companies, and the employees. It would be ideal if employees or their representatives also partici-

pated in this analysis, because if it shows that change is needed, the employees will have to have faith in the process of change.

- They can use the options approach discussed for visionary leaders (whom they may also be) to develop plans and strategies to use when the need arises. Because the cost of this approach is minimal, it would not affect their profits or stock prices significantly, so the institutional shareholders need not be aroused.

Government Officials

Officials of federal, state, and local governments may also be in awkward situations. Nobody wants to be the bearer of bad tidings. Elected officials and most who run for office treat bad news about the future like something the cat dragged in; nevertheless, they have responsibilities to the public.

Some elected and career officials are quite like corporate executives. Their jobs and their consciences require them to examine potential problems, and the SFR cycle can give them a bundle of problems.

For example, consider the head of a public retirement system that is committed to providing pensions to retired employees. Assume that the system uses stocks to increase the value of its portfolio and reduce the taxes that the jurisdiction's residents must pay to provide the system. If the SFR cycle is flawed, the system will face big troubles. Sometime in the future, the jurisdiction may have to choose between raising taxes or reneging on its commitments to its employees.

But there's another bug as well. Most jurisdictions borrow money continuously, if only to roll over their maturing bonds. When credit rating agencies eventually conclude that stock-based pension plans are weak, they will probably start to reduce credit ratings for long-term bonds because of potential pension liabilities. That could happen long before boomers start to retire.

Next, consider state, regional, county, and municipal planners. These are the people who will have to consider how to provide their jurisdictions' share of the facilities, which will be like creating three additional New Yorks, Chicagos, and Houstons. They should expect that many of the older people who will need these facilities will have very limited means. On top of that, they should be aware of the possibility of a serious economic downturn.

At the federal level, there is the Pension Benefit Guarantee Corporation (PBGC). This agency underwrites at least part of the pension liabilities of company defined benefit pension plans. It was created after the stock market slump of 1973–74, when the stock portfolios of company pension plans shrank to a fraction of their former value. If the SFR cycle does have a fatal flaw, the size of PBGC's job could make the savings and loan bailout look like child's play.

In the next chapter, we will explore ideas for new types of organizations and financial instruments to meet real needs. Many of these approaches will be slow to develop unless government officials cooperate and use their waiver authorities to permit experiments.

Finally, although government officials probably can't be expected to take the lead in examining the SFR cycle, they should certainly be aware of it. Shortly before Lawrence Summers was confirmed as Secretary of Treasury, he was asked at a meeting what he thought would happen when baby boomers shift from buying stocks to selling them. He answered that he hadn't thought about it. As a person in the audience was heard to comment, "He'd better."

Professors

Professors of business, economics, and government perform at least three vital functions. They teach students how to think and prepare for professional careers. They conduct research to advance knowledge. And as consultants, they advise governments and businesses.

I think that too often business school professors in particular teach, do research, and provide advice on a level that is narrow and superficial. As just one example, there is nothing profound in asking, as this book does, what good are stocks for retirement accounts if they will not be sold for gains. But few business professors or business school deans seem willing to consider that question.

In the physical and life sciences, research goes two ways: down into ever-greater detail and up toward ever-broader understanding. It goes wherever the probing of humans has never gone before.

In contrast, much of what business schools call research involves going out to companies and observing what they are already doing. The research does not lead, it follows.

I could expand this section into several chapters, but that is beyond the scope of this volume. Rather, in the next chapter I'll suggest examples of the type of work that pioneering professors can do to make a huge contribution.

Heads of Philanthropic Foundations

The typical foundation has two sides—the program side, which pursues the organization's mission, and the portfolio side, which provides money for the program.

The portfolios of some of America's largest foundations contain billions of dollars worth of stocks. These portfolios are as vulnerable to a failure of the SFR cycle as are the baby boomers' retirement accounts. If there is an economic dislocation or a depression, requests for assistance from foundation programs will probably increase just as their portfolio values collapse. But as we will discuss in the next chapter, in addition to foundations having a dual need, the senior executives who are responsible for both sides of these foundations' operations are in a unique position to help develop solutions.

Five Whys (or Hows)

As many historians have explained, America grew quickly because it had plenty of land and resources to support an influx of people. Things were done fast without much planning. Land and resources were used extravagantly to save labor, which was scarce. Thought and action occurred simultaneously.

The so-called new economy is expanding today in a similar manner. But some things will be different for Americans during the 2000s. As we have already discussed, people will have to think things through more thoroughly than they did in the past. Japanese manufacturers offer a good lesson in this.

In their drive to increase exports, the Japanese concentrated on quality. One way to do this was developed by Taiichi Ohno, who is generally credited with inventing just-in-time production. Ohno said that to really understand something you have to ask "why" five times.

Here's an example. Why is the gap between the doors so much wider on one side of a car than on the other side? Answering that question can lead to the stamping plant that makes the door panels. Asking why at the stamping plant can lead to the steel supplier. Asking the steel supplier can lead to questions about variations in the mix of materials that are used to make each batch of steel. And asking what the steel supplier can do to remove the variations can lead to realizing the need for real-time process control of the content of steel batches. Question sequences just like this led to better ways for Japanese and eventually American companies to produce steel and build cars.

When I used this technique to develop many of the points included in this book, I found that "how" often produced a better question than "why." And I don't think there is any magic in the number five. But the principle is important. Superficial explanations do not help people to understand and solve complex problems.

Press conferences by public officials sometimes permit followup questions. In practice, the follow-ups are just the first whys or hows. They can't go deep enough to convey real understanding or show what the official does or doesn't really understand.

Similarly, if readers of this book try to test its contents and advance their own understanding by asking the right questions, they will often encounter superficial answers. They must persist by asking why and how until they are given an answer that satisfies their need to find causes, not just effects.

Readers are likely to find that on these issues the experts are often not able to answer beyond the first or second level. Pursuing these questions may be discouraging, but doing so will show how much more we all have to learn.

Summary

We all have a stake in America's future. Some—like the baby boomers, younger workers, parents of baby boomers, wealthy people, visionary leaders, financial professionals, corporate leaders, government officials, professors, and heads of philanthropic foundations—are in a strong position to influence the future.

There are many things that people in each group can do that is in their own interest to help shift the country away from its phantom wealth structure. But the most fundamental thing to do is to understand, more deeply than many do today, *why* things are happening as they are and *how* they can be improved.

CHAPTER 11

What Organizations Can Do

HIGHLIGHT 24: The most important steps that organizations can take are to evaluate the national stocks-for-retirement cycle and, if they find that it is unreliable, to evaluate retirement portfolios realistically.

Due-Diligence Analyses of the Stocks-for-Retirement Cycle

The most immediate need is for responsible due-diligence analyses of the risks of the national stocks-for-retirement cycle, similar to the analyses that investors and companies routinely carry out before making productive investments. A due-diligence analysis starts with the question, "What could happen to make this investment go bad?" and proceeds to look for answers.

We know there is a Social Security problem because the law requires the trustees to publish a seventy-five-year projection for the program annually. This annual report is, in effect, the result of a due-diligence analysis. There has never been a corresponding, publicized analysis of the sum of all the country's organizational and individual retirement plans that considers the effects of millions of people following the same retirement investment strategy at the same time.

The core of this due-diligence analysis is not rocket science. Little more than back-of-the-envelope arithmetic is needed to estimate the potential domestic demand for stocks using available population and income projections to identify the most likely buyers and estimate how much they will be able to spend. (Chapter 2 presents a rough version of such an analysis.)

If the step shows that there will not be enough domestic buying power, the next step should be to examine potential foreign buying power. That will be less precise, but a fairly clear picture will probably emerge.

This two-step approach, based on system-failure analysis (also discussed in Chapter 2), will not predict what will happen. It will just warn if the system can't work as intended.

If the analyses show that adequate demand to make the SFR cycle work cannot be expected, the critics and the public will have many questions about who did the analyses, their interests, and the margin of error. The way the analyses are communicated will be critical to their acceptance.

For that reason, it is important for many organizations—particularly organizations of actuaries, accountants, auditors, and other financial professions—to do their own analyses and compare their results. That is consistent with good research practice, and it will reduce concerns about bias and methodology.

Evaluate Retirement Portfolios Realistically

If the due-diligence analyses show that stocks probably can't be sold from retirement accounts at the prices necessary to make them good investments, the next step should be to look at how retirement accounts are evaluated.

The normal process for determining the condition of a retirement account is to multiply the types and numbers of securities in the portfolio by their current market prices, add the amount by which the portfolio is expected to grow each year (based largely on the historical data), and compare the result with the retirement payments it will eventually have to make. If the projected assets are greater than the projected liabilities, the account is in good shape. (Of course, the process is more complicated, but this is the general idea.) Two things should be noted:

- The starting point is the market price of the securities in the portfolio. The process makes the portfolio seem like a stone wall, with each stone staying where it is put as more are added on top.
- The growth projections are largely based on stock price history, which is often viewed over ten-or twenty-year time spans.

But stock prices aren't stones. They don't just wobble, they change size. Using ten-or twenty-year spans to show stock price growth smooths out bumps that can happen during shorter periods. The smoothing obscures what a repeat of even historical fluctuations could do to a portfolio. It could be argued that this process seems to have been designed more to justify stock-based retirement accounts than to evaluate them.

The convention of taking the most recent stock prices, particularly during times of record high prices, and using them to project the amounts that retirement portfolios will be worth years hence, is spurious accuracy. As we have seen, stock prices are not created for this purpose and they are not up to the task. The convention builds anticipated price gains into the value of a stock inventory in a way that violates the accounting principles used to keep track of nearly all other inventories that are held for resale. It is a highly speculative treatment of what should be very safe portfolios.

There are other lessons to be learned from stock market history. Take, for example, the idea that stock values (if not prices) are driven primarily by earnings—past and anticipated. But market prices have varied widely in relation to earnings. Figure 7-1 showed that during the twenty years ending December 31, 1998, the total of all corporate earnings in the country rose by 212 percent while the market price of all stocks rose by 1,457 percent—seven times as much.

One way to gauge whether a stock price is high or low is to examine its price-to-earnings ratio. This same measure can be applied to indices that measure the price level of the whole market.

Market history tells us that the p/e ratio of the S&P 500 Index has ranged between about 37 and 7.5. That is, the price of the stocks in the Index was between 37 and 7.5 times what they earned.

On March 6, 2000, the S&P Index earned $43.96. If you multiply that by the historical p/e ratio range of 37 to 7.5, it shows that in the past, those earnings might have supported prices between about 1630 and 330. This is a range of nearly 5 to 1. The price of the Index on that date was 1409, near the upper end of the range.

Retirement portfolios that track the Index were valued on the basis of 1409 on that date. But should that price have been used for long-term projections? During the 1973–74 market decline, stock prices were cut almost in half. If that drop, which had no underlying demographic cause, were to be repeated, the Index could drop to about 705. And even that number assumes the earnings won't go down, which of course they would do in a recession or a depression. Treating the stock value of the portfolio as being somewhere on a range between 1630 and 330 would be much more realistic than saying that the value is 1409.

Other methods could also be used to calculate the value ranges of retirement portfolios. What all methods would appear to lose in precision, they would gain in realism. You can be far more confident saying that the future value of a portfolio will be within a range of 5 to 1 than projecting a particular value within that range.

This is not a trivial detail if you think about how the people who are putting their retirement savings into stocks will react when they learn that the monthly incomes they can expect to receive from their portfolios may be somewhere in this 5 to 1 range, or between $5,000 and $1,000. As that sinks in, stocks will lose their appeal as a sure thing, the drive to buy them will wane, fixation on prices will decline, pension and mutual funds will find it harder to sell their shares, corporations will be under less pressure to inflate their stock prices, the country will look for ways to make more dependable and sustainable investments, and the phantom wealth leak will be reduced.

An even more conservative approach would be to value stocks in retirement portfolios in the way almost all other inventories of things that are held for future sale are valued: at their *cost or market price, whichever is lower.* Think how appealing stocks would be if they could never be valued at more than was paid for them until they were sold. That's the way the inventory in Mom's and Pop's store is valued.

After performing due-diligence analyses of the SFR cycle, the next important step is to reflect the results of the analyses when evaluating retirement portfolios. It is also one of the easiest steps. Once the flaw in the cycle is understood, there are not likely to be insurmountable hurdles that prevent the flaw from being considered by those who have, manage, or evaluate retirement portfolios.

Develop Active Aging Programs Rather Than Just Retirement Programs

The Organization for Economic Co-operation and Development (OECD) discusses active aging in its publication *Maintaining Prosperity in an Ageing Society.*[1] It explains that peoples' disabilities are often concentrated in the last two years of life; productive life spans vary from individual to individual; educational limitations are often more important than the availability of jobs for people of all ages, including older people who can still work; and work and leisure should be distributed more evenly over a person's life rather than concentrated in phases as they tend to be today.

In contrast, typical corporate retirement plans are based on the assumption that older people will work full schedules until they retire or change employers. The plans assume that there will be a clean break between work and retirement at full benefits. In part, this is because federal laws require it.

But today, companies and older employees alike are finding that this kind of plan may not fit their needs or wants. Having gone through rounds of downsizing that urged older employees to take early retirement, some companies are finding that they chased away too much knowledge. Several years ago, a senior manager of a large company whose name is (was?) a household word, lamented to me that he didn't think its electronics division had retained enough experienced engineers to introduce a new product. Not long after that, the division was disbanded and sold.

Legalities aside, companies and employees need ways to shift gradually from full-to part-time employment, perhaps in different career fields. They should have access to full health benefits and partial retirement income payments to supplement their declining employment income. In addition, company retirement plans could help older employees pay for other changes that many of them will have to, or want to, make.

Congress took a step in the right direction in 2000 when it revised Social Security to allow people to receive their full retirement benefits even if they continue to work. Before that, retirement benefits were reduced if working income exceeded certain limits.

Companies can develop active aging programs to provide financial advice and other services to help both themselves and their employees make the transition from work to retirement. These programs could even provide ways to pool the employees' self-managed retirement accounts and help them avoid having to make the Impossible Decision about how long each of them will live.

Active aging programs could meet a wide range of needs. They could be as accessible as the employees' jobs. They could encourage companies and employees to develop mutually beneficial work and retirement arrangements, perhaps years in advance. Depending on the range of services provided, older employees and retirees might find that many of the problems that worry them the most could be worked out with the help of their employers' active aging programs.

These arrangements would help companies build loyalty and retain critical employees at affordable costs. They might also help reduce companies' contingent liabilities of having to make good on their retirement commitments if the SFR cycle does not work.

From the national standpoint, active aging programs could help meet needs of older people at local levels before the needs cascade into demands for government action. In addition, by helping older people continue to work longer and draw smaller amounts of retirement pay, they might help avoid a collapse of the SFR cycle. Even if the cycle does fail, these plans would be a nucleus around which to build recovery efforts.

There are three more important points to make about active aging programs.

- Unions could play vital roles. In some cases, companies may decide to let unions run the programs.
- Companies that don't want to become involved in the lives of their employees can make a huge contribution by arranging at arm's length for other organizations and professionals to provide the services. They have more buying power and savvy to make sound arrangements than most employees and they can monitor the quality of the services that are provided.
- Companies could work together to develop community-based active aging programs, which might provide beneficial links and services for aging employees while keeping a distance between employers and the lives of their employees. Working together with community leaders to develop these programs might induce large corporations to return to their former practice of helping communities as good corporate citizens.

Although this discussion is directed primarily at companies with defined benefit retirement plans, there is an even greater need for defined contribution plans to become active aging programs or feed accumulated savings into them. Today, individually managed plans put the full risk and responsibility for investment and retirement decisions on individuals, many of whom have little ability to make them. Millions of these people are being encouraged to buy into the SFR trap. They will need help, and active aging programs could provide it.

State and local governments should also develop active aging programs. Many jurisdictions have defined benefit pension plans with stock portfolios that are underfunded even by current evaluation techniques. If stocks fail to live up to their promises, more of these plans will become underfunded. To make matters worse, few state and local government employees are covered by Social Security.

When bond-rating agencies use ranges and other more conservative approaches to evaluate the financial condition of state and local pension plans, they will find that perhaps thousands of the plans will not be able to meet their obligations. The jurisdictions might be forced to reneg on commitments to their employees, increase taxes, borrow, or all of the above. These evaluations can lead to lower ratings for long-term bonds and higher borrowing costs, which of course will exacerbate the jurisdictions' problems.

There are real opportunities for state and local governments to work with their employees to develop programs that provide for the individual needs of the employees while reducing the chances that the current plans could end up hurting everybody.

Form Active Aging Clubs

There are thousands of investment clubs whose primary purpose is to help their members learn more about investing. These clubs are an outstanding model for voluntary, community-based organizations that could help people learn more about their needs and options, make preparations, and enjoy their later years. Active aging clubs might be primarily educational or they could provide services, much like the employer-or community-based active aging programs described in the previous section.

There are several ways to foster active aging clubs. They could be organized through the community colleges, most of which already provide courses geared to older people. Unlike universities that are tightly bound by academic requirements, traditions, and schedules, community colleges are remarkably agile in detecting and taking advantage of opportunities to serve their communities. Many of them have close ties to local employers so they can train people for available jobs.

Or a nonprofit organization might be formed to serve the clubs, much as the National Association of Investors Corporation (NAIC) helps investment clubs. Ideally, the supporting organization would not have close ties to the insurance or mutual fund industry or to others that might influence its actions or present the appearance of a conflict of interest.

Develop Ways to Avoid the Impossible Decision

Many retired people are already facing the problems caused by retirement self-sufficiency that were discussed in Chapter 4 and in the Vanguard Group's *Guide to Investing During Retirement.*[2]

Although many baby boomers and younger workers believe that they can manage their own affairs better than anyone else can, there is simply no way that most retired people, who will have to sell their assets to live, can know how long to stretch them. It is much easier to anticipate the aggregate needs of large groups of people. Thus, people need ways to pool their assets and spread the risk. Portfolios can be managed and liquidated to meet the needs of groups of people far more realistically than for individuals.

Some annuity plans work this way today, but more options are needed. One possibility might be to allow employees who are covered by employer-sponsored pension plans to convert them to active aging programs and let retirees add assets to these plans.

If people think about it, they can come up with countless other ideas. For example, it may be useful to create pools for people who have different size retirement portfolios and different objectives, such as those who want to preserve wealth and transfer as much as possible to their heirs.

The government, the securities industry, and many employers today promote self-sufficiency. But despite its appeal to traditional American values, the concept is fundamentally unsound and will have to be replaced with something that can work if millions of tragedies are to be avoided.

New Financial Instruments and Institutions

HIGHLIGHT 25: There are vast opportunities for organizations There are vast opportunities for organizations that pioneer new types of sustainable investments, investment instruments, financial institutions, and business organizations.

I believe that during the first quarter of the twenty-first century, growing pressures will force the country to realize that its financial institutions should exist to serve people, and not the other way around. (The situation will be much like when this country decided that the people, and not the King, should be sovereign.) In an article in *The Economist,* Peter Drucker explained why he thinks the financial services industry will have to reinvent itself, and he didn't even mention the SFR cycle problem.[3]

Whether or not the cycle fails, much of the emphasis that is now being put on stock prices will decline, and nearly all investment firms that are involved with stocks will have to change or go out of business. Drucker says that they have a big opportunity to provide smaller companies with services that are readily available to large companies. He mentions cash management as an example.

I agree with him, but take it a step further. After World War II, the Japanese accomplished much of their recovery through powerful clusters of companies that they built around major banks. Eventually they created a bubble economy that burst, but we should not allow their mistakes to cloud the positive aspects of this model, which showed how financial institutions can help clusters of companies. General Electric has a division that finances many of the company's sales, much as the Big Three auto makers and some large retailers do with their own credit operations.

In *The Post-Corporate World,* David Korten explained why the country needs more community-based companies.[4] One way to foster their development is to provide a wide range of services that they need to get established and run efficiently. In addition to providing financial services, local organizations could form pools that provide services for almost every type of function that is not directly related to a company's proprietary operations. This can include purchasing, insurance, some recruiting, employee training, and even representation in governmental rule-making processes. There are precedents for all of these types of clustered activities.

Financial institutions that undertake tasks like these could obtain money from individuals and retirement plan portfolios and invest it in small companies that are presently denied access to the primary lode of personal savings. Buying the stock of a little company is indeed risky for someone who has no connection with that company. But putting savings into a fund that takes friendly equity positions in dozens of companies, all of which the fund helps to achieve success, would be an entirely different proposition.

Managerial Strategic Investment Companies (MSIC)

Little companies represent the largest concentration of need for additional capital. More often than not, however, they need more than just money. They also need strategic and expert advice, business contacts, and often managerial skills that they don't have. Only a fraction of them offer investment opportunities that approach the pinnacle of today's productive investment pyramid.

Investing in these companies requires high administrative costs. Often they are privately held and their stocks don't trade on any exchange, so portfolio managers can't just sell the stocks if the companies don't do as well as hoped. Furthermore, both federal and state laws limit these companies' abilities to sell stock to most people because of rampant fraud that occurred in the past. These limitations have been relaxed to a degree, but equity markets are still inefficient for smaller companies.

In 1993, legislation was proposed to amend the Investment Company Act of 1940 to allow what are called Managerial Strategic Investment Companies.[5] An MSIC would raise capital like a closed-end mutual fund. Then it would take friendly, long-term, minority positions in small and medium-size companies and provide additional services that the companies need—much as angels do.

Because an MSIC would not buy and sell its companies' stocks, it and the companies would avoid much of the regulatory baggage that goes with arm's-length trading. An MSIC could provide small or medium-size companies with the best of both worlds—a private company's freedom to act and a large public company's access to resources. MSICs could become intermediaries that would channel personal savings that are managed by pension and mutual funds to small companies that want to make productive investments. The MSIC approach is used in Sweden, where about 10 percent of all public company stocks are owned by intermediaries of this type.

The legislation was not enacted, and the Securities and Exchange Commission did not use its waiver authority to allow an MSIC experiment. Yet, the idea is a good one.

Royalty-Based Financing

Another approach is royalty-based financing. Here, instead of conventional dividends or interest, companies pay their investors a royalty based on their total sales, total employee earnings, or some other operational measure, much as some authors and inventors are paid.

Not intended for trading, royalty-based financing instruments or bundles of them could be ideal investments for retirement accounts that will need future earnings streams instead of securities to sell into a falling market. They could be used by active aging programs to invest in human capital like education and training so that workers prosper, and they could also do well for retirement savers and eventually for retirees. Approaches like this have been used in several states to help small businesses get started.[6] In 1999, legislation was also proposed to allow small business investment corporations to use royalty financing, but it did not pass that year.

There is no reason why these two approaches could not be combined to create MSICs that would provide capital to smaller companies through royalty-based financing. And these approaches barely scratch the surface of what could be done once the need is realized.

There are huge opportunities for the financial organizations that pioneer new investment instruments and institutions of this type. These organizations will require a different mindset. They will need patience, where less than five years is short term, to build up trust in smaller companies, help the companies with their individual financial and operational needs, serve all stakeholders, and renounce the goal of parasitic returns. The institutions that do this will serve communities much as bankers used to do.

Finally on this point, several state pension plans have gotten into trouble by investing too heavily inside their borders—such as buying stock in a steel plant (now defunct) that probably shouldn't have been in the state in the first place. Retirement portfolios that invest in MSICs or organizations like them should spread their investments over a number of them in different regions to gain the portfolio effect of distributed risks.

New Investment Instruments

Today, public companies raise money by selling stocks, bonds, and promissory notes. Each type of instrument has its own characteristics. There are hybrids, such as participating preferred stocks that pay scheduled dividends and share in earnings increases, but they are not widespread. In the main, an investor either lends money that will earn interest until it is repaid or buys equity whose value fluctuates.

Both long-term bonds and stocks are widely used for speculation. Bond prices go up when interest rates go down and vice versa, whereas stocks do their own thing. But most of the stocks that retirees used to cherish because of their large, predictable dividends, with perhaps modest increases from time to time, are gone. Older people held these stocks primarily for their real returns, not for trading. When the baby boomers realize the SFR problem, there will be a renewed demand for instruments with these attributes.

Another type of instrument is also needed, one that aligns the interests of employees, investors, retirees, and managers. Today, a typical way to increase earnings and stock prices is to squeeze employees. As stocks are used today, they are almost perfectly designed to cause conflict between investors and employees.

But it is not carved in stone that instruments can't be developed to pay predictable real returns to investors like interest and a royalty that is based on the company's business success and its total payroll. With such instruments, investors would see employee compensation as something to encourage, not a cost to reduce. The company would be encouraged to make productive internal investments that add jobs, not discouraged from making them.

Financial institutions such as MSICs could raise money with instruments like these in the same way that closed-end mutual funds raise their capital portfolios. But unlike the stock of closedend funds, the instruments would be intended to raise long-term capital, provide the continuing flows of real returns that retirees need, and encourage the companies to maintain jobs, particularly for older people who will want or need to work. The instruments could be bought and sold if necessary, but they would be designed to discourage trading. They would be long-term, win-win instruments.

New Business Organizations: Collaboratives

This approach extends the principle of win-win investing to small companies themselves. It combines elements of corporations, cooperatives, and old whaling ship agreements. The primary emphasis of these organizations would be on labor because the largest component of national income is salaries and wages. Workers, managers, and investors would all be *members* of a *collaborative* (with the emphasis on "co" and "labor").

Under a whaling ship agreement, after a voyage was completed and the costs were recovered, the proceeds were distributed as shares. The owner got so many shares, the captain so many, and on down to the ship's boy. It was a royalty-style arrangement.

Similarly, the managers and workers of a collaborative would receive specified amounts as their basic salaries or wages. Investors would receive a specified basic amount as interest. A new business might delay its payments to investors until sales begin and other costs are being recovered. At the end of each accounting period, after all costs, including the basic amounts, have been paid to workers, managers, and investors, the remainder would go into a total earnings pot. Some of the pot would be kept for continued operations, contingencies, and reinvestment. The rest would be distributed by formula to the workers, managers, and investors.

The agreement could provide that if jobs are eliminated, any savings would go primarily to the remaining workers for several years, not to the investors.

All members of a collaborative would have a common interest in keeping the business healthy, expanding it, and increasing the returns to all. The returns to investors would be real. Because all members would understand that what they receive in the future will result from what they accomplish, they would have a strong incentive to serve their customers, suppliers, and the community. Phantom wealth would not be a consideration.

Investor members could sell their shares, perhaps back to the collaborative, but the membership certificates would not be instruments for trading or speculation. Another exit strategy for investor members could involve intermediary organizations that would accumulate the investment instruments of collaboratives in pools as long-term holdings for retirement accounts. This would provide diversity, the stability of community-based businesses, and long-term future earnings streams.

New Objectives for Corporate Governance

The principles of corporate governance that grew out of the shareholders' rights movement are a mixed bag. Some, such as making sure that managers don't enrich themselves at the expense of their companies, are sound under any conditions. *But the idea that corporations exist almost entirely to benefit their shareholders through stock price increases cannot survive after the flaw in the SFR cycle has become widely recognized.*

When baby boomers understand that they need companies to make sound long-term commitments, conduct responsible businesses, and reward owners with real returns based on what they actually accomplish, there will be less pressure for higher stock prices.

The country's major financial institutions and its public corporations should be thinking seriously about how to make the transition from driving corporations for stock price gains to driving them for the benefit of all stakeholders and society. The institutions that make the transition best will be the survivors and winners.

Economics, Accounting, and Transactions

There is a fascinating disconnect between phantom returns and the way economists and accountants usually think. From the Gross Domestic Product down to the smallest company, virtually all economic data are based on transactions. Sales, material, and labor costs, investments, and virtually everything that goes into the economy are recorded or estimated as transactions. The transactions are combined and summarized by calendar period. Then they are turned into accounting statements that show how things stood at the beginning of the period (a balance sheet for a company, outstandings for the economy), how the transactions affected things (the profit-and-loss statement for a company, flows for the economy), and how things wound up (the next balance sheet or outstandings). All the numbers are checked, crosschecked, and made as consistent as possible.

Except, that is, for the phantom wealth that is supposedly created by stock price gains. When Yahoo! stock jumped over 60 percent after its inclusion in the S&P 500 Index, there was absolutely no way to cross-check the validity of its surge in capitalized value (which was driven by the convention of marking all shares to market) that made it appear to be a larger company than General Motors. Nor was it possible to follow the effects of that surge as it worked through stock portfolios, retirement plans, and the consumer wealth effect. Throughout the economy, the value of assets just appeared to grow for no traceable reason.

One of the country's greatest needs is for a realistic way to measure the effects of real and phantom returns from investments. As the discussion of young growth and rapid growth companies in Chapter 5 showed, stocks make a vital contribution to the economy. The country needs to preserve some aspects of stocks but it also needs to develop a better way to understand when these investments are useful and when they are destructive. This parallels the need to develop better measures of the economy than the Gross Domestic Product.[7]

Foundations, Experiments

It is one thing to toss out ideas but something entirely different to show how to make them work. Unfortunately, the legal and fiduciary limitations on the pension fund and mutual fund managers who handle most of the country's retirement savings prevent them from changing their strategies until good alternatives have been developed. The idea of valuing their portfolios with ranges will make them squirm, and more willing to consider alternatives perhaps, but it is not realistic to expect them to pioneer the alternatives.

The situation cries out for others to test new ideas.

Large foundations are in an ideal position to experiment with new investment approaches. Their missions vary widely, but many of them are helping communities, improving health and social conditions that frequently include meeting the needs of older people, advancing education, and protecting the environment.

There is a "Chinese wall" between the program and portfolio sides of a foundation. The wall obscures the fact that, to varying degrees, the portfolio side may be contributing to the pressure on corporations that causes them to create the conditions that the program side is trying to change. This wasn't planned, it just works that way.

Foundations are unique because of their wide discretion over what they can do with billions of dollars. They must adhere to their charters and meet certain tax requirements. But unlike pension and mutual funds, few parties have the right to second-guess their investments or sue them for fiduciary reasons.

They also have a hole in the Chinese wall. They are authorized (by federal tax regulations, at least) to make what are called *program-related investments.* This means they can make investments from their portfolio side to fund projects on their program side. Foundations use this technique, for example, to make what are really subsidized loans to help community-based organizations become self-sufficient. Unlike a grant, a program-related investment loan can help put the recipient on a business-like basis while it makes money for the foundation.

So what do we have? On one hand, we have foundations that invest billions of dollars to earn money that they will use to meet philanthropic objectives. The objectives of some foundations are closely aligned with meeting the needs of the country's aging population. They have authority to provide grants and to make experimental investments.

On the other hand, let's assume that we have state or local governments that might like to run experiments with ideas like active aging programs or setting up MSICs to make productive investments and provide other services to smaller companies. Let's also assume these jurisdictions are willing to serve as test platforms but they can't justify risking their taxpayers' money.

Voilà! A basis for practical experiments emerges. A foundation can make a program-related investment that provides the capital for a state or local government to run the experiment. If it works, everybody is a hero and a new investment model is demonstrated. If it doesn't work, the foundation just funded another community-based project and everybody learned something.

Indeed, if the SFR cycle is destined to fail, foundations are going to need alternative investments to protect their own portfolios. Thus, they would not only help the country by helping jurisdictions that want to try new models but also be working toward meeting their own long-term investment needs.

On top of that, some foundations have standing as large institutional investors. If their experimental models work and foundations begin using them as sound investments of their own, they will set examples that pension and mutual fund managers can follow.

Multipliers of multipliers.

Virtuous Cycles

Typical economic analyses sometimes miss important cause-and-effect relationships. For years, what the Japanese call the *virtuous cycle* was an example of this.

Perhaps the easiest way to explain virtuous cycles is with the one that General Electric ran for decades. One side of the company made products to generate and distribute electricity. The other side made products to consume electricity. As power companies grew and bought more generation and distribution equipment, the cost of power came down, so more products were invented to use it, which of course created more demand. The two sides of the company fed off each other, and large profits from some divisions were used to subsidize new products and even new industries. This went on until the oil embargoes changed ideas about energy use and large stockholders began to demand even larger phantom returns.

As Paul Kennedy explained, one of the earliest virtuous cycles drove the Industrial Revolution in Britain.[8] In describing the factory system, he says: "The massive increase in productivity, especially in the textile industries ... in turn stimulated a demand for more machines, more raw materials (above all cotton), more iron, more shipping, better communications, and so on."

Several virtuous cycles played a big part in America's development. An early one involved using railroads as the dominant mode of transportation, wood and coal as the dominant fuels, wood and iron as the dominant materials, developing northern manufacturing and finance centers as industrial drivers, and westward expansion as a dominant goal.

This gradually grew into a cycle that included air and highways as the dominant modes of transportation, petroleum and electricity as the dominant fuels, steel, aluminum, and concrete as the dominant materials, expanding southern and western manufacturing and finance centers as the industrial drivers, and suburban expansion as the dominant goal.[9]

We have already discussed Japan's situation after World War II, so we need only add that they used British and American models to design their virtuous cycle of importing low-cost materials, using various types of knowledge, including technology, worker skills, and design to add value to them, and then selling the high value-added products on world markets.[10] This development didn't just happen, it was deliberate.

Although many economists said it couldn't work, the Japanese used their cycle to build the world's second largest economy in just a few decades. In the process, they showed the rest of the world how well it could work. Japan's subsequent troubles cannot detract from that accomplishment.

The fundamental contribution of all virtuous cycles is to help companies, investors, and ordinary people understand at least part of what is happening and figure out how they want to participate. To varying degrees, each of the virtuous cycles mentioned came about through foresight and planning.

These and other cycles teach us an important lesson. In the past, strong economies didn't just grow because of uncoordinated efforts of countless players who were constantly in motion. There were patterns for the players to recognize and use to their advantage.

States and communities all around the United States today have an opportunity to think about what they want to become as the country and its investment institutions adapt to the aging population. They can define what they mean by *growth* and set broad outlines for the cycle that can take them where they want to go. This is not conventional thinking, but it has a more solid historical foundation than growth based on stock prices.

In fact, a large cycle is running in the United States today. It is driven primarily by computer, communications, and medical technology; scientific and technical training; entertainment and the market for diversions; retirement savings; and investment processes that provide huge phantom wealth rewards for hopes and expectations.

At the national and probably at the international level virtuous cycles and many subcycles could be built by combining some or all of the elements in the following list:

- Sustainable energy, manufacturing, and transportation
- Conservation and materials recycling
- Healthy economic regions
- Education, training, and communications
- Fulfilling opportunities for all types of people of all ages, including the less advantaged
- Converging financial, economic, environmental, and social objectives

SEC1 AND SEC2

The federal government aids, abets, and even promotes short-term stock trading, primarily through the Securities and Exchange Commission. One way to understand its effects is to compare it with a theoretical organization that would be its opposite.

Let's call the Securities and Exchange Commission SEC1. Let's assume that its mirror twin or foil is the Sustainable Economy Commission, or SEC2. The job of this organization is to guide the economy toward meeting the real needs of all Americans in ways that can continue indefinitely without depriving generations that will follow.

Before we begin thinking about the differences between SEC1 and SEC2, let's review again the main messages of this book as they were listed in the Introduction:

1. Much of the country's economy and many of its retirement plans are built on a structure of phantom wealth that depends on stock prices.
2. Stock prices are based on projected future events or what people hope will happen, not on actual corporate accomplishments. Using stock prices to measure wealth is like counting chickens before they've hatched.
3. The drive to create phantom wealth by inflating stock prices helps some people, but it distorts the economy and hurts society as a whole.
4. Demographic trends and retirement plans are helping to build the phantom wealth structure. But unless the structure is replaced with one that is more sustainable, those same trends will eventually make it fail, and that in turn will drag down the retirement plans and the economy.
5. Individuals and organizations can help prevent retirement plans and the economy as a whole from collapsing—or protect themselves in case there is a collapse—by creating real wealth based on work, earnings, and solid accomplishments,

instead of just hopes. But doing this requires a different mindset that includes new values, goals, and ways of thinking about living, aging, investing, and running companies.

SEC1 is running flat-out to expand the phantom wealth structure that the fourth message says will fail and must be replaced. A classic illustration of this was provided by Jack Willoughby in his article in *Barron's* titled "Burning Up."[11] Willoughby listed 207 Internet companies, all of which lost money in the fourth quarter of 1999. In total, they lost $29.7 billion. Their total revenues were $4.8 billion. Their combined market capitalization as of the end of February 2000 was $493.3 billion. Just 21 of these companies had a combined capitalization of $278.1 billion. If that were real instead of phantom money, it would be more than the country's military expenditures proposed in the budget for fiscal year 2001!

SEC1 does very little that is consistent with the fifth message to meet the real-world needs of people and communities while preventing the phantom wealth structure from failing. Instead, it supports the current cycle that was described in Parts I and II.

Developing ideas for SEC2 can be a powerful learning exercise for students of business, economics, and government. But it can be much more than that. Many observers in and out of government believe the economy is a level playing field that allows sound investments to be made in the balanced best interests of all concerned. Comparing the two SECs, even as summarily as we have just done, however, shows that SEC1 exerts a strong bias in favor of just using money to make money in the short run at the expense of most interested parties, the long run, and sustainability.

To begin to identify what SEC2 would do, look at the points discussed in this chapter and the list of elements in the previous section that could be used to start a new, sustainable, virtuous cycle. What new rules of the game could be developed to encourage such a cycle? How could those who manage most of the country's retirement savings be encouraged to invest in these activities?

This is the kind of inquiry that people undertook in the mid-to late-1700s.

Summary

Organizations of financial professionals should first analyze the national stocks-for-retirement cycle to see if it can work for future retirees. If it can't, the next step should be to evaluate all retirement plans on a more realistic basis.

Financial organizations should develop new types of financial instruments and institutions that channel personal savings to community-based, small companies that will provide secure jobs and pay investors on the basis of what they accomplish.

Companies and state and local governments should promote the concept of active aging and help develop programs and organizations to help people make the transition to this approach to life.

Large foundations are in a unique position to help the country make the transition to a more sustainable future because they have both the program interests and the investment need to develop new models for themselves and other large investors.

Finally, at the broadest and most general level, it is important to expand economic understanding by developing realistic ways to measure and trace the effects of phantom wealth. In addition, it is important to learn how to channel money away from the pursuit of phantom wealth and into investments that will lead to a more sustainable economy.

CHAPTER 12

Conclusion: How to Change a Very Big System

HIGHLIGHT 26: The key is to change a few critical things that will cause many other changes to ripple out and eventually to cascade.

I recommend the classic approach to changing large systems, which is to identify a very few critical actions that, if taken, can lead to a plethora of cascading changes. One change leads to three other changes, which make nine other things happen, and so on. A disadvantage of this approach is that there is no way to know in advance all that will happen. An advantage is that it can work.

Thus, I urge three seemingly mundane steps:

1. Avoid the trap of trying to "save" Social Security with stocks.
2. Analyze the national stocks-for-retirement cycle.
3. Base the evaluation of retirement plans on the results of that analysis.

If taking these three actions does what I think it will do, many things will change of their own accord. To some, this approach may seem very hit-or-miss. The first step may seem rather passive. But if a congressional review finds that stocks can't really help

Social Security, the country will become "a little bit pregnant." It will be almost impossible to avoid the next logical question, which is, What can stocks do if they can't help Social Security?

The Role of the Federal Government

Except for urging that it keep Social Security money out of stocks, I have avoided suggesting federal government actions for three reasons.

- Too many people might not like some of my ideas and say, "If that's how we have to fix the problem, I don't agree with the problem!"—the find-a-more-comfortable-diagnosis response.
- The government reacts to emergencies and pressure. Despite growing awareness of the Social Security problem, it is not yet seen as an emergency, and most people have never even thought about phantom wealth as a weakness of all retirement plans. Furthermore, financial pressure in the form of campaign contributions from corporations and others with large interests in maintaining the status quo will prevent the government, including Congress, from considering remedial actions until an emergency is imminent or its possibility is widely recognized. In contrast, we are trying to prevent an emergency.
- Nobody knows what to write into new laws, regulations, or tax policies.

We must be realistic about what we expect government to do. For example, in theory, changing tax policy should be like a surgical operation to encourage desirable actions and discourage undesirable ones. But in practice, when you look at new tax laws as they roll out of the operating room, you can't tell whether the doctors used a scalpel, a chain saw, or a bulldozer.

For example—and *this is not a recommendation*—consider what might happen to a proposal to treat parasitic investing like all other gambling: tax the gains as current income but don't allow the losses to be deducted. From a theoretical standpoint, this idea might (or might not) make sense. But from a political standpoint, it would not be considered.

There is also the Law of Unintended Consequences. The noble goals of home ownership and an efficient road system during the Eisenhower era largely destroyed the inner cities, led to suburban sprawl, and resulted in massive traffic congestion. Although I favor planning to meet the needs of the aging population, there is a limit to what it can accomplish on a national scale, at least as a first step.

Part of what we can learn from the founding of this country, the home ownership-road system experience, and many other lessons of history is that it is wise to run local experiments to see what works before setting a national agenda. It may not seem like an efficient approach in theory, but in practice it can lead to better use of proven solutions and fewer unintended consequences.

Americans Are Not Alone

In Chapter 2 we discussed that population aging is a global phenomenon. The economic and social issues vary widely from country to country, but probably no industrialized country in the world can escape them. Other countries may be willing and able to help American boomers retire. But it would be foolish to count on them until sound analyses show how they can help and international agreements ensure that they will do it.

Productive Investments and Merging Interests

When, as Paul Harvey says on his radio program, people "know the rest of the story," they will realize that parasitic gains are no substitute for productive investments, real returns to investors, adequate employee compensation, or sustainability. Long-term thinking and freedom will be recognized as compatible, complementary, and absolutely necessary.

Instead of being forced to choose between competing interests—as kids in camp used to say, "Clean mind or clean body; take your pick"—most people will see that the United States can't be successful in the long run without satisfying all of them. Major issues that are treated today as either-or choices will be seen instead as vital *and* opportunities. Here are a few examples.

Workers and Retirees

Discussions of America's aging population often oppose interests in emotionally laden terms. It is said that workers will be *taxed* to pay *lazy, politically powerful,* and *selfish* retired baby boomers. Social Security investments in government bonds (which most financial institutions treat as the safest possible investment) are *meaningless IOUs.* Generation Xers may have to *revolt* and *fight* for themselves.

This conflict-oriented language is consistent with the country's political system, which produces winners and losers, its legal system, based on adversarial confrontation, its view of the world as being like a continuing series of sporting events, and its media that use conflict to sell their products.

But let's look at the situation another way. When millions of baby boomers realize that the SFR cycle won't work for them, they will need a Plan B. Many will no longer want the portfolio managers of their retirement accounts to force large companies to cut jobs and benefits to increase stock prices because stock prices won't mean much to them, but they will need the jobs and benefits. They will stop putting money into mutual funds that create pressures for higher stock prices.

Once they and younger workers understand that phantom returns can actually come back to haunt them, they will see that they have complementary, not opposing interests. When this happens, they will want companies to once again become stable operating entities and employers, not just stepping-stones to phantom wealth.

Environmentalists and Companies

Many environmentalists appear to (or actually do) oppose economic growth. At national and international levels, their pleas for large companies to consider long-term environmental effects are often drowned out by the demands of institutional investors for stock price gains and claims that too many jobs would be lost if companies took a longer view. In smaller communities, environmentalists have opposed developers that they thought were needlessly destroying rural and urban spaces. These battles have primarily been fought on legal turf because the economic landscape usually seems hostile to the environmental cause.

We will not consider the merits of the environmentalists' arguments here. But when public companies discover that stock prices don't mean very much because aging investors want jobs and stable dividend streams for decades instead of phantom wealth, their time horizons will double, triple, or quadruple. This is because retirement savings will no longer flow into parasitic investments that are expected to double in four years or less and that set the standard for all investment returns.

After companies and institutional investors make these discoveries, many of the investments that are avoided today because they are in the productive investment gap will be seen to have merit. The gap will narrow. Advocates of investments in more sustainable processes will find an entirely different climate, and more of their recommendations will be accepted. As expectations of stock growth wane, companies will be able to shift from trying to make their internal investments double in four years or less to opportunities that may take ten years or longer to double. Then environmentalists with good ideas will find themselves more in demand to help the companies.

Communities and Local Developers

Many communities have responded to the demands of companies whose expansion was driven by the steroid-like effects of stock prices. They have had to compete to attract and then retain companies in bidding wars. Many of them provided tax incentives, made expenditures for transportation and education, and even lowered environmental requirements.

Local real estate developers were usually the big winners in communities that were successful in the bidding wars. Throughout all of this, the role of cities and communities as places to live, grow, work, raise families, enjoy full lives, help immigrants and minorities merge into the larger society, and eventually retire has been overshadowed by the demands for growth.

Now there is an impasse. Large companies that have not moved their operations to other countries have deserted cities for the suburbs. But the pressure to build around cities is being resisted by those who oppose sprawl. Traffic congestion is becoming more costly in time, money, fuel, and civil order. Yet, the Census Bureau projects that growth in some form must continue as the population continues to grow and the number of people over age 65 doubles by 2030 (see again Table 1-1).

Obviously, population growth will be diffused around the country, but nobody knows how it will be spread. As Peter Peterson explained in *Gray Dawn,* by the year 2023 the whole country will resemble Florida, with nearly a fifth of the population over age 65.[1]

Now is the time for communities to start charting their futures. They cannot all be havens for financially secure retirees who will be supported by retirement plans and investments. Millions of baby boomers know they will have to be employed because they will not have enough income to retire comfortably, and many others who think they will be financially secure are likely to be surprised when their phantom wealth disappears. Where will all these people live and work?

Communities should base their plans on real needs and financial realities such as those we have discussed. They should attract companies that will be good corporate citizens, not absentee landlords. They will find this is easier to do when companies realize that stock-driven growth is no longer the name of the game.

Stockholders and Stakeholders

As Ralph Estes explained in *Tyranny of the Bottom Line,* years ago corporations were granted charters to accomplish public purposes.[2] Many parties or stakeholders had interests in what they did, including customers, employees, suppliers, creditors, communities, stockholders, and managers. In theory, the managers served and balanced the interests of all the stakeholders.

But more recently, and particularly since the 1970s, stockholders gradually gained power at the expense of all others. Dominated by large investors who demanded portfolio gains, they shifted the primary emphasis of corporations to managing stock prices. As unions did before them, the investors overplayed their hand. When the effects of the impending sales of baby boomer retirement accounts are more widely understood, stock prices are destined to decline and become less important. That will reduce the power of portfolio managers to demand higher stock prices. As happened with the unions, their magic will fade.

Power will then shift to the other stakeholders. Reforms, such as the accounting systems that meet the needs of all stakeholders that Estes advocates, will become more obvious and corporate resistance to them will diminish. Articles like the one about Ben & Jerry's that was discussed in Chapter 6 will become historical artifacts.

Idealism and Realism

Is all this idealistic? Sure it is.

Is it realistic? I think so, for three reasons.

1. Much of America's history from before the Revolution through the post-World War II recovery shows that those who built this country were a bunch of tough cookies who were guided by a mix of idealism and realism. That is our heritage. possible to replace the structure without a crisis.
2. It is realistic to say that the days of the phantom wealth structure are numbered. It seems realistic to say that it ought to be
3. I don't think it is realistic to believe that only bad things can happen.

We'll see.

Summary of This Book

There is a limit to how much workers will pay to support retired older people. Despite the appeal of schemes to buy stocks so their gains can pay incomes to retired baby boomers, all the schemes have the same problem as Social Security does: any gains must come from workers who buy the stocks when retirees sell them.

At a more basic level, the most that financial retirement schemes can do is stockpile money for retirees to use to buy real goods and services when they are ready to consume them. But the national pie of most real goods and services is produced shortly before it is consumed. The pie doesn't keep, and it can't be stockpiled.

If retirees are going to sell their stocks for gains, most of the gains will have to come from workers' incomes. For this to happen, workers must get hit twice—first when they use part of their income to buy the stocks and then when they use the remainder of their income to buy their slice of the pie of goods and services at prices that have been inflated by retirees' purchases.

At the national level, it takes current earnings to pay for consumption. The consumption of retirees who do not have current earnings (from work, interest, and dividends) will somehow have to come from workers' earnings.

Half of America's stocks have been accumulated in retirement plans in a deluded attempt to escape these basic facts. The attempt to use stocks to stockpile future purchasing power has created trillions of dollars of phantom wealth that can, and probably will, just disappear if too many boomers try to live on workers' incomes. If the system fails, it is likely to depress stock prices for years and could lead to a depression.

Without repeating the litany of social and economic ills caused by the drive to create phantom wealth, it will be years before the country understands the full costs of doing so. The irony is that the costs are being paid to pursue an impossible goal.

It is like an Ancient Greek tragedy in which there are no villains. All the players do the best they can with their limited abilities and knowledge. Yet in the end, they all lose.

America's play doesn't have to end that way. We can be the audience and the players. We can use our knowledge of what is happening to change what is going to happen.

Most of the suggestions in Part III of this book are offered as examples only. They show that solutions can be found if people and organizations want to find them. They are intended to function like the most significant achievement of the Wright brothers, which was to show that man can fly. Once that was done, the question shifted to how to do it best and that is still being worked on. What America eventually does will be the sum of what its people and organizations do.

In retrospect, all of this seems pretty straightforward. Which leads to a big question: If it's so easy to understand, why doesn't everybody already know it?

I leave you with that question.

Appendixes

Appendix A presents a list of questions that baby boomers can ask while thinking about how this book may apply to them. Each question is at the first level; that is, it can lead to a subsequent chain of questions that lead to real understanding, as discussed in Chapter 10.

The following appendixes (B, C, and D) present sample letters. Readers may wish to use them as they are written or as a guide for composing their own letters. Permission is granted to quote, copy, or reproduce any or all of them on the condition that their source, *What If Boomers Can't Retire?* by Thornton Parker (Berrett-Koehler, 2000) is mentioned.

Each sample letter refers to this book in order to advise the recipients of the manner in which their answers will be evaluated. If they explain how stocks can work for Social Security and the baby boomers' retirement accounts in terms of the issues this book raises, then readers can be more confident that today's conventional wisdom is well founded. If they don't provide good explanations, however, it will become clear that the situation is as the book describes.

Appendix B presents a letter that can be sent to Senators and Representatives asking that, before they vote on any proposal to use Social Security funds to buy stocks, they explain how it would work.

Appendix C presents a letter that can be sent to brokers, accountants, financial advisers or planners, or anyone else who helps with retirement investments. It asks that individual to explain how stocks can help provide people with retirement income and if there are any other types of investments that would be better suited to providing such income.

Finally, Appendix D presents a letter that can be sent to a mutual fund or other organizations that manage retirement accounts. The letter asks that organization to provide an analysis of how stocks can help boomers retire.

Appendix A

Questions for Readers to Ask Themselves

Many books and Web sites offer checklists and forms to help people anticipate their retirement income needs and sources. This list is different. It is intended to help readers think about and ask deeper questions about what they want the rest of their lives to mean.

To begin, look down the list and pick a category or a few questions that are of greatest interest to you. Don't try to deal with all the questions at once, but return to this appendix later and think through a few more of them. If you jot down your answers and review them in the future, you may find that your thoughts change over time.

The questions are intended to spur thinking, learning, and preparing. If you expect to age with someone, change the noun "I" to "we."

Chapter 10 discussed the five "whys" that the Japanese asked to refine their industrial processes. Similarly, cub newspaper reporters were traditionally taught to ask who, what, where, when, and how. Each of the following questions can lead to its own array of five or more levels of who, what, where, when, how, and why.

None of the questions or subsequent questions have answers that are right or wrong in the abstract. Your answers are important only to you.

Questions About This Book

- Does this book seem reasonable, or does it seem wrong in some way?
- How can I resolve what it says about stocks and retirements with everything else I know, believe, think, or have heard?
- Should I send letters or ask questions like those shown in Appendixes B, C, and D?
- What should I say or do if I get answers that are based on the past performance of stocks or the reply, "It's too hard to predict"?
- With whom can I discuss the book?
- Should I be active in the Social Security debate, perhaps by sending a letter like that shown in Appendix B?

Questions About My Mindset

- Can I honestly say that I think I will enjoy or be content to continue living as I am now during my later years?
- Am I interested more in what I can get from society or what I can contribute to society?
- Do I expect to work hard, build a retirement kitty, and enjoy years of retirement?

- Do I think of my work as something I would only do if paid?
- What fields or subjects would I most enjoy continuing to learn about?

Questions About My Situation

- Into which of the seven classes of boomers discussed in Chapter 2 am I most likely to fall?
- Do I expect to grow older with someone or by myself?
- What are my health prospects?
- Will others depend on me as I grow older?
- If I plan to manage my own affairs as I age but then become incapacitated and unable to do so, who will manage my affairs for me?

On Finding Satisfaction and Fulfillment

- What do I do that is really satisfying and fulfilling?
- What would I like to do that I think would be satisfying and fulfilling?
- Whom do I know who has aged well (or not aged well)?
- Whom do I admire and respect who has led a long life that I would like to emulate?
- How will my interests change and what will become particularly important as I grow older?
- Can I prepare for my later years as I prepared for my career?

Questions About Retirement Income

- Do I expect to have adequate income when I retire?
- Do I expect to receive income from a pension, annuity, or defined benefit plan?
- Does the provider of that income expect stocks to help provide it?
- What backup is available to the provider if the stock market declines?
- Do I expect to receive income from 401(k), IRA, or other tax-advantaged portfolios that would be produced by stock gains?
- What would I do if any of the sources of retirement income that I anticipate were to have disappointing results or fail?

On the Impossible Decision

- If I manage my retirement portfolio and it contains securities that will have to be sold for income, should I decide how long to make them last or should I put them into a pool to get "longevity" insurance?
- If I decide to manage the sale of my retirement assets as I grow older, how long should I try to make them last?
- What will I do if my decision turns out to be wrong and I outlive my assets?

Questions About Work in Later Years

- Do I have job security?
- Can I expect to continue to work in my same field or job as I get older?
- Will I become obsolete if I don't keep on learning and adapting?
- Will I want to stay in this field or job?
- What will I want from my job in later years in addition to income?
- How can I anticipate and prepare for the employment opportunities that will be open to me?

Questions About Consumption

- Am I living on my income, or do I borrow against future income to pay for my consumption today?
- Why do I buy most things—because I really need or want and will use them; because I am responding to advertising and promotion; to get what is currently in style; or to replace things that I am tired of?
- Do I usually enjoy the things I buy and consume, or have I often found that anticipation was greater than the fulfillment?
- Do my possessions work for me, or am I working to get and maintain my possessions?

- Do I have physical or medical disabilities that will require significant levels of expenditures and consumption?
- If my income declines as I grow older, how will I adjust my consumption to match?

Questions About Where to Live

- Will I want and be able to afford to stay where I am living now as I grow older?
- If I own my own home, will it be serving me in later years, or will I be serving it?
- If I move, will I want to live in a community of older people or with people of all ages?
- If I will want to or have to move, will I stay in the same general area or go to a different part of the country?
- Before I move to a different region, how can I be sure I will like it?
- If I consider a retirement community, how can I be sure I will have enough income to afford it?
- Can I expect to be relatively fixed in what I want, or am I generally flexible and able to adapt to what comes along?

On Sources of Advice

- Whom can I ask about how peoples' lives and outlooks change as they grow older?

- Do I have friends or associates with whom I can have open, candid discussions of these types of questions?
- If I think this book may be right about the risks of stocks and managing retirement incomes, how can I find advisers or professionals to manage my affairs who agree with its premise?

Appendix B

Questions to Ask Senators and Representatives

Dear Senator [or Representative]:

It would be a mistake to buy stocks with Social Security funds unless there is a clear understanding of how doing so could help solve the Social Security problem. Before you vote for any legislation that would use these funds to buy stocks, please provide answers to the following questions.

1. Is there any way that stocks could help Social Security obtain cash to pay retirement benefits if the stocks are not sold?
2. If the program buys stocks that will eventually have to be sold, whom do you believe might be the primary buyers other than people who are still working?
3. If the primary buyers will have to be workers, why would Social Security not continue to be a pay-as-you-go, passthrough, intergenerational transfer program that requires workers to pay retirement benefits?
4. If the burden of paying retirement benefits would still fall on workers who buy the stocks, how would stocks help Social Security?
5. If workers must buy most of the retired baby boomers' stocks, to whom would the workers sell

them when they retire? Why would that not be a pyramid scheme that would eventually fail?

Please do not base your answers to these questions on the history of the stock market or tell me that it has done so much better than other types of investments. As Thornton Parker explained in *What If Boomers Can't Retire?* (Berrett-Koehler, 2000), no event in the history of the stock market has ever come close to the planned waves of selling that nearly all boomers' pension plans and retirement accounts are designed to do.

The book explains that history does not provide a precedent for the current situation. The only relevant answers to my questions must explain who will be able to buy the stocks when Social Security needs money to pay beneficiaries. Nothing else matters. If the primary buyers must be workers, the Social Security problem will be worsened because the program will have to sell its stocks at the same time that other retirement plans are selling theirs. To help you consider my questions and your answers, you might want to ask the General Accounting Office to evaluate the analyses in the first four chapters of that book.

I look forward to your reply.

Sincerely,

Appendix C

Questions to Ask Brokers and Financial Planners

Dear _____:

I am concerned that stocks may not be able to provide adequate income when I expect to retire and begin selling my stocks in _____. I bought my stocks primarily to provide gains, but to convert any gains into income, I will have to sell them. Because the price I will receive will be determined by the market supply and demand conditions for stocks when they are sold, I have several questions about those conditions that I would like you to answer for me.

1. Whom do you anticipate will be the primary buyers of the stocks that baby boomers will sell at the time when I expect to retire?
2. If you expect the primary buyers will be people who are still working, what is the projected ratio of worker-buyer to retireeseller during that period?
3. Because workers buy most of their stocks during their peak earning years, how many workers are expected to be in their peak earning years in relation to the number of boomers who will probably be selling during my retirement years?
4. Do you know of any studies or due-diligence analyses of the market conditions that are likely

to prevail for stocks, including the buying potential of other countries, at the time when I expect to be selling them?

5. If you have no information that can be used to anticipate what will happen when the baby boomers try to sell their stocks for retirement income, do you still recommend the purchase of stocks for my retirement accounts?
6. If you do recommend purchasing stocks, why? What risks are inherent in the recommendation? (Note that a discussion of the history of stock prices will not answer this question unless it refers to a specific period when market conditions approximated those that can be expected at the time when I sell my stocks.)
7. Can you recommend other investments that would be safer for my retirement portfolio—that would preserve my capital, use it for productive purposes, pay my income from then-current earnings, and increase the payments if the company does well, as utility companies used to do?

The reasons why I am asking these questions are discussed in *What If Boomers Can't Retire?* by Thornton Parker (Berrett-Koehler, 2000). I would appreciate your views on the first four chapters of that book.

Sincerely,

Appendix D

Questions to Ask Mutual Fund Organizations

Dear _____:

Reference Account No._____

I own shares of _____ Fund (in my IRA, 401[k], or other retirement account). I am concerned that when I plan to retire in _____ and will need to sell them for income, many other boomers will also be selling stocks and the prices may fall. Please send me any projections or analyses that you have of the market supply and demand conditions for that time period.

If you do not have a projection or analysis that shows how large amounts of stocks can be sold at prices high enough to provide retirement incomes, do you still advise buying stocks for retirement accounts? If you do, why?

Please do not answer that question on the basis of stock price history or how stocks have compared with other investments. As Thornton Parker explains in *What If Boomers Can't Retire?* (Berrett-Koehler, 2000), there has not been a published due-diligence analysis of how the full stocks-for-retirement cycle can work. The book says that retirement accounts have created an unprecedented situation where trillions of dollars of stocks will have to be sold to what appears to be a relatively smaller number of buyers. If you advise buying stocks for retirement accounts, please explain how your advice relates to the first four chapters of that book.

Sincerely,

Notes

Foreword

[1] Anthony B. Perkins and Michael C. Perkins, *Internet Bubble* (New York: HarperCollins, 1999), p.239.

[2] Hazel Henderson, *Creating Alternative Futures* (New York: Berkeley Publishing, 1978, 1996), p.193.

Introduction: Beware of Phantom Wealth

[1] David C. Korten, *The Post-Corporate World: Life After Capitalism* (San Francisco: Berrett-Koehler, and Hartford, Conn.: Kumarian Press, 1998).

[2] Robert A.G. Monks, *The Emperor's Nightingale: Restoring the Integrity of the Corporation in the Age of Shareholder Activism* (Reading, Mass.: Addison-Wesley, 1998).

[3] Peter G. Peterson, *Gray Dawn: How the Coming Age Wave Will Transform America—and the World* (New York: Random House, 1999).

[4] William Strauss and Neil Howe, *The Fourth Turning: What the Cycles of History Tell Us About America's Next Rendezvous with Destiny* (New York: Broadway Books, 1997).

Chapter 1: Social Security: The Tip of the Retirement Iceberg

[1] American Academy of Actuaries, "Financing the Retirement of Future Generations—The Problem and Options for Change," *Public Policy Monograph No.1* (Washington, D.C.: Author, 1998).

[2] U.S. Bureau of the Census, *Resident Population of the United States: Middle Series Projections* (Washington D.C.: Author, March 1996).

[3] Social Security Administration, *Annual Report of the Board of Trustees of the Federal Old-Age and Survivors Insurance and Disability Insurance Trust Funds* (Washington, D.C.: Author, March 2000), Table II.F19, p.122.

[4] Social Security Administration, *Annual Report of the Board of Trustees,* Table III.B3, p.181.

[5] Board of Governors of the Federal Reserve System, *Flow of Funds Accounts of the United States, Second Quarter 1999* (Washington, D.C.: Author, September 1999), p.13.

[6] John B. Shoven, "The Retirement Security of the Baby Boom Generation," *TIAA CREF Research Dialogues,* no.43, March 1995, p.2.

Chapter 2: Can Stocks Help Baby Boomers Retire?

[1] Twila Slesnick and John C. Suttle, *IRAs, 401(k)s & Other Retirement Plans: Taking Your Money Out* (Berkeley, Calif.: Nolo Press, 1999), p.6-1.

[2] A number of publications discuss the problem of selling stocks to pay for baby boomers' retirements, including Miriam Bensman, "The Baby Boomer Boomerang," *Institutional Investor,* September 1994, p.53; Craig S. Karpel, *The Retirement Myth* (New York: HarperCollins, 1995); Thornton Parker, "What Will Happen When the Baby Boomer Retires?" *IRRC Corporate Governance Bulletin,* January – March 1995, p.17; Thornton Parker, "Today's Stock Investment Dilemma," *Perspectives on Business and Global Change,* June 1997, p.67; Thornton Parker, "Boomers' Time Bomb," *Barron's,* November 16, 1998, p.57; Thornton Parker, "Can the Stocks-for-Retirement Cycle Work," presentation at the Retirement 2000 Multi-Disciplinary Symposium, Society of Actuaries, Washington D.C., February 23–24, 2000; Peterson, *Gray Dawn;* Shoven, "The Retirement of the Baby Boom Generation"; William Sterling and Stephen Waite, *Boomernomics: The Future of Your Money in the Upcoming Generational Warfare* (New York: Ballantine Books, 1998);

"Early Retirement Isn't in the Boomers' Future," *Wall Street Journal,* May 6, 1996, p.A1.

[3] Financial Executives Institute's Committee on the Investment of Employee Benefit Assets (CIEBA), *Implications of Investing Social Security Funds in Financial Markers,* a report prepared by Goldman, Sachs, Morgan Stanley Dean Witter, J.P. Morgan Investment Management, and INVESCO Global Strategies. The peak buying years are discussed primarily in the INVESCO portion of the report, starting at about p.110.

[4] Organization for Economic Co-operation and Development, *Maintaining Prosperity in an Ageing Society* [policy brief] (Paris, France: Author, 1998).

[5] Peterson, *Gray Dawn,* p.5.

[6] Niall Ferguson and Laurence J. Kotlikoff, "The Degeneration of EMU," *Foreign Affairs,* March – April 2000, pp.110–121.

[7] Donald Lee Rome, "Tomorrow's Jobless: Will Private Investment Yields Support the Swelling Ranks of Retirees?" *Barron's,* June 8, 1998, p.53.

[8] Interest and dividend data are from *Flow of Funds Accounts of the United States, Fourth Quarter 1998* (Washington, D.C.: Board of Governors of the Federal Reserve System, 1999).

[9] Ibid.

[10] Richard Mahoney, "Unshackling Corporate Profits," *New York Times,* December 28, 1997, pp.3–12.

[11] Henry Petroski, *Design Paradigms: Case Histories of Error and Judgment in Engineering* (Cambridge, U.K.: Cambridge University Press, 1994).

Chapter 3: Views from Eight Other Books

[1] Harry S. Dent, Jr., *The Roaring 2000s Investor: Strategies for the Life You Want* (New York: Simon & Schuster, 1999).

[2] Strauss and Howe, *The Fourth Turning.*

[3] Bambi Holzer with Elaine Floyd, *Retire Rich: The Baby Boomer's Guide to a Secure Future* (New York: Wiley, 1998).

[4] James P. O'Shaughnessy, *What Works on Wall Street: A Guide to the Best Performing Investment Strategies of All Time* (New York: McGraw-Hill, 1998).

[5] Jeremy J. Siegel, *Stocks for the Long Run: The Definitive Guide to Financial Market Returns and Long-Term Investment Strategies* (New York: McGraw-Hill, 1998).

[6] Edward Chancellor, *Devil Take the Hindmost: A History of Financial Speculation* (New York: Farrar, Straus and Giroux, 1999).

[7] Edward Chancellor, "When the Bubble Bursts...," *Wall Street Journal,* August 18, 1999, p.A18.

[8] Charles R. Morris, *Money, Greed, and Risk* (New York: Random House, 1999).

[9] The Vanguard Group, *The Vanguard Guide to Investing During Retirement,* 2nd ed. (New York: McGraw-Hill, 1998), pp.78–79.

[10] Slesnick and Suttle, *IRAs, 401(k)s & Other Retirement Plans,* p.6–3.

[11] Siegel, *Stocks for the Long Run,* pp.38–42.

[12] Robert L. Brown, *Impacts on Economic Security Programs on Rapidly Shifting Demographics* [CD-ROM] (Schaumburg, Ill.: The Society of Actuaries, 2000), pp.14–15.

[13] Francisco Bayo, "Measures of Actuarial Balance for Social Insurance Programs," *Record of the Society of Actuaries,* 1998, 14(1), pp.161–179; cited in Brown, *Impacts on Economic Security Programs,* p.15.

[14] Nicholas Barr, *The Economics of the Welfare State* (London: Weidenfeld and Nicolson, 1993); cited in Brown, *Impacts on Economic Security Programs,* p.15.

[15] Irving M. Copi, *Introduction to LOGIC* (New York: Macmillan, 1961), p.79.

Chapter 4: How Baby Boomers' Later Years Will Unfold

[1] Brown, *Impacts on Economic Security Programs,* pp.6–7.

[2] F. Levy and R.C. Michel, "Are Baby Boomers Selfish?" *American Demographics,* April 1985,

pp.39–44; cited in Brown, *Impacts on Economic Security Programs.*

[3] Vanguard Group, *The Vanguard Guide to Investing,* pp.168–169.

[4] Jonathan Clements, "Playing the Right Retirement Cards," *Wall Street Journal,* November 19, 1999, p.C1.

Chapter 5: Stocks, Wealth, and Phantom Wealth

[1] David L. Birch interview, "Thinking About Tomorrow," *Wall Street Journal,* May 24, 1999, p.R30.

[2] Mark Heinzl, "Nortel to Buy Maker of Optical Switches for Internet in $3.25 Billion Stock Deal," *Wall Street Journal,* March 15, 2000, p.B6.

[3] Don Clark, "E.piphany Agrees to Pay $3.18 Billion for Maker of Web-Customer Software," *Wall Street Journal,* March 15, 2000, p.B6.

Chapter 6: The Drive to Create Phantom Wealth

[1] The AOL purchase of Time Warner was widely covered in the popular and financial presses from the day following its announcement. The *Wall Street Journal* devoted page B1 of its January 11, 2000 issue to the subject, as did the *Washington Post* with its business section, starting at page E1. Both ran additional arti-

cles during the next several days, particularly to examine the changes in stock prices and how they affected the wealth of individuals who owned large amounts of AOL and Time Warner stock.

[2] Jerry Useem, "New Ethics or No Ethics?" *Fortune,* March 20, 2000, pp.82–86.

[3] Paul Hawken, *The Ecology of Commerce* (New York: Harper-Collins, 1993), pp.89–90, 138–39.

[4] Joseph M. Abe, Patricia E. Dempsey, and David Bassett, *Business Ecology* (Boston: Butterworth-Heinemann, 1998), pp.163, 169–170.

[5] Matthew M. Stichnoth, "Just Deserts: An Acquirer Could Unfreeze Ben & Jerry's Value for Neglected Stockholders," *Bloomberg Personal Finance,* March 2000, pp.22–24.

[6] Shawn Tully, "America's Wealth Creators," *Fortune,* November 22, 1999, pp.275–284. This article was the latest of the annual articles in *Fortune* on EVA and MVA as this book was being written.

[7] Martha M. Hamilton, "Exxon Mobil Plans Deeper Cuts," *Washington Post,* December 16, 1999, p.E3.

[8] Stern Stewart advertisement, *Fortune,* September 22, 1999, p.303.

[9] Based on personal communication with Stern Stewart staff, April 11, 2000.

Chapter 7: Why Stock Prices Don't Create Real Wealth

[1] Greg Schneider, "A New Economy Nightmare," *Washington Post,* March 5, 2000, p.H1.

[2] David Streitfeld, "Tangled in a Web of Net Losses," *Washington Post,* March 5, 2000, p.A14.

[3] Jerry Knight, "What Michael Saylor Is *Really* Worth," *Washington Business* section of the *Washington Post,* March 6, 2000, p.7.

[4] Chancellor, *Devil Take the Hindmost,* p.45.

[5] Fred Barbash, "Market Guru Put Acolytes on Wild Ride," *Washington Post,* March 5, 2000, p.H1.

[6] Andrew Bary, "How to Fix GM," *Barron's,* July 5, 1999, pp.18–19.

[7] Carol Loomis, "Mr. Buffett on the Stock Market," *Fortune,* November 22, 1999, pp.212–220.

[8] E.S. Browning, "Yahoo! Flies Higher on S&P Effect at the Expense of Blue-Chip Stocks," *Wall Street Journal,* December 12, 1999, p.C1.

Chapter 8: How Phantom Wealth Hurts the Economy

[1] Scott Thurm, "Thunder on Wall Street Shakes Silicon Valley," *Wall Street Journal,* April 3, 2000, p.A-1.

[2] Gene Epstein, "There's a Minor Upside to Corporate Downsizing," *Barron's,* November 8, 1999, p.52.

[3] Hamilton, "Exxon Mobil Plans Deeper Cuts."

[4] Korten, *The Post-Corporate World,* p.83.

[5] Alan Greenspan, remarks before symposium, Federal Reserve Bank of Kansas City, Jackson Hole, Wyoming, August 27, 1999.

[6] Shannon Henry, "AOL's Stock Plunge Has a Deep Impact," *Washingon Post,* August 6, 1999, p.E-1.

[7] Paul Hawken, *The Ecology of Commerce* (New York: Harper-Collins, 1993).

[8] Ralph Estes, *Tyranny of the Bottom Line* (San Francisco: Berrett-Koehler, 1996).

[9] Monks, *The Emperor's Nightingale.*

[10] Korten, *The Post-Corporate World.*

Chapter 9: How We Can Meet Our Real Needs

[1] Gordon S. Wood, *The Creation of the American Republic 1776–1787* (Chapel Hill: University of North Carolina Press, 1998).

[2] Organization for Economic Co-operation and Development, *Maintaining Prosperity in an Ageing Society,* pp.83–101.

Chapter 10: What Individuals Can Do

[1]. Organization for Economic Co-operation and Development, *Maintaining Prosperity in an Ageing Society,* p.84.

[2] Strauss and Howe, *The Fourth Turning.*

[3] Stephen Fox, "I Like to Build Things," *Invention & Technology,* Summer 1999, 15(1), pp.20–30.

[4] Graham R. Mitchell and William F. Hamilton, "Managing R&D As a Strategic Option," *Research and Technology Management,* May– June 1988, 31(3), pp.15–22.

Chapter 11: What Organizations Can Do

[1] Organization for Economic Co-operation and Development, *Maintaining Prosperity in an Ageing Society,* pp.83–101.

[2] Vanguard Group, *The Vanguard Guide to Investing,* pp.168–169.

[3] Peter Drucker, "Innovate or Die," *The Economist,* September 25, 1999, pp.25–28.

[4] Korten, *The Post-Corporate World.*

[5] *Proposed Amendment of the Investment Company Act of 1940 to Facilitate Operations of Managerial Strategic Investment Companies* (Boston: Foley, Hoag & Eliot Attorneys, June 1993).

[6] Jerry Useem, "Info-Age Companies Shun Debt and Equity, Embrace Royalties," *Inc.,* December 1996, p.25; and Julie Sturgeon, "Need Capital? Hate Debt? Afraid of Equity? Try This Option," *Indianapolis C.E.O.,* June 1995, p.48.

[7] Clifford Cobb, Ted Halstead, and Jonathan Rowe, "If the GDP Is Up, Why Is America Down?" *Atlantic Monthly,* October 1995, pp.59–78.

[8] Paul Kennedy, *The Rise and Fall of the Great Powers* (New York: Random House, 1987), p.145.

[9] This explanation of America's experience with virtuous cycles is based in part on *U.S. Industry and Trade—Trends and Perspectives* (Tokyo: International Trade Institute, Japan Foreign Trade Council, 1988). For additional information, see Thornton Parker, "Harnessing the Power of Growth Cycles," *Perspectives on Business and Global Change,* December 1997, 11(4), pp.21–34.

[10] Thornton Parker and Theodore Lettes, "Technology, Knowledge, and Value Added (or Making Something From Almost Nothing)," *National Estimator,* Spring 1993, pp.52–56.

[11] Jack Willoughby, "Burning Up," *Barron's,* March 20, 2000, pp.29–32.

Chapter 12: Conclusion: How to Change a Very Big System

[1] Peterson, *Gray Dawn.*

[2] Estes, *Tyranny of the Bottom Line.*

Glossary

Capitalized value—the result of multiplying the number of shares that a company has outstanding by the market price. Also called *market capitalization* or *market cap.*

Closed-end fund—a mutual fund that raises the capital it uses to manage its portfolio by selling its own stock at one time. Its shares are then traded on an exchange. This is distinct from an open-end fund that is normally willing to sell or buy back its own shares. Most mutual funds are open-end.

Defined benefit—a type of retirement plan offered by an employer where the retirees' payments or benefits are established or defined by contract. The benefits are often called pensions and set as a percentage of an employee's later years of work. In general, the employer bears the risks of meeting its obligations for as long as the retiree lives.

Defined contribution—a type of retirement plan where the employer contributes a set amount or percentage of an employee's earnings to an account. The employee bears all the risks and responsibilities for investing the money and drawing it down after retirement.

Dilution—the term used to indicate that when a corporation issues additional shares of stock, its future profits will be spread over the larger number of shares.

Due diligence—a type of analysis that is usually done to identify the possible risks before making a productive investment. It starts from the question, "What could happen that could turn this into a bad investment?" It follows that question wherever it leads, and if the risks are too great, the investment is not made.

Equity—ownership of a corporation. Shares of stock are certificates of equity or ownership.

EVA—Earned Value Added, a technique used by large corporations to ensure that each investment they make is likely to produce a return that is high enough to contribute to profits and increase the stock price.

Exit strategy—the plan of an early investor in a young company to recover his or her investment and profits.

IPO—initial public offering, the first time that a corporation raises capital by offering its stock for sale to the public.

Indexing—the practice of maintaining a portfolio that includes shares of the same company stocks in the same quantities as an index. A portfolio indexed to the S&P 500 Index is intended to perform almost the same as that Index. (See *stock index.)*

Mark to market—the practice of treating all outstanding shares of a company's stock as being worth the same price as the last shares traded.

MVA—Market Value Added, which some believe is the object of running a corporation. It is the amount that the market increases the capitalized value of a corporation over the amount of capital that was paid in and returned from operations.

Hurdle rate—a rate of return that companies use to analyze and select from among investment opportunities. It is a rate that an investment is expected to exceed in order to be considered successful.

Nonfinancial assets—tangibles that can be used to produce or store real wealth, such as land, minerals, buildings, and tools, and various types of intangibles, such as technology.

Parasitic investing—the use of money to buy financial assets like stocks or mutual fund shares to make money. Parasitic investors are passive. They don't think of themselves as having any responsibilities as owners. They are rarely aware of, much less involved in, the normal operation of a business other than to look out for their interests. If things do not go well, their normal reaction is to sell their stocks rather than find ways to help the business overcome its troubles.

Price earnings ratio (p/e)—the price of a share of a company's stock divided by the company's earnings per share.

Private sector—a widely used term for the world of business, as distinct from the public sector, or the world of government.

Productive investing—the practice of using money to buy nonfinancial assets like materials, tools, technologies, and employee skills that companies must have to make the products or services that they sell to earn profits. Productive investors are often actively involved in the business and provide more than just money. Most of the country's productive investments are made by large companies using the cash they have produced through their operations.

Secondary market—exchanges of various types where outstanding stocks are traded. Most stock buying and selling is done on secondary markets through transactions that do not provide money to the corporations.

Secondary offering—a corporation's offer to sell additional shares of stock to the public after its initial public offering.

Stock index—a measure of stock prices used to gauge the overall level of the market, trends in market prices, and comparisons of particular company stocks with the broad market. Widely used indices include the Dow Jones Industrial Average, Standard and Poor's 500 Index, Russell 3000, and the Wilshire 5000 Index.

Then-current earnings—earnings that a company or an investment will produce from routine operations in the future.

About the Author

Most people specialize in one or a few fields and progress up through them in what are often called stovepipes or fence pickets. Thornton (Tip) Parker has done the opposite by deliberately working on tasks that require knowledge of multiple fields. He is a generalist with more than forty-five years of widely diverse government and business experience in management, strategic planning, finance and accounting, manufacturing, marketing, personnel administration, transportation, technology management, large computer and information systems, intergovernmental relations, assistance management, and policy development.

After receiving his bachelor's of science degree in business administration from the University of Maryland in 1953, he served two years in the Air Force, where he rose to the rank of and separated as a first lieutenant. He then entered General Electric's Business Training Course, a business training program where he earned the equivalent of a master's degree in management accounting and learned to program computers—at a time when it was done with plugboard wiring and in machine code on rotating drums. At GE, Parker worked on large data systems for manufacturing military electronic equipment. Later, he was assigned to GE's television receiver division—a division whose sales alone made it big enough to have qualified to rank fifty-sixth in the *Fortune* 500 listing—whose accounting system he computerized.

In 1961, Parker joined the Federal Systems Office of RCA's electronic data processing division, where he marketed computers to the government and advised government agencies on how to use computers in large financial and logistics systems. He became one of RCA's senior systems people while concurrently serving as a regional personal administrator. He was a member of the threeperson team that completed a business planning study showing why RCA would fail in the computer business unless it changed its strategies; these recommendations were adopted eventually, but too late to prevent the failure.

In 1967, Parker joined the government and helped establish the Computer Science Center in what was then the National Bureau of Standards. He led the government's in-house computer management consulting division, which helped agencies design systems, select computers, and fill management positions.

He then moved to the Office of Economic Opportunity in the Executive Office of the President, where he headed the Information Center's systems planning staff. He was involved in planning systems to support the War on Poverty, working with most federal agencies and many state and local governments. He also made the initial plans for automating the federal budget preparation cycle (which was run on OEO computers in 1969).

Parker was invited to join the ADP Management Staff of the Bureau of the Budget (now the Office of Management and Budget), also in the Executive Office, in 1970. There, he was responsible for the data standards program and led an interagency team that proposed ways to improve the effectiveness of the government's thirty-two thousand systems analysts and programmers.

Based on his experience, he was transferred to the Intergovernmental Relations Division of OMB, where he helped coordinate programs and improve the flow of information among federal agencies, states, and units of local government. He became the deputy leader of the only governmentwide study of federal assistance that has ever been done and wrote the report on the study.

He transferred to the Commerce Department in the early 1980s. There, he helped develop policies to encourage industry to use the results of federal research and was one of the authors of the Federal Technology Transfer Act of 1986, which fostered industry collaboration with federal laboratories and growth of many of the country's high-tech industries.

Parker has always been interested in the deeper meaning of his work. After helping make it easier for industry to use technologies created with federal funding, he was among the first to see that many of the technologies were being used more by foreign competitors than companies in this country. He organized a series of roundtables on financing technology that were hosted jointly by the Secretaries of Commerce and Treasury to learn why this was so. As a result, he realized that the demands of large institutional investors for stock price increases were forcing managers of public companies to concentrate on short-term returns. The more he studied and discussed what was happening with industry leaders, the more he was convinced that parts of America's investment system were no longer working (had become dysfunctional) and that the national emphasis on stock prices was a major weakness.

After finding that other government agencies including the Department of Labor, the Securities and Exchange Commission, the Pension Benefit Guaranty Corporation, and the National Economic Council were not interested in considering the implications of the issues, he retired in 1993 to devote himself to them.

While at the Commerce Department, Parker worked with an associate to help local organizations, often community colleges, establish shared teaching facilities. These facilities used state-of-the-art, computer-controlled manufacturing equipment to help managers of small manufacturing companies learn about new technologies and how to manage their own businesses after they had been modernized. (This concept was endorsed in 1992 by candidate Bill Clinton, who proposed establishing two hundred of these facilities; the idea was subsequently rejected by Congress.)

After they retired, he and his associate established Growth Cycle Design, Inc. (GCD) to help organizations that help small manufacturing companies. Under contract with the Electric Power Research Institute, the company developed ways for utility companies to help their small manufacturing customers prosper.

But industry deregulation forced power companies to concentrate on retaining their large customers and reducing costs in order to increase their stock prices, and small manufacturing customers and their communities were largely left to shift for themselves. GCD was subsequently disbanded. Parker has written articles for the *Corporate Governance Bulletin* of the Investors Responsibility Research Center, *Perspectives on Business and Global Change,* and *Barron's.* His letters-to-the-editor have been published in *Barron's, Fortune,* and the *Washington Post.*

Berrett-Koehler Publishers

BERRETT-KOEHLER is an independent publisher of books, periodicals, and other publications at the leading edge of new thinking and innovative practice on work, business, management, leadership, stewardship, career development, human resources, entrepreneurship, and global sustainability.

Since the company's founding in 1992, we have been committed to supporting the movement toward a more enlightened world of work by publishing books, periodicals, and other publications that help us to integrate our values with our work and work lives, and to create more humane and effective organizations.

We have chosen to focus on the areas of work, business, and organizations, because these are central elements in many people's lives today. Furthermore, the work world is going through tumultuous changes, from the decline of job security to the rise of new structures for organizing people and work. We believe that change is needed at all levels—individual, organizational, community, and global—and our publications address each of these levels.

We seek to create new lenses for understanding organizations, to legitimize topics that people care deeply about but that current business orthodoxy censors or considers secondary to bottom-line concerns, and to uncover new meaning, means, and ends for our work and work lives.

Other books from Berrett-Koehler Publishers

The Divine Right of Capital

Dethroning the Corporate Aristocracy

Marjorie Kelly

Marjorie Kelly argues that focusing on the interests of stockholders to the exclusion of everyone else's interests is a form of discrimination based on property or wealth. *The Divine Right of Capital* shows how to design more equitable alternatives—new property rights, new forms of corporate governance, new ways of looking at corporate performance—that build on both free-market and democratic principles.

Tyranny of the Bottom Line

Why Corporations Make Good People Do Bad Things

Ralph Estes

Estes shows that all of us are stakeholders in the corporation—with an investment, an interest in its performance, and a right to accountability—and lays out a plan to reform the corporate system to serve all stakeholders.

When Corporations Rule the World

David C. Korten

David Korten offers an alarming exposé of the devastating consequences of economic globalization and a passionate message of hope in this well-reasoned, extensively researched analysis. He documents the human and environmental consequences of economic globalization, and explain why human survival depends on a community-based, people-centered alternative.

Berrett-Koehler Publishers
PO Box 565, Williston, VT 05495-9900
Call toll-free! **800-929-2929** 7 am-9 pm Eastern Standard Time
Or fax your order to 802-864-7627
For fastest service order online: **www.bkconnection.com**

D

E

F

M

P

Q

R

S

T

U

V

Books For ALL Kinds of Readers

At ReadHowYouWant we understand that one size does not fit all types of readers. Our innovative, patent pending technology allows us to design new formats to make reading easier and more enjoyable for you. This helps improve your speed of reading and your comprehension. Our EasyRead printed books have been optimized to improve word recognition, ease eye tracking by adjusting word and line spacing as well as minimizing hyphenation. Our EasyRead SuperLarge editions have been developed to make reading easier and more accessible for vision-impaired readers. We offer Braille and DAISY formats of our books and all popular E-Book formats.

Made in United States
Orlando, FL
04 November 2026

90202366R00223